Computer Incident Response and Product Security

Damir Rajnović

D0813998

Cisco Press

800 East 96th Street

Indianapolis, IN 46240

Computer Incident Response and Product Security

Damir Rajnović

Published by:
Cisco Press
800 East 96th Street
Indianapolis, IN 46240 USA

Printed in the United States of America

First Printing December 2010

Library of Congress Cataloging-in-Publication Data:

Rajnović, Damir, 1965-
    Computer incident response and product security / Damir Rajnović.
       p. cm.
    Includes bibliographical references.
    ISBN 978-1-58705-264-4 (pbk.)
  1. Computer networks—Security measures. 2. Computer crimes—Risk assessment.
  3. Data recovery (Computer science) I. Title.

    TK5105.59.R35 2011

    005.8—dc22

                                                                    2010045607

ISBN-13: 978-1-58705-264-4

ISBN-10: 1-58705-264-4

Warning and Disclaimer

Trademark Acknowledgments

Corporate and Government Sales

The publisher offers excellent discounts on this book when ordered in quantity for bulk purchases or special sales, which may include electronic versions and/or custom covers and content particular to your business, training goals, marketing focus, and branding interests. For more information, please contact:

U.S. Corporate and Government Sales   1-800-382-3419   corpsales@pearsontechgroup.com

For sales outside the United States, please contact: **International Sales**   international@pearsoned.com

Feedback Information

At Cisco Press, our goal is to create in-depth technical books of the highest quality and value. Each book is crafted with care and precision, undergoing rigorous development that involves the unique expertise of members from the professional technical community.

Readers' feedback is a natural continuation of this process. If you have any comments regarding how we could improve the quality of this book, or otherwise alter it to better suit your needs, you can contact us through email at feedback@ciscopress.com. Please make sure to include the book title and ISBN in your message.

We greatly appreciate your assistance.

Publisher: Paul Boger	**Manager, Global Certification:** Erik Ullanderson
Associate Publisher: Dave Dusthimer	**Business Operation Manager, Cisco Press:** Anand Sundaram
Executive Editor: Brett Bartow	**Technical Editors:** Yurie Ito, Derrick Scholl
Managing Editor: Sandra Schroeder	**Copy Editor:** Apostrophe Editing Services
Development Editor: Andrew Cupp	**Proofreader:** Water Crest Publishing, Inc.
Senior Project Editor: Tonya Simpson	**Editorial Assistant:** Vanessa Evans
Book Designer: Louisa Adair	**Cover Designer:** Sandra Schroeder
Composition: Mark Shirar	**Indexer:** Tim Wright

CISCO.

Americas Headquarters	Asia Pacific Headquarters	Europe Headquarters
Cisco Systems, Inc.	Cisco Systems (USA) Pte. Ltd.	Cisco Systems International BV
San Jose, CA	Singapore	Amsterdam, The Netherlands

Cisco has more than 200 offices worldwide. Addresses, phone numbers, and fax numbers are listed on the Cisco Website at **www.cisco.com/go/offices.**

CCDE, CCENT, Cisco Eos, Cisco HealthPresence, the Cisco logo, Cisco Lumin, Cisco Nexus, Cisco StadiumVision, Cisco TelePresence, Cisco WebEx, DCE, and Welcome to the Human Network are trademarks; Changing the Way We Work, Live, Play, and Learn and Cisco Store are service marks; and Access Registrar, Aironet, AsyncOS, Bringing the Meeting To You, Catalyst, CCDA, CCDP, CCIE, CCIP, CCNA, CCNP, CCSP, CCVP, Cisco, the Cisco Certified Internetwork Expert logo, Cisco IOS, Cisco Press, Cisco Systems, Cisco Systems Capital, the Cisco Systems logo, Cisco Unity, Collaboration Without Limitation, EtherFast, EtherSwitch, Event Center, Fast Step, Follow Me Browsing, FormShare, GigaDrive, HomeLink, Internet Quotient, IOS, iPhone, iQuick Study, IronPort, the IronPort logo, LightStream, Linksys, MediaTone, MeetingPlace, MeetingPlace Chime Sound, MGX, Networkers, Networking Academy, Network Registrar, PCNow, PIX, PowerPanels, ProConnect, ScriptShare, SenderBase, SMARTnet, Spectrum Expert, StackWise, The Fastest Way to Increase Your Internet Quotient, TransPath, WebEx, and the WebEx logo are registered trademarks of Cisco Systems, Inc. and/or its affiliates in the United States and certain other countries.

All other trademarks mentioned in this document or website are the property of their respective owners. The use of the word partner does not imply a partnership relationship between Cisco and any other company. (0812R)

About the Author

Damir Rajnović finished his education in Croatia where, in 1993, he started his career in computer security. He started at the Croatian News Agency Hina, then moved on to the Ministry of Foreign Affairs, and finally to the Ministry of Science and Technology. During that time, Damir became involved with the Forum of Incident Response Teams (FIRST) and established the Croatian Academic and Research Network Computer Incident Response Team (CARNet CERT), which, until recently, was not only handling computer incidents for CARNet but was also acting as the Croatian national CERT. Damir then moved to the United Kingdom to work in EuroCERT which was a project that aimed to coordinate CERTs within the European region. After EuroCERT, Damir moved to the Cisco Product Security Incident Response Team (Cisco PSIRT), where he is still working. Cisco PSIRT is the focal point for managing security vulnerabilities in all Cisco products.

Damir remains active in FIRST, where he created Vendor SIG, and currently serves as liaison officer to the International Organization for Standardization (ISO) and International Telecommunication Union (ITU). Damir was an invited lecturer for the MSc Information Technology Security course at Westminster University, London. He was one of the core people who dreamed up and formed the Industry Consortium for the Advancement of Security on the Internet (ICASI).

His nonsecurity-related work includes working as a sound engineer on Radio 101 (http://www.radio101.hr) while living in Zagreb, Croatia. Damir lives with his family in Didcot, UK.

About the Contributing Author

Mike Caudill is a program manager within the Cisco Security Research and Operations team, a larger organization that includes the Cisco Product Security Incident Response Team (PSIRT), which he joined in 2001. while in PSIRT, Mike worked as an incident manager driving the resolution, coordination, and disclosure of product vulnerabilities within Cisco products. Before joining the Cisco PSIRT, Mike spent three years in the Cisco technical assistance center providing application support as an engineer in the Network Management team and as a manager for the Enterprise Voice team supporting IP telephony applications.

Before joining Cisco, Mike spent five years doing system administration for North Carolina State University's multiplatform "Eos" academic network and administrative computer systems. Mike graduated from N.C. State University with a BS in mechanical engineering and a certificate in computer science.

Mike currently serves as the executive director for the Industry Consortium for the Advancement of Security on the Internet (ICASI), a nonprofit consortium of industry vendors whose purpose is to enhance global IT security through proactive collaboration to drive excellence and innovation in security response, ultimately helping to reduce the impact of security threats.

Previously Mike served for four years on the steering committee of FIRST and the board of directors of FIRST.org, a nonprofit organization composed of international response teams dedicated to promoting best practices, information sharing, and collaboration within the incident response community to further computer and network security.

About the Technical Reviewers

Yurie Ito joined ICANN in April 2008 as a director of global security programs, where she leads ICANN's involvement in collaborative response activities and works with ICANN partner organizations and stakeholders at global and regional levels in implementing ICANN security, stability, and resiliency programs. Before joining ICANN, she was a director of technical operation at JPCERT/CC, Japan's National CSIRT, where she still works as a global coordination director. Yurie served as a steering committee member and a board director of Forum of Incident Response Security Teams (FIRST) from 2005 to 2011. She also is an active leader in the Asia Pacific Computer Emergency Response Teams (APCERT) where JPCERT/CC participates on the steering committee and provides the secretariat.

Derrick Scholl is the director of security engineering and response at Sun Microsystems. He is responsible for all aspects of security engineering and response across the entire Sun Microsystems product line. During his tenure as head of the security response team, Derrick has been instrumental in a number of improvements to Sun's handling of security vulnerabilities. With focuses on speed, quality, and constant communication with customers, Sun is a recognized leader in security response. Derrick began his career at Sun more than 12 years ago as a service engineer. He has also held positions as a sustaining engineer and a program manager before taking the reins of the security coordination team in 2000. Derrick is also the current president and chairman of the steering committee of Forum of Incident Response and Security Teams (FIRST), which is a global forum of member teams who work together on multiple aspects of security. Derrick holds a B.S. degree in computer and electrical engineering from Purdue University and an MBA degree from Santa Clara University.

Dedication

Dedicated to Ljiljana and Adela. Thank you for your support.

Acknowledgments

This book would not be possible without the help of many people who influenced and helped me learn throughout the years. The complete list would be too long to mention, so here are only a few names.

Damir Delija, Nevenko Bartolinãiç, Davorin Bengez, and Samuel Polenus—we started learning together and remained friends all these years.

Thanks to my current and former teammates in Cisco PSIRT, for we went through a lot together. Many times we were making up things as we went, guessing and blundering, but we were always there to help each other.

A big thank you to Ilker Temir and Paul Oxman for providing comments on early versions of this book. Also thanks go to Tara Flanagan, legal counselor at Cisco; Terrence Palfrey, prosecutor at The Crown Prosecution Service in London; and Etsuo Doi, managing partner at the Tokyo office and the Japan Practice Group of Foley & Lardner LLP, who provided advice on legal aspects of computer incident response in the USA, UK, and Japan.

Special thanks to Mike Caudill, who provided some of the material included in this book.

Although all these people helped in the creation of this book by providing advice and content, any errors that might have remained are mine.

Contents at a Glance

Contents

Introduction

This book is actually two books in one. The first six chapters are about forming and running a computer incident response team. Starting with Chapter 7, "Product Security Vulnerabilities," the book is devoted to managing product security vulnerabilities. The reason these two subjects are combined into a single book is that they are connected. Attackers use security vulnerabilities to compromise a device. Remove vulnerabilities from the product and it becomes so much more resilient to attacks.

For many companies, incident response is new territory. Some companies do not have incident response teams (IRT). Some would like to have them but need guidance to start, and others would like to improve existing practices. Today, only a handful of companies have mature and experienced teams. For that reason, this book provides guidance in both creating and running an effective incident response team. Organizations that are evaluating whether to invest in an IRT, or that are starting to build one, will find the information in this book to be invaluable in helping them understand the nature of the threats, justifying resources, and building effective IRTs. Established IRTs will also benefit from the best practices highlighted in building IRTs and information on the current state of incident response handling, incident coordination, and legal issues. In an ideal world, this book can provide all the right answers for how to handle every incident; however, because every situation is unique, this book strives instead to help you ask the right questions.

Similarly for managing product security vulnerabilities, the sad truth is that many vendors prefer to live in denial rather than face the truth—vendors who would rather cover up information about vulnerabilities than remove the problem. Only a handful of responsible vendors do the right thing and face the problem and not hide from it. Other vendors should follow their lead and establish their product security teams, join the community, and start making a difference. This is especially important because the protocols underpinning the Internet are starting to show their age. We are now witnessing a rise in the number of vulnerabilities that affect these basic protocols (such as DNS, TLS, and TCP), and these vulnerabilities affect virtually every device that can be connected to the Internet. Vendors without product security teams cannot react properly, or at all, on these vulnerabilities and leave their customers exposed. Ultimately, vendors ignore product security at their own peril, as customers will move away from them and go to vendors who know how to manage vulnerabilities.

Goals and Methods

This book has several goals; the two main ones follow:

- To help you establish computer incident response teams, if you do not have them, and give you ideas how to improve operation of the existing ones.

- To help vendors in understanding that their products will contain security vulnerabilities no matter how hard they try to avoid them and to form a team and processes to manage these vulnerabilities.

Accepting problems might not be easy, and other factors, such as organization culture, can make this acceptance even more difficult, but it must be done. Interestingly, when the organization accepts the existence of the problems, it can benefit, as some examples in the book show.

When talking about a particular aspect of either an incident response or vulnerability management, this book always tries to formulate a problem, present options, and discuss relative merits of the options. This presents a balanced view on the matter. In some instances, the book offers suggestions on how things should be done. Apart from a few cases in which these actions may be dictated by laws, these suggestions are mine. Both of the areas (incident response and vulnerability management) are largely unregulated, so you are not forced to act according to these suggestions. Finally, there are cases in which there is no right or wrong answer and you are free to explore. In such instances, the book offers hints, usually in the form of questions, on how to define boundaries and parameters of the action or requirement.

Topics Not Covered

In the incident response part of the book, the biggest area not covered is forensics. Despite the fact that forensics is a large part of daily routine of many teams, I refrained from covering that topic. There is a plethora of good sources on forensics, so this book will not try to replace those. Other major topics not covered are malware analysis and operating system (OS) hardening for the same reason.

In the products security part of the book, areas that are not covered are secure (defensive) programming, product development lifecycle, negative (robustness) testing, and other development-related topics. Each of these areas deserves a book unto itself, and in many cases there already are several published books, so it is better to focus on an area that has not received as much exposure.

Who Should Read This Book?

In the same way both subjects are multifaceted, so is the target audience. Some chapters contain more technical information, whereas others deal with legal or managerial issues. Although the overall tone is closer to team managers and the level or two above, I strongly believe that each team member must be cognizant of all issues described in this book. Because security touches organization at so many points and deals with many intertwined things, it is impossible to perform a good job from a narrow view. Only by having full awareness of as many aspects of incident handling and product security (as the case might be) will the team be able to deliver outstanding performance.

There is no prerequisite knowledge for understanding this book apart from general knowledge about computers, operating systems, networks, and network protocols. In parts that demand deeper technical knowledge, sufficient information is provided to aid understanding to make the book as accessible to nontechnical decision makers as it is to security professionals.

How This Book Is Organized

Although this book can be read cover-to-cover, it is designed to be flexible and enable you to easily move between chapters and sections of chapters to cover just the material of interest.

Chapters 1 through 6 deal with computer incident response and cover the following topics:

- **Chapter 1, "Why Care About Incident Response?"**—This chapter covers the various reasons an organization should set up an incident response team (IRT). Some of the reasons are simply to protect the organization, but others are legal in nature.

- **Chapter 2, "Forming an IRT"**—If you want to form an IRT, this chapter provides ideas on how to go about it: how to make your case to upper management, how to defend your budget, where to place the team within the organizational hierarchy, and what policies you might want to put in place.

- **Chapter 3, "Operating an IRT"**—This chapter provides ideas about how to operate a successful IRT. It does not discuss technical details about how to address a particular incident but instead covers how to prepare the team for effective incident handling. It also gives information on what other groups within the organization should be involved and when and why.

- **Chapter 4, "Dealing with an Attack"**—After an attack has been detected, how do you handle it effectively? That is the question this chapter answers. Again, it does not provides concrete answers on how to deal with compromised passwords, for example, but what process to follow to manage an attack situation well.

- **Chapter 5, "Incident Coordination"**—Rarely, an incident is limited to only a single organization. Miscreants routinely use compromised computers to mount further attacks. This chapter deals with the issues of incident coordination. What are the important issues when working jointly with other IRTs? And what about when law enforcement gets involved?

- **Chapter 6, "Getting to Know Your Peers: Teams and Organizations Around the World"**—Sometimes it might feel that you alone are fighting all the badness in the world, but that is not the case. There are many IRTs around the globe, and they work with each other. This chapter presents some of them and some more significant forums where various teams are coming together. This knowledge helps greatly when dealing with an incident that involves someone from the other side of the globe or to understand the latest attacks that you have discovered in your network.

Chapters 7 through 13 deal with managing product security vulnerabilities and cover the following topics:

- **Chapter 7, "Product Security Vulnerabilities"**—This chapter introduces the theme of product security vulnerability. It talks about defining what vulnerability is, differences between a vulnerability and a feature, and their severity.

- **Chapter 8, "Creating a Product Security Team"**—Discusses details pertinent to the creation of a product security team. Issues common to forming the IRT, such as budget considerations, are not discussed again here because they are covered in detail in Chapter 2, "Forming an IRT." This chapter deals only with issues specific to forming the product security team.

- **Chapter 9, "Operating a Product Security Team"**—Gives details on what is needed to operate a successful product security team. Irrespective of a vendor, every product security team must have resources to test reports and record the information. It also must establish a relationship with key partners, such as third parties that provide components for the products. This chapter describes some of the issues that will be encountered in this process.

- **Chapter 10, "Actors in Vulnerability Handling"**—No single team or vendor exists in isolation. This chapter provides an overview on who can be involved in the whole product vulnerability space and what their motivations might be. This chapter also lists key forums that vendors can use as a vehicle to establish contact with each other.

- **Chapter 11, "Security Vulnerability Handling by Vendors"**—This chapter describes in detail steps to deal with a vulnerability—starting from receiving a report on potential vulnerability all the way to publishing a notification. Even though the exact steps each vendor will make while dealing with the vulnerability are unique for that vendor, the overall process is common for everyone. This common process is the focus of this chapter.

- **Chapter 12, "Security Vulnerability Notification"**—After a remedy is produced, a vendor wants to notify its customers about the vulnerability and its remedy. This seemingly simple document requires much more effort than many initially assume. This chapter discusses various issues related to the notification, from what types a vendor may need and why, to language and dissemination, and finishes with the document maintenance.

- **Chapter 13, "Vulnerability Coordination"**—More and more, a vulnerability can affect multiple vendors. This chapter talks about issues related to vulnerability coordination. Why would a vendor consent to be coordinated by an external party? Who can be a coordinator and what would be required to be a good one? These and other questions are covered in this chapter.

Chapter 1

Why Care About Incident Response?

Some organizations think that, given the right technology, computer security is something that they do not have to worry about too much. After all, maybe they just purchased the best firewall on the market and its installation is complete. Is there anything more to do? There is. Technology is not a panacea, so knowledgeable people are needed to understand what is going on with an incident and to make considered decisions.

You need people who will know whether a series of events is just a sequence of unrelated occurrences or a clever attempt to subvert the security of the organization—and they need to know how to counteract it. Without this knowledge, the organization will remain vulnerable to attacks and represent an easy target. And attacked it will be.

These same people from the incident response team can tell you that the organization can be targeted for any number of reasons. Financial gain is always the biggest motivation, but you might become a target for a host of other reasons. Knowing these reasons and who may perpetrate attacks can help you prepare and defend the organization. The organization can invest in effective security measures rather than expending resources on the newest fads.

Before this book delves deeply into the details of computer incident response, this chapter introduces the threats and reasons to have a dedicated incident response team.

Instead of an Introduction

Early in the morning, around 3:00 a.m., a telephone wakes you up. While you are trying to regain your faculties, an excited and anxious voice on the other end of the line explains to you that someone is stealing data from your company database. He tried to stop this incident but was unsuccessful. He called you because you are a "senior IT guy" who knows "security stuff" and now expects you to tell him what to do. What would you tell him? Can you recommend some specific technical measures? Do you want to take the database offline? If you take the database offline, what business consequences would that have on the organization? Or do you even know what database he is talking about? And why did he call you? There must be someone else to take care of that problem. You do not know who that someone is but, surely, there must be someone else because you are only a senior network designer. And while this conversation is ongoing, the organization is leaking data, company secrets, and intellectual properties. Years of work and investment are now stolen and available for anyone to buy cheaply.

The way to prevent this imaginary scenario from becoming your reality is to realize that computer incidents can happen to you and that you must be ready to deal with them when they happen. Apart from wanting to be prepared, are there any other reasons you must pay attention to incident response? In fact, there are multiple reasons for that. Let's list the main ones.

Reasons to Care About Responding to Incidents

Following are several of the most compelling reasons to formulate a considered and clear response to security incidents:

- Business impacts

- Legal reasons

- Being part of a critical infrastructure

- Direct costs

- Loss of life

Business Impacts

Computer security incidents can, and do, have impact on your business or organization. These impacts can manifest in various ways. You might be unable to conduct normal business, such as receiving orders or providing a service to your customers. You might find that an incident can affect the confidence in your product or your brand. Additionally, attacks can have a negative effect on the stock price of publicly traded companies. In the study, "The Economic Cost of Publicly Announced Information Security Breaches," a correlation was found between a decrease in the stock price of companies that suffered an incident in which company confidential information was lost. The study also found that the effect on the stock price depended on the type of the incident. Incidents in which a company asset was lost and viewed as nonrecoverable had a much higher impact than other types of incidents, such as a short-lived denial-of-service attack. Although a dedicated incident response team cannot prevent all incidents from happening, its work can limit an incident's severity and damage to the organization.

A great example of negative brand impact is facing some members of the financial services industry. One type of attack, known as phishing, often targets customers of large banks. A phishing attack typically involves a fabricated email that appears legitimate to convince an unsuspecting victim to visit a rogue website to "confirm" personal account information. Behind the scenes, an attacker is harvesting the information provided for later criminal activity, such as credit card fraud, withdrawing funds from accounts, or identity theft.

Given that cost savings are realized via Internet banking as opposed to paying human bank tellers, those savings, revenues, and profits can change if customers move to a different institution over concerns regarding the safety and well-being of their accounts. Additionally, in most cases, if customers prove that they were victims, the bank will refund stolen money, thus realizing additional loss.

Legal Reasons

Legal concerns can also dictate actions required in response to an incident. In the United States, various laws might be applicable to the organization or the data handled by the organization.

For example, the State of California enacted SB 1386, which went into effect on July 1, 2003. SB 1386 requires:

> ...a state agency, or a person or business that conducts business in California, that owns or licenses computerized data that includes personal information, as defined, to disclose in specified ways, any breach of the security of the data, as defined, to any resident of California whose unencrypted personal information was, or is reasonably believed to have been, acquired by an unauthorized person.

In 1996, the United States Congress passed the Health Insurance Portability and Accountability Act, or HIPAA, which describes the protections that must be in place for organizations that process healthcare-related information. Violation of HIPAA can have direct consequences on individuals held accountable under the act via both fines and or prison sentences.

Under the Sarbanes-Oxley act of 2002, individuals within corporate executive leadership are held personally accountable for the accuracy of financial reports for their organization.

These are examples of United States laws; other countries have enacted similar laws. For example, the Canadian government enacted the Personal Information Protection and Electronic Documents Act (PIPEDA) on April 13, 2000, which specifies rules governing the collection, use, and disclosure requirements for personal information by Canadian organizations.

Many of these data protection requirements not only require organizations to take proper steps to protect the data, but also respond to any incidents and report any breaches of confidentiality or integrity of the data. No matter where you are located or doing business, be sure to investigate the legal requirements for data protection that could apply. You will need to ensure that your incident response team is aware of any applicable laws and that any necessary actions to comply with those laws are part of the incident response plan for your organization.

Being Part of a Critical Infrastructure

On May 22, 1998, United States President Bill Clinton issued Presidential Decision Directive 63 (more commonly referred to as PDD-63) in which critical national infrastructure was defined as the following:

> ...those physical and cyber-based systems essential to the minimum operations of the economy and government. They include, but are not limited to, telecommunications, energy, banking and finance, transportation, water systems, and emergency services, both governmental and private.

PDD-63 instructed the federal government, state and local governments, and the private sector to take steps to ensure that

> Any interruptions or manipulations of these critical functions must be brief, infrequent, manageable, geographically isolated, and minimally detrimental....

As of December 2003, the PDD-63 has been superseded by Homeland Security Presidential Directive/HSPD-7, which expands on PDD-63 but does not change things fundamentally. It still calls for protecting U.S. critical national infrastructure.

The PDD-63 specifically called for the establishment of Information Sharing and Analysis Centers (ISAC) within each identified critical infrastructure segment for quicker and more efficient analysis and dissemination of information that could be used for minimizing the impact of an incident. At the time of publishing, 15 ISACs exist in the United States.

In the United Kingdom, the National Infrastructure Security Co-ordination Centre (NISCC) was established in 1999, with a charter to minimize the risk to the UK Critical National Infrastructure (CNI) from an electronic attack. In 2007, NISCC became a part of a larger organization now known under the name Centre for the Protection on National Infrastructure (CPNI), which provides advice on physical, personal, and computer-related aspects to business and organizations that make up UK CNI. The UK's definition of CNI is fairly similar to the U.S. definition:

> Within the nine national infrastructure sectors there are critical elements (these may be physical or electronic), the loss or compromise of which would have a major detrimental impact on the availability or integrity of essential services, leading to severe economic or social consequences or to loss of life. These critical elements of infrastructure comprise the nation's critical national infrastructure.

These are two examples of countries that have established partnerships between government and the private sector to minimize the risk and impact on components of critical infrastructures within those countries. Effective incident response is a key element in minimizing detrimental effects.

Following are other countries that have similar approaches (the list is not exhaustive):

- Australia
- Austria
- Canada

- Finland

- France

- Germany

- India

- Italy

- Japan

- Republic of Korea

- Malaysia

- The Netherlands

- New Zealand

- Norway

- Russia

- Singapore

- Sweden

- Switzerland

If the service provided by your organization currently falls within a CNI sector or could be a part of the CNI in the future, you should seriously consider forming a dedicated team to deal with computer incidents. If you are not in one of the countries listed here, there is a chance that your government is thinking about protecting its CNI, and you could be part of that plan.

Direct Costs

Many times, incidents have direct costs that might not be immediately recognized. There is a cost for having staff deal with incidents as opposed to doing their normal job. Your organization might be liable for paying additional fees for extra bandwidth utilization, staff payroll (both during business hours and after business hours, especially if overtime pay is involved), and the cost of time wasted while control is established. And, in rare cases, this cost can be even higher.

One such incident involved an Internet service provider in the UK named CloudNine. In January 2002, CloudNine was the victim of a massive denial-of-service attack. In an online news article dated January 24, 2002, ZDNET reported:

> Cloud Nine closed down on Tuesday morning, blaming a vicious DoS attack that it claimed had disabled its servers and caused serious damage to its business. The ISP told its customers that because its insurance would not cover the cost of bringing its servers back online, it was forced to sell up.

Another example, from May 5, 2006, involves an Israeli security firm named Blue Security. Blue Security offered an antispam service for dealing with unsolicited bulk email. In a message sent to the Internet Storm Center at SANS.org, Guy Rosen from Blue Security described the attacks:

Monday: Spam-based threats and accusations.

Tuesday: Our website www.bluesecurity.com is cut off from outside of Israel by a mysterious routing change.

—Later on, huge DDoSes lash out at our service's servers (but NOT the www, note!), with adverse effects to several different hosting facilities in which they were located.

—To restore access to our inaccessible www site and keep our users informed, we restore an old blog we had and point www there.

—Within about an hour, a DDoS attacks the blog site on which that blog was located.

Wednesday: Massive DDoS goes out at our domain's DNS provider, causing a service outage that affected their customers.

Thursday: DoSes continue as we relocate our service to bring it back up. One estimate was of something of the order of 10 million packets/sec coming in.

Friday: Today we are slowly coming back up and hope to see the service working soon.

Ultimately, Blue Security went out of business. The May 17, 2006 online edition of *The Washington Post* reported that Blue Security

...will wave a virtual white flag and surrender. The company will shut down this morning and its website will display a message informing its customers about the closure.

Loss of Life

Normally, people do not consider that computer incidents can directly lead to a loss of life, but they can. On September 7, 2001, a team of surgeons successfully completed a gall bladder removal from a patient in Strasbourg, France. What made this surgery different was that the surgeons were on the other side of the Atlantic Ocean in New York City. They were performing the operation remotely on a patient in France using a technology known as remote surgery or telesurgery.

Various organizations are working to bring telesurgery to the mainstream. One such idea is to have a "medical pad" that could be deployed remotely. A person in need of surgery will be placed in it, and a surgeon will perform the operation remotely. If realized to its full extent, this idea could save many lives because it is much easier to deploy such multiple pads in an area hit by an earthquake than to fly tens of surgeons from multiple countries. The stakes in telesurgery are high. If the network comes under attack, the information telling the robotic hand to stop cutting can be delayed. A delay of a fraction of a second can make a difference between cutting only an affected tissue and cutting an artery.

Another example how computer incidents can directly put lives in danger is air travel. An investigation into the crash of Spanair flight 5022 in 2008 brought to light evidence that the plane's central computer system was infected with malware. At this time, it is not certain what role, if any, malware played in the crash, but an idea of hijacking a plane via malware is not far fetched—especially if the innovation brought by Boeing's 787 Dreamliner airplane is accepted by other manufacturers.

In Boeing's Dreamliner, passengers will be able to use a computer network during the flight. Not only that, but some elements of that network are shared with the airplane's flight-safety, control, and navigation system. Although in the Spanair case, it is suspected that malware was brought into the system via a USB stick, which assumes physical access, in Dreamliner there is a potential for attacks using a local network that increases the number of people who might be tempted to plant malware into an airplane's system. Boeing Dreamliner can seat from 210 to 290 passengers, so the potential for loss of life is great.

How Did We Get Here or "Why Me?"

Computer and computer assisted incidents are nothing new. As soon as a new technology is developed, malicious people will find ways to abuse it. If we recall that the first commercial computers were put into operation in 1951, we should not be too surprised that some of the first documented cases of computer misuses are from the early 1960s.

It is interesting to note how common knowledge says that computer incidents are associated with hackers and script kiddies—that these hacker and script kiddies were attacking devices on the Internet first for fun and, only later, for profit. But the sad truth is that it was always about money. Some of the early computer cases were quite profitable, as is the case with James Harlowe, who embezzled almost $1,000,000 USD from 1963–1969. Those miscreants who were attacking for fun were just an aberration. People were misusing computers to gain money from the beginning. The stakes have grown from the 60s because organized crime has now joined the game.

Usually the answer to the question of why someone would attack me and my organization is that you have something that can be monetized. But occasionally, there might be some other reasons, as listed here.

Corporate Espionage

Corporate espionage is nothing new. It existed almost from the time when trade itself was invented. The difference is only how it is being done, which is by someone who can walk into a building and walk away with a big pile of papers or, what is more likely to happen nowadays, just send documents via email or take them home on a memory stick or iPod. Dependence on physical access to the documents to steal the information is not a requirement anymore because much of the intellectual property today exists in electronic form. New product designs, financial data, information on mergers and acquisitions that have not been announced, customer lists, and source code are all just examples that an attacker might be after. Another option is to steal a device that contains data. That can be a laptop computer, PDA, or mobile phone. All are small and each can store an amazing amount of data.

Corporations and government agencies are the most usual targets for espionage. Some of the more known cases are theft of the source code for Cisco IOS and Microsoft's Windows 2000 and NT. Example of alleged espionage in government agencies is theft of nuclear weapons data from Los Alamos Nuclear Laboratory and selling them to China.

Unintended Consequences

Not all attacks are maliciously or financially motivated. Such was the case in 2003, when the University of Wisconsin suffered a denial-of-service attack due to a flood of Network Time Protocol (NTP) requests. The source of the NTP traffic was generated by up to 707,147 Netgear brand routers around the world that were configured to synchronize their clocks once a second with the network time server located at the University of Wisconsin. The result of an unintentional configuration error in the manufacturing of those routers ended up being a very serious situation for the university because it experienced high traffic loads on its network and time servers.

A scenario like that is not necessarily a one-time occurrence. In April 2006, the Danish Internet Exchange (DIX) contacted D-Link, accusing the company of creating a denial of service against its NTP servers due to a large number of D-Link routers querying its servers directly. For a network designed to have approximately 2000 legitimate users of a service, an exponential increase in usage can create a denial of service (sometimes a long-lasting one) to be dealt with.

Government-Sponsored Cyber Attacks

Governments are also jumping into the fray and are actively developing cyber-warfare capabilities. Two governments widely known to have such capabilities are the United States (Joint Functional Component Command—Network Warfare, JFCC-NW) and China. There should be no doubts that other countries are also developing their capabilities.

It is also alleged that some of the governments use their cyber capabilities not to attack but for intelligence purposes, as is the case with malware-based electronic surveillance of the Office of His Holiness the Dalai Lama. Incidents with Google also illustrate how, allegedly, China has used its cyber capabilities to attack Google corporate infrastructure and steal intellectual property.

Terrorism and Activism

Depending on what business your organization is in, who you are, or what you symbolize, you might be targeted by terrorists and organizations that employ terror methods to achieve their goals. This category contains not only organizations such as Hizballah and al-Qa'ida, but also animal rights extremists. All of them are known to use cyber attacks in lieu of physical attacks.

Summary

There are numerous reasons why you should form your own incident response team. Technology on its own, no matter how sophisticated, cannot solve problems. People are needed to solve problems. The costs of attacks in any form are real and can have a serious impact on an organization. And you can become a target for any number of reasons.

The ability to take precautions early and respond quickly to an incident is critical. This is only possible with a dedicated incidence response team, and the aim of this book is to help you form one. If you already do have such a team, this book can help you improve it.

References

2002. H.R. 3763, Sarbanes-Oxley Act of 2002. Available at news.findlaw.com/cnn/docs/gwbush/sarbanesoxley072302.pdf. [Accessed September 27, 2010].

2003. Homeland Security Presidential Directive 7: Critical Infrastructure Identification, Prioritization, and Protection. Available at http://www.dhs.gov/xabout/laws/gc_1214597989952.shtm. [Accessed September 27, 2010].

Anderson, R. and Nagaraja, S., 2009. "Computer Laboratory—Technical reports: UCAM-CL-TR-746." Available at http://www.cl.cam.ac.uk/techreports/UCAM-CL-TR-746.html. [Accessed July 31, 2010].

Arrest in Cisco source code theft, BBC News, http://news.bbc.co.uk/1/hi/technology/3672242.stm, Sept. 20, 2004.

Cloud Nine sells up after DoS attack, ZDNet UK, Graeme Wearden, http://news.zdnet.co.uk/internet/0,39020369,2103098,00.htm, January 24, 2002.

The Collapse of Barings Bank, TIME, Howard Chua-Eoan, http://www.time.com/time/2007/crimes/18.html.

Computer Capers: Tales of Electronic Thievery, Embezzlement, and Fraud, Thomas Whiteside, published by Thomas Y. Crowell, 1978.

CPNI, http://www.cpni.gov.uk/.

Department of Justice Canada, 2000. Personal Information Protection and Electronic Documents Act. Available at http://laws.justice.gc.ca/en/P-8.6/FullText.html. [Accessed September 27, 2010].

Drummond, D., 2010. Official Google Blog: A new approach to China. Available at http://googleblog.blogspot.com/2010/01/new-approach-to-china.html. [Accessed August 1, 2010].

The Economic Cost of Publicly Announced Information Security Breaches: Empirical Evidence from the Stock Market, Campbell, K., L.A. Gordon, M.P. Loeb, and L. Zhou, *Journal of Computer Security*, 11(2003), pages 431–448.

Email from Guy Rosen at Blue Security, SANS, Guy Rosen,
http://isc.sans.org/diary.php?storyid=1311, May 5, 2005.

FBI: Cyber Blackmail by Animal Rights Hackers, The Blotter, ABC News,
http://blogs.abcnews.com/theblotter/2006/04/fbi_cyber_black.html, April 28, 2006.

FBI Makes Arrest in Windows Source Code, eWeek.com, Ryan Naraine,
http://www.eweek.com/article2/0,1895,1724978,00.asp, November 11, 2004.

Flawed Routers Flood University of Wisconsin Internet Time Server, Dave Plonka,
http://www.cs.wisc.edu/~plonka/netgear-sntp/, August 21, 2003.

Huston, C., "UNIVAC in Pittsburgh 1953–1963—Folklore." Available at
https://wiki.cc.gatech.edu/folklore/index.php/UNIVAC_in_Pittsburgh_1953-1963.
[Accessed July 31, 2010].

In the Fight Against Spam E-Mail, Goliath Wins Again, The Washington Post, Brian
Krebs, Wednesday, May 17, 2006; Page A01, http://www.washingtonpost.com/wp-
dyn/content/article/2006/05/16/AR2006051601873.html.

Information Operations and Cyberwar: Capabilities and Related Policy Issues, CRS
Report for Congress, Clay Wilson, http://www.fas.org/irp/crs/RL31787.pdf, September
14, 2006.

Infosecurity (USA), "FAA Plays Down Boeing 787 Security Concerns." Available at
http://www.infosecurity-us.com/view/1196/faa-plays-down-boeing-787-security-
concerns-/. [Accessed August 25, 2010].

*International CIIP Handbook 2006, Vol. I, Comprehensive Risk Analysis and
Management Network*, Isabelle Abele-Wigert and Myriam Dunn, May 2005,
http://www.crn.ethz.ch/projects/current/detail.cfm?id=15165.

ISAC Council Home Page. Available at http://www.isaccouncil.org/. [Accessed July 31,
2010].

Meredith, L., "Malware Implicated in Fatal Spanair Plane Crash," LiveScience. Available at
http://www.livescience.com/technology/malware-spanair-plane-crash-100820.html.
[Accessed August 25, 2010].

Military and Security Developments Involving the People's Republic of China 2010,
US Department of Defense, Secretary of Defense,
http://www.defense.gov/pubs/pdfs/2010_CMPR_Final.pdf, 2010.

Nature, "The cutting edge in surgery," Vicki Brower. Available at
http://www.nature.com/embor/journal/v3/n4/full/embor175.html. [Accessed July 31, 2010].

Net clocks suffering data deluge, Mark Ward, BBC News,
http://news.bbc.co.uk/2/hi/technology/4906138.stm, April 13, 2006.

Presidential Decision Directives/NCS 63, Critical Infrastructure Protection,
http://www.fas.org/irp/offdocs/pdd/pdd-63.htm, May 22, 1998.

Teen Hackers Crash Hizbollah ISP, Newsfactor Network, Robyn Weisman, http://www.newsfactor.com/perl/story/6880.html, January 22, 2001.

Wen Ho Lee Reporters Held in Contempt, *The Washington Post*, Neely Tucker, http://www.washingtonpost.com/wp-dyn/articles/A13508-2004Aug18.html, Thursday, August 19, 2004; Page A02.

Chapter 2

Forming an IRT

Like it or not, attacks do happen. Not all attacks are successful in a way that they result in a compromise, but they do happen. That is a fact of life, and it cannot be ignored. Attackers, in general, are opportunistic. They do not care whether you are a big company or just a small family business with a single computer or if you are an international bank or local charity. If your computers can be compromised, they most probably will be.

After you are attacked, you need to react fast to limit potential damage and, if the worst happens, to prevent further compromises. Any such reaction cannot be the result of an ad-hoc process. Not being prepared will only lead to confusion and an inadequate response. Not having dedicated people and proper procedures in place will practically make an efficient response impossible. If nobody looks for signs of compromises, how can the organization know that it has been compromised? Without a dedicated team to handle computer incidents, it is much harder to fulfill that obligation.

The definition of a team is a group tasked with dealing with attacks to the organization from outside or inside and attempts to attack other systems from within the organization. Depending on the organization's actual size, the team might be composed of only a single person or have more than 100 people.

When talking to people who work in this field, you might encounter the following acronyms: CERT, CIRT, IRT, and ERT. CERT stands for Computer Emergency Response Team, CIRT is Computer Incident Response Team, IRT is simply Incident Response Team, and ERT is Emergency Response Team. Occasionally, you might see an "S" (for "Security") in these acronyms, so we also can have CSIRT, SIRT, or SERT. For our purposes, we treat all these acronyms as equal and use mostly IRT or IR Team. The assumption is that a dedicated team of people exists and that their primary job is (or, at least, the major portion of their time is devoted to) fighting computer-related incidents.

This chapter provides useful guidelines and outline options for the process of establishing an Incident Response Team. Examples illustrate some points or options, but these examples must not be taken as exclusive of other possibilities. There are no universally correct or universally incorrect ways to do something. Hundreds of IR teams exist worldwide, and each has some unique characteristics and others shared with other IRTs. You can decide how to apply the guidelines to your situation.

This chapter is tailored to present a situation in a sizable organization and to encompass fairly complex interactions. This is not to say that small organizations do not need to cover the same ground—they do. It is just that, for the small organization, the interaction between different parts of the organization is less complex. As the size of an organization and complexity of the interaction increases, you can easily revisit this chapter at a later stage and see what else you can take away from the text.

Steps in Establishing an IRT

Establishing an IRT is a process in which we can identify several distinct steps:

Step 1.   Define the constituency.

Step 2.   Ensure upper-management support.

Step 3.   Secure funding.

Step 4.   Place the IRT within the organization's hierarchy.

Step 5.   Determine whether the team will be central, distributed, or virtual.

Step 6.   Develop policies and procedures.

The order of the steps is not necessarily linear as it appears here, and often the steps overlap each other or are taken in a different order. What's more important is the meaning of each step and what you are trying to accomplish by it, because that is what all incident response teams must go through in their formative stages. Some of the steps will have to be revisited even after the team's formation; for example, the IRT might want to change the scope of its constituency, or a new incident response team might be created within the constituency. Revisiting steps is not specifically pointed out in the rest of the text because each team should be able to decide this by itself. Let us now examine these steps in more detail.

Define Constituency

Defining the constituency is the first step in the process. Who will the IR team serve? Will the IRT cover only the organization or also entities external to the organization? Will that be only a part of the host organization or all of it? If external entities will be included, how will they be selected? Here is how some of the existing teams define their constituency:

■   **Internal to the organization:** The team handles only attacks directed toward the organization or originating from it. In many organizations, this kind of team is usually known as IT Security. One example is the Cisco Computer Security Incident Response Team (CSIRT).

- **External to the organization:** The team handles attacks only if they are not directed to or from the organization. An example is the Cisco Product Security Incident Response Team (PSIRT), which handles attacks to Cisco customers but not ones to and from Cisco itself because they will be handled by the Cisco CSIRT.

- **Mixed constituency:** This can encompass all entities somehow related but not necessarily under the organization's direct management. There are several ways in which this relationship can be defined. The next two examples present some of them:

  - **Belong to a common Autonomous System (AS):** An AS number, used in routing to denote an administrative domain that covers all institutions under AS559 (for example, Swiss Education and Research Network CERT [SWITCH-CERT]).

  - **Common domain name:** JANET is a network that connects educational and research organizations within the United Kingdom to each other and to the rest of the world. JANET CSIRT's constituency is all institutions that have .ac.uk in their domain name; in other words, all education and research institutions in the UK.

- **National team:** All citizens and organizations operating within a country are entitled to ask their national team for help. In reality, it is usually only organizations that use the service. Japan CERT Coordination Centre (JPCERT/CC) is an example of such a team.

- **National critical infrastructure:** These teams work only with organizations that are part of a critical national infrastructure (CNI). Usually that includes the financial sector, utilities (electricity, gas, water, and so on), transport, government institutions, military, police, and others as defined by that nation.

- **Organizations that subscribe to a service:** IBM Managed Security Service (IBM MSS) is one example. Whoever buys managed security service from IBM automatically receives the IBM MSS team's services.

Defining the constituency is a prime example of where no universal recommendations exist for what must be done when forming an IRT. The constituency can depend on your mission (for example, "to protect critical national infrastructure"), your geographic location, or your ambition (that is, trying to capture the market). Whatever your constrains and ambitions are, you must address two further issues:

- Overlapping constituencies

- Asserting your authority over the constituency

Overlapping Constituencies

What will happen when one constituent is part of the constituency of multiple IRTs? Take, for example, Balliol College in Oxford, UK. On one hand, as one of the oldest colleges in Oxford, it is covered by Oxford University CERT (OxCERT). According to its domain, balliol.ox.ac.uk, it is also part of the JANET CSIRT constituency. Providing that the college has some Cisco equipment, it is also entitled to receive help from Cisco PSIRT.

If multiple IRTs claim or assert themselves on a part of your chosen constituency, an agreement must be reached to determine the role and rules of engagement. An organization can be part of the constituency of multiple teams as long as all involved teams have a clear picture of their respective role and influence on the organization. Occasionally, it can be beneficial for the institution to use another IRT as a backup if its primary IR team does not have sufficient coverage (for example, the primary IRT does not have 24×7 coverage, whereas the other does).

Two things must be done here. The first is to open a dialog with other IRTs that claim your constituent, and the second thing is to talk with the constituent. Dialog with other IRTs can clarify the roles of each of the IRTs involved, such as when and how they plan to be engaged and what services they can provide. Work with these other IRTs to develop rules of engagement acceptable to all.

Talking with the constituent will provide you with a picture of how and when it engages with other IRTs. You should not be surprised if the constituent is completely oblivious that it can use services from multiple teams! Your job is to present the engagement rules to the constituent and explain what services it can expect from each of the IRTs it belongs to.

Asserting Your Authority Over the Constituency

It is not sufficient to select only your constituency; you must make sure that constituency knows about the team, and the team must be accepted by it. At first, the IRT must advertise its existence and services that it provides. This part of the process is ongoing because there will always be new organizations that might not know about the IR team. The next step is to be accepted by the constituency. You can claim to represent your constituency, but if it uses another IRT to handle its security incidents, your claim is without any validity. This situation can arise not only when multiple IR teams are claiming the same constituency, but also when the constituency satisfies its needs by itself.

If the IRT is to handle only incidents internal to the organization, this might not be a problem. The authority issue can be resolved by a memo sent by the higher management declaring that your team is in charge.

When dealing with the constituency that is either external to your organization or that your organization does not have direct influence over, the situation becomes more delicate. One of the best ways to become accepted by your target constituency is to be useful and show results. This approach is valid no matter whether your constituency is internal or external to your organization. Everyone likes to see concrete results, and if your team can show that it brings value, chances are the constituency will accept you and start dealing with you.

The key here is to select some relatively easy reachable goals and communicate to your target constituency when you reach them. One possible starting point can be handling an incident within your organization. After handling a few incidents, make a showcase of your capabilities and present that to the target constituency. Show that the IRT is successful in defending the host organization and how your capabilities and expertise can be used by the constituency.

Obviously, this is not a guarantee that your constituency will accept you. It is quite possible that some of your constituents might already have mature incident handling teams and that they genuinely do not need someone else to "take over" from them. Recognize that, and work with these teams instead of trying to undermine them. Miscreants are already cooperating, so why wouldn't you?

Ensure Upper-Management Support

The next crucial step in forming an IRT is to ensure management support in its mission. That must be done to, among other things, establish authority of the team. One of the usual ways to accomplish that is to have an executive sponsor, someone who believes in the importance of the team and its services and has a presence in the upper-management circles. It's even better if more than one person is convinced of the idea; however, one must be an official team representative.

If the phrase *executive sponsor* sounds too commercial for places such as universities or not-for-profit organizations, it can be substituted with any other suitable title or position. It can be a professor or department head or anyone who is sufficiently high in the organization's hierarchy. For simplicity, we will continue using terms *sponsor* or *executive sponsor* in the remainder of the text.

Generally speaking, the sponsor's task is to provide the nucleus of the team's authority to represent the team in front of the executives and act as a link between the upper-management and the IRT. The following list expands on these roles:

- **Authority:** Can be addressed in a way that upper management sends a message throughout the constituency describing the new situation. The sponsor or upper management needs to periodically repeat that message (for example, on a yearly basis). That can enforce the organization's commitment to support the IRT, remind the existing constituency of that, and for new additions in the constituency, introduce them to the situation.

- **Management handling during the crisis:** Because security incidents can have a profound impact on the host organization, it is the sponsor's duty to keep upper management informed of the situation and be ready to take decisive actions. A worm outbreak, for example, can severely disrupt the organization for a while. In situations like that, the sponsor's role can be to keep other executives apprised of the situation and guide them on what decisions and actions need to be done. In moments of crisis, people tend to overreact and start ordering actions that might not contribute to the solution. The sponsor's role can be to calm down the management and allow the team to handle the situation. Although the IRT should formulate the message, it is the sponsor who can explain it to the management so that the team has more time to deal with the issue.

- **Expert opinion:** In the time of formulating new services or strategies for the organization, it is the sponsor's task to make the management aware of potential security implications. If, for example, the organization would like to open an office at a remote location, what would that mean from an incident handling standpoint? Allowing employees to work from home can significantly alter the organization's security exposure. Things like that should be communicated to the management by the sponsor. To do so, the sponsor must pass some of the plans and ideas to the team, collect the team's situation assessment, and formulate the response to the rest of the management. A good sponsor will also allow individual team members to present in front of the executives. That adds to the team's and the individual's visibility and recognition.

- **Budget:** Last, but not least, the sponsor fights for the team's budget.

Secure Funding and Funding Models

Appropriate funding of an IRT is necessary for its successful operation. It is necessary for the team to have secured premises, required equipment, books, and the opportunity to learn new skills and to travel. Each of these items cost money, and a successful IRT requires a lot of resources.

For most employees, it might be sufficient to possess only a single computer. IRT members might require two to three on average so that suspected malware can be analyzed in an isolated environment. The IR team might also need additional routers and switches if it wants to operate honeynets and honeypots to capture malware samples. Books and courses are also mandatory. Team members must keep pace with new developments and try to be as close to the current state-of-the-art as possible; that means constantly acquiring new skills and keeping them honed.

Travel can be a significant item in the team's budget, but it is unavoidable. This is true even with the broader use of video teleconferencing capabilities. Services such as Cisco WebEx or Skype are a poor substitute for direct contact. Even the top-end solutions, such as Telepresence, cannot completely remove the need for face-to-face meetings. Having said this, video teleconferencing is good to maintain relationships after they are established. There are two main reasons why IRT members must travel: one is to meet with their constituency, and another is to meet their peers from other IRTs. That is essential to establishing a positive rapport that then enables smooth and efficient communication when required. Furthermore, travel must not be limited only to one or two team members but available to all.

As you can see, a successful IRT does needs a budget that can be, in relative terms, larger than most other teams and groups within the organization. The question is, where will that money come from? In the subsequent sections, we look at some funding models and main issues associated with them. The models will not tell you how large a budget you need but will give you ideas of potential sources for the budget. As always, there are no "better" or "worse" models; there are only different models. All funding models described here are used by some of the existing IRTs, which is the testimony that all of them are viable. All you need to do is to select one that suits your situation the best.

The models are as follows:

- IRT as a cost center
- Selling the service internally
- Selling the service externally
- Mixed model

IRT as a Cost Center

This is probably the most common funding model. The budget for the IRT is carved from the overall organization's budget. The biggest issue with this model is that the IRT is treated as a cost center. The IR team does not bring money into the organization but spends it, so nobody is willing to give up part of their budget for the IRT. That perception can make it hard to justify an adequate budget. What can help here is not to look at how much money the IRT brings but how much it saves the organization.

The money for the organization is saved by preventing incidents from happening and, if they do occur, handling them efficiently. Less damage translates into speedier recovery, which means less money required to restore the original state before the compromise. Until the organization establishes a baseline of how many incidents represent a "normal" situation, the only way to gauge a number of incidents the IRT has prevented is to compare its number with the industry average. This average can be estimated from the two surveys that we will look at later. And if because of the IRT your organization experiences fewer attacks, you can easily estimate how much money has been saved. That leads us to the question of how to estimate the cost of an incident.

Cost of an Incident

Unfortunately, there is no single answer to this at the moment. The main reason is that the total cost of an incident is multifaceted. We can first divide it into direct and indirect cost that can be refined even further, as demonstrated in Table 2-1.

Table 2-1 *Direct and Indirect Costs of an Incident*

Direct Cost

Cost Type	Description
Working hours spent by the IRT to work on the incident.	While handling an incident, the IRT staff cannot be proactive and improve the security posture. Overtime hours must be paid.
Working hours lost by the staff whose computers/applications were unusable because of the incident.	Employees' computer can be taken to be cleaned. Databases and other resources might be taken offline. Data must be restored from the backups.

continues

Table 2-1   *Direct and Indirect Costs of an Incident*   *(continued)*

Direct Cost

Cost Type	Description
Failure to pay, or collect payment, ship goods, or deliver services. Some of this can be subject to contract and can carry additional financial consequences if not fulfilled.	If key resources were not accessible, or an employee did not have the equipment, some actions might happen later.
Equipment damaged due the incident.	Rarely, but not impossible, equipment can be damaged during the incident and needs to be replaced.

Indirect Cost

Cost Type	Description
Organization's loss of image.	The organization might be perceived as unreliable. If it cannot protect itself, how can it protect your information, money, and so on?
Loss of opportunity.	Because of resource unavailability (for example, a database offline or an employee without a computer), a sale might not be realized or a new client acquired.
Loss of morale among employees, which can lead to lower efficiency.	Business interruption because of incidents and negative publicity because of compromises can lead to morale loss. Less motivated employees have lower productivity and are more prone to making mistakes.
Purchase of additional hardware, software, or services to cope with further attacks.	Reaction on a compromise can result in purchasing unnecessary equipment (over and beyond what is planned), as management is compelled to "do something." This wastes resources (money and time) and accomplishes little.
Stolen intellectual property and the organization's sensitive information.	This information can be used by competitors to undermine the organization. Some possibilities of how a competitor can misuse this information are adjusting the pricing model to win deals, speeding up its research by using stolen information, patenting ideas as its own, and so on.

Estimating indirect cost is almost impossible. How can you be sure that employees have less enthusiasm because the organization was criticized by the press rather than what is happening in their private life? How can you determine that potential customers decided not to approach your organization because they learned about the incident? The study "The Economic Cost of Publicly Announced Information Security Breaches: Empirical Evidence from the Stock Market" suggests that it is also the type of the incident that can influence losses. It suggests that compromises that involve theft of personal data can have a bigger negative impact than compromises in which no personal data was disclosed. But can you really be sure that a dip in stock price is due to an incident or because of expected slow growth of the organization? You cannot directly measure indirect cost.

The organization can try to collect data on indirect cost through surveys and try to estimate losses based on that information. The survey should probe how important is information on security incidents to the clients when making purchasing decision. This survey should be performed not only when a sale was not realized but also on a regular basis. There are two caveats: one for the survey and another on purchasing. A survey does not need to be a long document that someone must fill in; it can also be in the form of an informal chat. As long as the right questions are asked, the form is of secondary importance. The term "purchasing" is used here to simplify writing. In this context, it encompasses not only the buying and selling of goods, but also of service and investing (for example, opening an account with a particular bank or partnering with an organization).

After the organization collects sufficient information, it can estimate the indirect cost of an incident. Until then, you need to be cognizant that indirect costs exist and calculate only what you can toward the cost of an incident. What you can calculate toward the loss because of an incident is a direct cost.

An estimate of the direct cost, although much easier than an indirect cost, proves not to be straightforward in a general case. The cost depends on a particular organization and value it gives to its assets. It seems also to depend on the geographic region of the organization. Following is a framework of how to calculate direct cost and then three examples to illustrate the range of direct cost. The three examples are

- Incident Cost Analysis and Modeling Project II (I-CAMP II).

- Data from Computer Security Institute's "Computer Crime and Security Survey for 2009." (This book went to print before the survey for 2010 became available.)

- Data from BERR's[1] "2008 Information Security Breaches Survey." (It is a biennial survey, so there is no data for 2009, and this book went to print before the survey for 2010 became available.)

[1] Department for Business, Enterprises & Regulatory Reform, United Kingdom Government.

Framework for Direct Cost Calculation

The framework for calculating the direct cost of an incident is rather straightforward. The following information needs to be available:

- Number of hours spent in dealing with an incident

- Hourly wage of the people involved in handling an incident

- Number of people affected by an incident

- Hourly wage of the people affected by an incident

- How long the affected people were unable to use computer resources

- Overtime and equipment and software purchased to deal with an incident

If you know all this information, it is a simple matter of multiplying and adding these quantities. If you do this for all incidents within a certain time period, dividing the grand total with the number of incident can give you the cost estimate for a single incident.

The framework is simple enough, but the numbers are still hard to come by. One of the biggest obstacles is to account for all the time spent handling an incident and also the number of people affected by it and how long they were not productive. In other words, you are missing the key information.

In reality, the organization can estimate the missing pieces after the IRT is established and starts handling incidents, but what you want is an idea of how much an incident can cost before the IRT is established. Now look at the three examples that provide this estimate.

I-CAMP II Study

The I-CAMP II study focused on the university environment. It had three objectives:

> [...]First the study provides guidelines to cost analyze IT-incidents in the academic environment. Through the use of a template, IT personnel are able to identify true costs and follow a guide in analyzing them....
>
> Second, the study analyzes the status of the databases of the participating institutions and their categorization schemes for classifying incidents. It also begins the examination of the frequencies of occurrence for specific types of incidents in three different periods of time (periods of high, medium, and low academic activity).
>
> Finally, the study provides a categorization scheme as a guide to encourage more incident data gathering and to encourage consistency in the classification process.

We will look only at the results related to the first goal: determining the price of an incident.

During the course of the I-CAMP II study, 15 incidents from 18 U.S. universities were analyzed. The universities that were part of the study experienced more than 15 incidents, and selected incidents were chosen specifically for the purpose of the I-CAMP II study. They are not an indication of how many incidents actually occurred in an individual university.

One of the challenges of the study was to estimate the amount of money that affected students' loss because of an incident. Although finding this cost was easy for the staff, because their wages are known, there is no "student wage" that can be used. This student wage is required for the cost framework because students are likely to be affected by an incident (that is, unable to use computer and network).

The way the I-CAMP study approached the issue of student's wage was to divide an average cost of studying ($10,000 USD) with the number of study hours per semester (672 hours)[2]. Dividing these two values gives a price of 1 hour of study. The price is $15.00 per hour. What is then assumed is that, if students are unable to study because of an incident, they "lose" $15.00 for every hour not studying. It is important to note that this is not a loss in a direct sense; that is, neither the students nor the university will earn less money or lose actual money. It is a virtual hourly wage created only to enable us to calculate a cost of an incident. Table 2-2 provides information of an average cost of an incident depending on an incident type.

Table 2-2 *Average Cost of an Incident in a University Environment*

Incident Type	Number of Occurrences	Cost per Incident in USD
Compromised Access	2	1800
Hacker Attack	3	2100
Harmful Code	3	980
Denial-of-Service	2	22,350
Copyright Violation	5	340

This table shows that a cost of an average incident is approximately $3950 USD. The I-CAMP II was finished in 2000, and the cost figure was valid at that time. Today, that figure will be somewhat higher if you adjust it for inflation—approximately $5500 USD in 2010 with inflation of 3.5%.

The different types of incidents have different price tags. In the university environment, denial-of-service (DoS) attacks are the most expensive, whereas the copyright violations are the least expensive. This is probably because DoS attacks affect many students, whereas the Recording Industry Association of America (RIAA) cease and desist notices about the copyrighted material are handled by a single member of the IRT staff and, possibly, affect only a few students.

Even though some of the numbers might seem low, it would be wrong to be tempted not to react to an incident. Some can have legal ramifications (for example, copyright violation), whereas others can compromise your intellectual property (for example, system penetration). Recall that Stoll Clifford managed to uncover a spy ring only because of a billing discrepancy of $0.75 USD.

---

[2] 12 hours/week per class, 4 class per term, 3.5 months in a semester, and 4 weeks in a month. Multiplying all these values yields the number of studying hours per semester.

CSI Computer Crime and Security Survey

CSI's Computer Crime and Security Survey (formerly known as the SCI/FBI Survey) is conducted on a yearly basis. The survey is sent to hundreds of computer security experts. These experts are employed to safeguard computer assets of organizations such as commercial corporations, financial organizations, government agencies, medical organizations, and universities. The survey is focused on situations in the United States. In 2009, 443 experts responded to the survey.

From the 2009 survey, it is not possible to deduce the cost of a single incident. What is given is an average loss of $234,244 USD per respondent. That figure, presumably, represents the sum of all losses during the year incurred because of computer incidents.

The cost of the top-three incident categories are singled out in the survey and appear in Table 2-3.

Table 2-3   *Average Loss per Respondent for U.S. Commercial Organization*

Incident Type	Average Loss per Respondent in USD
Wireless exploits	$770,000
Theft of personally identifiable or personal health information because of all causes other than mobile device theft and loss	$710,000
Financial fraud	$450,000

BERR's 2008 Information Security Breaches Survey

The Information Security Breaches Survey (ISBS 2008) is a survey sponsored by the UK Department of Trade and Industry and managed by PriceWaterhouseCoopers. In 2008, a little more than 1000 business were randomly selected from a register of UK businesses. The sample consists of very small organizations (fewer than 10 employees) to very large (500 and more) from all parts of the United Kingdom and from all sectors (for example, not-for-profit, government, educational, retail, telecommunication, technology, financial, and so on).

Similarly to CSI's survey, ISBS 2008 does not provide the cost estimate per single incident. Instead, it gives a cost range for the worst incident that an organization experienced in the previous year. This cost is presented in the Table 2-4.

Table 2-4   *Average Cost of the Worst Incident for a UK Organization*

Company Size	Average Cost of the Worst Incident in GBP
Overall (size independent)	10,000–20,000
Large organization (>250 staff)	90,000–70,000
Very large organization (>500 staff)	1,000,000–2,000,000

It is important to note that Table 2-4 provides the cost range for a single, worst incident. ISBS 2008 also gives an average number of incidents as follows:

- 100 incidents for small organizations (<50 staff)

- 200 for large organizations (>240 staff)

- >1300 incidents per year for very large organizations (>500 staff)

Selling the Service Internally

In this model, the IR team charges other departments for its service. For every action, the team provides specifications for what has been done, how long it took, and the cost. The department that received IRT's service then transfers the funds to the team's budget. Although this can also be considered as a variation of the cost center model (because a department will, effectively, give up part of its budget to the IRT), you can treat this model separately because it has some unique characteristics.

One of the setups in which this model can be suitable is where the IRT serves a constituency that is not under the direct host organization's control. An example can be a computer department at a university that helps different departments. The computer department might not have the direct authority over the other departments but possesses required skills and expertise to perform the job.

Following is what distinguishes this funding model from the pure cost center model:

- The IRT must have a price list so that the affected party can estimate how much it needs to pay for the support.

- Clear engagement rules must be established to prevent misunderstanding and wrong expectations.

- The IRT can have problems performing required tasks and asserting its authority.

Price List

Before the IRT starts selling its service, it must have a price list—how much it will charge for cleaning a computer, performing a forensics investigation, reconfiguring networking devices, and so on. The affected side must have a notion about how much an incident recovery might cost. Obviously, it is not always possible to predict the exact cost because the incident's scope might not be known before the investigation starts.

Although this requirement is shared with the fully commercial incident response service (see the upcoming "Selling the Service Externally" section), the pricing here is not as critical as with the fully commercial services. The IRT can afford to miss the right price because, after all, it is dealing with internal customers that are more forgiving than external clients.

Clear Engagement Rules

This is an important aspect of this model. The engagement rules describe what events the IRT will handle, when it can be engaged, when the IRT will automatically be engaged, and when it will disengage from the incident.

It is to be expected that the IRT wants its resources to be used effectively, so tasks such as regular network and system maintenance should probably be excluded from the tasks that the IRT is willing to perform. If the IRT becomes aware that a single computer has been probed, the team might just add this to its daily/weekly report but not act in any other way (unless it is explicitly asked by the affected party). If, on the other hand, the IRT handles a life-and-death situation, it can expand its investigation automatically to all computers under the contract without asking for the approval.

Disengagement from the case is also important. There is a certain tendency that after you start following one thread, you can go on and on with no end in sight. One thing can lead to another, and you need to know when to stop. For example, if a deficiency in an operating system's or a router's configuration is detected, the IRT can notify the networking department and stop its engagement at that place. It is also beneficial to put a time limit on how long an unknown piece of malware will be analyzed. Obviously, it would be good to know what each new piece of malware can do, but unless there are extraordinary circumstances, if no tangible results are accomplished within a day or two, it makes no sense to continue the analysis. The malware can be classified as "bad—unknown behavior—removed on the spot" and the case can be closed.

Authority Problems

Because the IRT does not have direct authority over the departments or organizations it provides for, the services can cause problems in certain cases. One example might be when one department has a few compromised devices scanning other parts of the organization—nothing major but annoying nonetheless. Because the department with the compromised devices does not experience any negative effects, it might try to block the IRT from cleaning the compromised devices (cost control again!). Another example might be where the IRT needs an access to networking devices to verify their configuration to prevent certain types of attacks. Because these devices were not compromised, the department that owns them might not allow access to them. In situations like these, the IRT must have the means and the authority to perform its tasks.

It is also necessary to allow sufficient time for the incident to be handled and damage put under control. The affected party might be tempted to force the IRT to stop its investigation to limit the expenses of handling the incident. This tactic to save money is not effective in the long run. If an incident has not been handled properly, the chances of it occurring again are increased. So, in the long run, it might be more expensive to not allow the IRT to properly finish the job.

Selling the Service Externally

This is the model in which the IRT sells its services to external customers. This model is associated with phrases such as "managed service" or even "outsourcing." Here, even more than in the previous model, it is crucial to agree in advance what level of services will be provided and to delineate roles and responsibilities of all involved parties. Because you will be contracted to perform only a specific service, it can be quite possible that there will be parts of the customer's network that you will not have access to. Therefore, knowing in advance what you can, and cannot, do is important.

Other things that must be defined in the contract are priorities of specific services or applications that your customer uses. Imagine that your customer has a mail server for which a new exploit has just been published. The exploit is destructive and is extremely hard to filter. There is no workaround, and the mail server's vendor will release the fix in several weeks. You have these options at your disposal:

- Wait for the official fix and, until then, keep on restarting the mail server every few hours.

- Try to filter, or quarantine, mail known to cause problems, wait for the official fix, and keep restarting the mail server every other day.

- Block all mail for a day or two until a replacement mail server, one that is not affected by the exploit, is brought online. Continue with the normal operation after that.

Blocking mail might be the best option from the security perspective, but it might not be acceptable from the customer's business standpoint. You, the IRT, must make sure that things such as this are covered in your contract—when you will engage, what are the priorities for the customer (for example, database access is more important than email), and when you will disengage. All that must be known in advance because when an incident is happening, there might not be time to have long discussions. A decision on how to handle an incident must be made, and it must be made as quickly as possible.

Although the contract must be as exhaustive as possible, it is not possible to specify all things in advance. To compensate for that, the IRT must have a designated contact within a customer who can be asked to make decisions during the crisis. That contact must have good technical knowledge, know the business side, and have sufficient authority to order actions to be executed. That person must be available on a 24×7 basis, so in reality there must be more than one person as a designated contact.

Mixed Model

As the title suggests, this is the mixture of any of the previously mentioned models; therefore, all previously mentioned caveats are applicable here.

One scenario how this situation can occur is if we start with an Internet service provider (ISP) where the IRT is treated as a cost center. The ISP then acquires another ISP but, instead of absorbing it completely, this acquired ISP is established as a subsidiary—not entirely part of the organization but also not completely independent. The IRT now can be asked to extend its services to the subsidiary ISP, which will have to pay for them.

Now we have a mix of two different funding models. The last step can be if the ISP decides to offer certain incident-related services to its customers as a pay-for service (for example, datacenter protection).

Placement of IRT Within the Organization

Placement of the IRT within the organization has two components: one is how deep in the hierarchy the team will be (how many managers to the top of the chain), and another is within which department it will be placed. Let's look at the "how deep" aspect first.

Given the pervasive nature of computer security and how much organizations, in general, tend to rely on computers, the IRT should not be placed too deep in the hierarchy. The team must have an easy and direct way to communicate with higher management and especially with its executive sponsor. From that standpoint, it might be best if the team's manager is directly reporting to the executive sponsor. Once removed is still acceptable, but the deeper you go, the potential for problems to operate efficiently increases. It is easy to keep one or two managers above apprised of the situation, but having to organize three or more every time there is some urgent matter can be a real challenge. Not being too deep down is also good for the team's morale. Being relatively high in the hierarchy can give the IRT members a feeling of being more empowered. That can certainly help when the team members need to have serious, and not always pleasant, conversations with managers of other groups.

The next facet is where within the organization structure the IRT will be placed. To whom will the IRT report? The concrete answer depends on the host organization, what it does, and its existing structure. You can still look at some of the options and list general comments on each of them. Whichever placement is considered, it is implicit that the IRT is a self-contained group with its own manager. The case of a virtual team is discussed in the next section.

The main message, again, is that there is no universally best place to situate the IRT, nor are there universally wrong places. Instead, you should approach this from the perspective of whether the IRT can be efficient and effective in its job. If it can, the actual placement of the team within the organization is of secondary importance. There are, however, a few places that tend to house the IRT more frequently than others:

- IT department
- Network support
- Help desk center
- Internal security

Some organizations combine the first three services into a single department, whereas some do not. Because arguments for situating the IRT in the IT department, network support, and help desk center are similar, they are covered in a single section. Also, for the simplicity sake, we use "IT" to denote all three functions.

Placement in IT Department, Network Support, and Help Desk Center

This is the place where many teams initially start. Many of them are still part of their respective IT departments and are successful. This looks like a natural place to start because the IT department has people versed in computer-related issues, and handling computer security issues can be viewed as another specialization.

Following are some of the arguments for the IRT to be part of the IT department:

- Computer security incidents depend on what operating system and applications are used and on the overall network infrastructure. That all tends to be under control of the IT department.

- The IT department already possesses a high level of knowledge and expertise in deploying and configuring all parts of the information infrastructure.

- Users tend to report incidents, and other strange issues, to "computer/network folks." The IT department is definitely part of that computer coterie, so IRT can receive the reports directly.

Internal Security

Another possible way the internal security group can evolve is within a group that handles only the physical security of the organization (for example, theft and illegal entry), assuming it is not outsourced. This is later extended to encompass network and communication security. Given that the internal security group also provides support during police investigations, computer forensics and incident handling is a natural extension of the group's mandate.

Following are some arguments for the IRT to be part of the internal security group:

- The internal security group handles all incidents that can compromise the organization, so computer incidents should not be an exception.

- A computer incident can be combined with physical intrusion (and vice versa) so both aspects of an incident should be handled by a single group as a single event.

- In some organizations, individual members of the internal security group have the right to arrest people. Although that does not directly help the IRT, it can add a weight to the IRT. Being a part of a "no nonsense" group can help the IRT be taken seriously by the constituency from the start.

Central, Distributed, and Virtual Teams

The next decisions that need to be made are whether the IRT should be a group with a common immediate manager (a "real" team) or a virtual team, and whether it should be centrally located or distributed.

When discussing the virtual team structure, the IRT often needs to seek help from individuals outside the IRT. In that sense the IRT will always be virtual to some extent. For the lack of a better phrase, *real team* means a team with a common immediate manager, a separate account, and a budget.

Virtual Versus Real Team

If you do not have sufficiently strong support from your executives to form a real IRT, a virtual team is good option. Generally, it can be easier to set up a virtual team because it is less formal and requires fewer bureaucratic hurdles.

A virtual team can be structured in several ways. It can be completely virtual (no permanent members in the team), it can have a small permanent core, and it can be virtual only in a sense that there is no single manager who team members report to. We start with analyzing the structure with no permanent members in the virtual team.

Following are positive sides of a virtual team:

- **Easy formation:** It is relatively simply to form a virtual team because it needs only minimal paperwork.

- **Size of the team matches the need:** The virtual team can shrink or grow as required. For small incidents, only a few people will be involved, so there is no overhead. The IRT will not have people who will not have something to do. When there are no incidents, the size of the team is zero—the team does not exist at all!

- **The best people are involved:** Anyone, at any time, can be a part of a virtual team. Therefore, it is natural that only the best people (for the occasion) will actually be part of a virtual team when they are needed.

Following are negative sides of a virtual team:

- **People have their daily jobs:** Participating in a virtual team is an additional function that employees can do if they have time to participate. If employees are busy with a high-priority task, they might not be able to take part in handling an incident; therefore, a virtual team will consist of the best available people at a time. The people who, under different circumstances, would be third or fourth choice will be involved but only because the others are tied with their daily job.

- **Learning processes and procedures:** Every time people join a virtual team, they need to be acquainted with how computer incidents must be handled—what processes and procedures must be followed in what cases. This is true even if that person was part of the virtual team in the past because processes could have changed since then. For extremely critical incidents, there will be no time for this learning process to happen. This can prolong the incident resolution or cause that evidence to become inadmissible in a court.

- **Slow team setup:** It can take time for a virtual team to assemble. This time can vary from several hours to multiple days. This time is spent on making a decision that the virtual team is assembled, selecting its members, and finally for the members to free their time and start participating in the virtual team. Faced with a critical incident, the organization might not have the luxury of waiting that long.

- **Loss of "team's memory":** Because there is no guarantee that the same people will always be part of the virtual team, each incident will be handled separately. Some incidents are related, and that fact might be completely missed because nobody from the current team is aware of the previous incidents. Additionally, the IRT might waste time reinventing a solution for an incident because nobody from the old team's incarnation is currently present.

- **Number of incidents:** When the number of incidents reaches a certain level, the virtual team will become, more or less, fully occupied with handling them. Members of the virtual team will be so busy that they will not have a chance to return to their "home" teams.

Overall, a completely virtual team is not a viable long-term option. Virtual team structure can be made viable in the long term if it would have permanent core members. A virtual team with a permanent core can help address many of the shortcomings listed. For example, the team setup is much faster because the core members will start handling an incident while the rest of the virtual team is being assembled. The IRT's collective memory is retained, and the permanent core members can guide auxiliary members through the incident handling processes and procedures. What is not addressed in this model is the sheer number of incidents. When that number reaches a certain level, the core team would need to grow. When the core team grows to more than a few people, it then becomes a real team and ceases to be virtual any more.

The last option in setting up a virtual team is where you have dedicated people whose time is completely spent handling computer incidents, but they do not have a common immediate manager to report to. This model addresses all concerns related to a virtual team. It also adds a specific concern on its own: managers.

As long as all managers, whose people form the IRT, are fully cognizant that the IRT personnel have different drivers, targets, and objectives from the rest of their respective teams, this model can work. If managers ever try to impose the same expectations on the IRT members as on the non-IRT members, this virtual model will collapse.

Central Versus Distributed Team

You need to know whether the team will be centrally placed or distributed. This decision, in practice, is made for you and is governed by the constituency. If the constituency is centrally placed, and it is easy to reach it from a single place, a central team is the perfect solution. A geographically distributed constituency generally requires the same from the IRT.

Trying to support a distributed constituency with a centrally placed IRT can be difficult. The same is true for the opposite, serving a centrally placed constituency with a distributed team. The main reason is that there is always a need for someone to be physically present on a site. This might sound strange because we have developed all this technology to enable us to do things remotely, but in practice we must have physical access to the devices to perform some actions. The prime example is when you need to handle cases in which an attacker compromised a device and changed its passwords.

The procedure for changing passwords on networking devices requires a device to be powered off and on while you are connected to the console. Turning the power off and on, in most cases, is not possible unless someone is actually physically close to the device. Although you can have setups where a device is connected to a special power switch or an uninterruptible power supply (UPS) that can be controlled remotely, an attacker might prevent you from accessing these devices either by blocking your access to them or by changing passwords on these devices too.

Given this need for an onsite person, you should plan to have someone either physically on the site or relatively close by (for example, someone can be onsite within an hour or two). That onsite person does not always need to be an IRT member; it can be someone to whom the IRT can ask to perform certain tasks. Obviously, the more security knowledge that a person has and the more tasks that can be handled autonomously, the better for everyone. The constituency will benefit from faster and better service, and the IRT will have fewer interruptions.

Developing Policies and Procedures

The IRT must have several basic policies and procedures in place to operate satisfactory. The main ones follow:

- Incident classification and handling

- Information classification and protection

- Information dissemination

- Record retentions and destruction

- Usage of encryption

- Engaging and cooperation with external groups (other IRTs, law enforcement, and so on)

Depending on the IRT's needs and requirements, these policies can be separated even further, so instead of having a single Incident Classification and Handling policy, the team can split this into separate policies for incident classification and another one for incident handling.

Some additional policies that can be defined follow:

- Hiring policy

- Using an outsourcing organization to handle incidents

- Working across multiple legal jurisdictions

More policies can be defined depending on the team's circumstances. Not all policies need to be defined on the first day. The main ones should be in place because they govern the daily operation, but the others can follow later when the time becomes ripe for them. Also, policies do not need to be perfect and all-encompassing from the beginning.

It is normal that certain aspects will be left uncovered because you have not thought about it yet or you were not in that situation before. The policies must be living documents. When the policy shows signs that it is not adequate or the team's circumstances change, you can go back and update the policy.

Policies and procedures governing operation of the IRT should not only be in harmony with other organizational policies, but also are subject to the same rules and requirements as any other similar documents in your organization, such as the same level of protection, means of storing them, and process of how to update them, audit them, their compliance, and so on.

Good sources of information when you are drafting your policy and procedure documents are the following documents published by International Organization for Standardization/International Electrotechnical Commission (ISO/IEC):

- ISO/IEC 27001:2005, Information technology—Security techniques—Information security management systems—Requirements.

- ISO/IEC 27002:2005, Information technology—Security techniques—Code of practice for information security management.

- ISO/IEC 27005:2008, Information technology—Security techniques—Information security risk management.

- ISO/PAS 22399:2007, Societal Security—Guidelines for Incident Preparedness and Operational Continuity Management.

- ISO/IEC TR 18044:2004, Information technology—Security techniques—Information security incident management.

The ISO/IEC Technical Report (TR) 18044 is currently being transformed into an international standard and, when adopted, it will be published as ISO/IEC 27033.

In the reminder of this section, we look at what these policies may contain. The text only highlights the main items that particular policy should deal with and is not meant to represent the full policy.

Incident Classification and Handling Policy

This is the first main policy that must be in place. It describes what constitutes an incident. How would you recognize one when you see it? How would an incident get prioritized? How would you mark them? Would you use sequential numbers or some other scheme? What is the criterion for closing an incident? What information would you like to see in the report? Who will receive the report[3] and what actions will be done on it? How is an owner assigned to a report? How do you escalate an incident if the other side is unresponsive? How do you escalate an incident if it is not handled satisfactorily by the IRT? What information will be collected for statistical purposes? What kind of statistics would the team like to produce? The following is an example of a fairly simple policy.

[3] A report is whatever information is reported to you. A report will become an incident if it satisfies your criteria for an incident.

Definition of an Incident

Any event that breaks confidentiality, integrity, and availability of the information system is considered a security incident. For this purpose, the information system encompasses applications, information, network, computers, and all other devices and programs used to process, store, and transmit the information.

Monitoring Incoming Reports

The incoming queue is monitored around the clock by a duty person. A day is broken into three shifts. Each shift last 8 hours. The task of the duty person is rotated among all members of the IRT.

Receiving Reports

Every report sent to the IRT will be accepted by the person on duty, who will assign it a random tracking number and enter it into the tracking database. Each report is tagged by a keyword (for example, virus, spam, compromise, phish, and so on) and assigned an initial priority.

When receiving a report, the on-duty person will make a decision whether a report represents an incident. If the report does not represent an incident, the original reporter is notified of that fact, and the report will be closed immediately.

Timelines

Within 5 hours from receiving the report, an acknowledgment will be sent back to the original sender. The response must be cryptographically signed. It will also be encrypted if the initial report were sent encrypted.

Within 24 hours after an incident has been received, it must be assigned an owner. An owner is a person who will handle the incident.

Incident with Special Treatment

All cases involving child pornography, illegal substances, and life-or-death situations within the constituency will be automatically reported to the constituent and to law enforcement.

Escalation Procedure

In the case of a noncooperating third party, either an original reporter or the party that causes the incident, attempts will be made to find an alternative contact point. This will be done using publicly accessible information (for example, websites and whois database) and open or closed forums (for example, FIRST or police contacts). If no alternative contacts, or viable contacts, were found and the third party does not respond to five notices (email, voice, or telefax) sent in 3-day to 5-day intervals from each other, the incident will be marked as unresolved.

Incident Closing

The incident will remain open until it is either resolved or no further progress can be made and is marked as unresolved.

Post Mortem

A post mortem will be performed after every significant incident irrespective of the incident's outcome (for example, incident solved or not). It will be performed as soon as practical after the incident closure. A significant incident is every incident that deviates in one or more aspects from incidents handled until that time. Deviation can be either in scope (for example, cooperation with significantly more other groups or groups with special requirements such as law enforcement, government, or intelligence services), technical details (for example, new technology), or novelty (for example, a new type of incident).

In the absence of significant incidents during a year, two incidents will be selected, and a post mortem will be performed on them. One of the selected incidents must be successfully closed, and another one must be unresolved.

Reporting

At midnight, a report will be made. It will contain information pertaining to the previous 24 hours. The following information will be included: number of received incidents, number of closed incidents, number of unassigned incidents, and number of incidents per each member of the IRT. The same report will also be generated on a weekly and monthly basis. The weekly and monthly reports will contain information on the minimum, average, and maximum time taken to send the acknowledgment to the reporting party.

One of the often-debated issues is labeling incidents. It is much easier if they are given some sort of a label instead of using incident-specific information. Using incident-related information for labeling will lead to information leakage. If an incident is labeled "Oxford-ssh-compromise," it is immediately clear what the incident is about. Unfortunately, using this label in emails, and especially in the Subject line, can also give strong clues to what the mail is about. The easiest way to mark an incident is to assign it a number. The number can be sequentially incremented for each new incident. The downside of this is that it leaks information on how many incidents have been created. It also indirectly gives away information when a particular incident was created and, consequently, how long it takes to close it. The other obvious solution is to use a date (either in the YYYYMMDDHHMMSS format or as a number of seconds or milliseconds from the epoch or some other preset time), but it suffers from the same problem as a sequential number: It leaks too much information. The only other choice is to use a random number. That prevents information leaking. To make the label unique, the IRT's name or designation is usually added as a prefix or suffix.

Information Classification and Protection

This policy describes how information will be classified and what, if any, protection methods will be used to safeguard it. If the organization already has an information classification policy, it can be either reused completely or used as a basis to create the policy for the IRT. If the organization does not have such a policy, this would be a good time to create it. This policy is vital so that people who are reporting an incident have confidence that information will not be made public. The policy must encompass all input media such as email, telefax, or CD/DVDs. The protection must be adequate for a given classification level. Information declassification should also be covered.

A sample policy may look like the following:

The IRT classification scheme consists of the following levels, starting from the lowest to the highest:

- **Public:** Information can be freely shared within and outside the team and organization.

- **Restricted:** Information can shared only with the employees of the organization (full time, part time, and contractors).

- **Confidential:** Information can be shared only with full-time employees of the organization.

- **Secret:** Information can be shared only on a need-to-know basis.

By default, all information received by the IRT is classified as Secret unless the sender explicitly sets a different level. Also, by default, all members of IRT have need-to-know rights on all incidents handled by the team.

The information classification can be decreased only by the information owner. If it originated from outside the organization, the sender is considered the owner. Classification can be increased by the IRT without consulting the owner.

Information classified as Restricted and above will always be stored on a computer in an encrypted form. If it is in a nonelectronic form (for example, paper, CD, or magnetic tape), it will be stored in a metal locker, and for the information marked Restricted or Confidential and above, it will be stored in a safe. For the information classified as Public, there is no specific storage method.

Information Dissemination

To handle an incident, information must be shared; however, sharing must not be haphazard but controlled and purposeful. The IRT must share incident information with different groups, some of which are inside the organization and some that are outside. Not all groups need the same kind of information or the same level of details. The timing when the information is shared is also different for different groups. Most important, the purpose of why the information is shared will vary among the groups. Information classification also must be taken into account. In some cases, this would require the recipient to sign a nondisclosure agreement or receive formal clearance to handle the information. If that is impractical or impossible, the information might not be shared. Table 2-5 contains some examples of what information may be shared with some of the relevant groups.

Table 2-5   *Examples of Information Dissemination Levels*

Group	Purpose	Level of Details	Timeliness
External IRT	Help in handling the incident.	Detailed information but only pertained to the constituency of that IRT.	As soon as possible; under some circumstances even in real time.
Local management	Statistics, team's appraisal, budgeting, and related purposes.	Aggregate numbers only.	The report is generated periodically (for example, monthly or quarterly).
	Post mortem of significant incidents involving the host organization with the goal of improving local security practices and posture.	Very detailed description of the incident, together with reasons why the incident was possible to happen and suggested steps to prevent its occurrence in the future.	Incident post mortems as soon as practical after the incident's closure.
Local legal department	Handling legal aspects of incident that involve host organization (for example, intellectual property cases).	Sufficient to grasp legal ramification; possibly omitting technical details but depends on the case.	As soon as legal assistance is required.
Local press relation	Promotional material.	Aggregate figures only; low level of details.	Upon request from PR department or periodically (for example, quarterly or biannually).
	Press inquires on a particular incident.	Low level of details. Usually without personal details but may depend on the case.	Upon request from PR department.

Record Retention and Destruction

Information retention will be mostly governed by the host's organization policy that, in turn, must follow applicable laws and regulations applicable to the country in which the IRT resides or operates. Following are a few general guidelines:

- The information should not be retained longer than necessary.

- Countries that are members of the European Union, in general, have more stringent laws governing data protection than the rest of the world[4].

- Operators of public networks (for example, Internet service providers and telephone networks) might have additional requirements on data collection and retention (for example, EU Directives 2002/58/EC and 2006/24/EC).

- Do not overclassify your data.

- Destruction of data must be appropriate to the classification level and the media the information resides.

Following is an example of a simple data retention and destruction policy.

Information Retention and Destruction

All information generated by the IRT is subject to the organization's retention and destruction policy. The exception from the retention policy is information related to open incidents.

The exception from the data destruction policy is that the IRT will possess its own capabilities to destroy documents.

Information Retention

Documents and information should be retained for the period of six years, after which they will be destroyed. Exceptions from this policy follow:

- Information pertaining to still active incidents.

- Information required for the IRT's operation.

- Information related to an active incident will be held for as long as the incident remains open. After that time, the information will be treated in accordance with the standard retention policy (that is, destroyed after six years).

- Information required to the IRT's operation will be retained for as long as the IRT exists, after which time the information will be treated according to the standard policy.

---

[4] This is changing with time, as more and more non-EU countries are adopting (more) stringent data protection laws.

Email Retention

If emails are stored on a personal computer (desktop, laptop, mobile phone, and so on), all emails should be deleted as soon as they are not needed anymore or after one year, whichever is sooner. The exceptions are still open incidents.

Emails stored on a server are subject to the six-year rule.

Information Destruction

All information must be destroyed securely and in an environmentally friendly way. The IRT will have full control over the destruction process. The way the information will be destroyed depends on the classification and the media:

- **Public information:** No specific procedure required. Paper documents and information on other recyclable media will be recycled as they are. Nonrecyclable media will be disposed of in an appropriate manner.

- **Restricted and confidential information:** Paper documents, magnetic tapes, CDs/DVDs, and other media that can be shredded will be destroyed using a cross-cut shredder. Hard drives will be demagnetized and then disposed of according to the organization's disposal policy.

- **Secret information:** Paper documents and other flammable, but nontoxic media, will be destroyed using a cross-cut shredder and then incinerated. CD/DVD media and hard drives will be physically destroyed. For hard drives, the magnetic platters will be removed from the drive casing and then destroyed. The drive casing and the associated electronic will not be destroyed.

Usage of Encryption

The IRT must be capable of sending and receiving information securely. In most cases, that involves cryptography. The main reason why you might want to use encryption is to protect information exchange. In some cases, attackers can have access to communications channels (for example, access to emails, intercepting phone conversations [voice over IP] or access to spooled Short Message Services [SMS] messages) and can learn whether they have been discovered and learn about plans drawn up to catch them.

One interesting mistake related to information confidentiality that people tend to commit occasionally is to send an encrypted email with a Subject line such as "Host 1.2.3.4 is attacking 5.6.7.8 using old ssh exploit." Obviously, with the subject like this, there is no need to read the mail. The interesting part is that this mistake can be committed even by experienced people who should know better. Luckily, that happens rarely.

Whatever the case might be, this means that IRT must decide which algorithms and software will be used. The first requirement is that whatever is chosen is acceptable for the constituency. Mandating an expensive software package or use of uncommon hardware platform might not be the best choice because it can require the constituency to expense additional amounts of money. Therefore, if the constituency already has something in place, the team might consider whether that can be used.

Another issue to keep in mind is that the team is not isolated. It will need to exchange the information with other teams. Therefore, the selected encryption system must be such that this information exchange is possible. This requirement can lead to the situation in which the IRT uses several encryption systems to communicate with all required parties. That, by itself, should not be a big issue, but the team must accept that possibility. If indeed that ends up being the case, the team might consider buying, or developing, a special encryption gateway. Something that can accept a message encrypted in any legitimate format and then either re-encrypt it into the desired other format or decrypt it into cleartext. If the number of messages increases to a level in which a significant amount of time is spent only in decrypting and re-encrypting messages, such an automatic system can be a sound investment.

For the majority of teams, programs such as Pretty Good Privacy (PGP) or its open-source incarnation GNU Privacy Guard (GPG) can fulfill most of the needs. Although they are not the same, they do interoperate well. For brevity, throughout the remainder of this text, GPG is used, but that can be either PGP or GPG. Indeed, Forum of Incident Response Teams (FIRST), the biggest global forum of IRTs, prescribes GPG as mandatory, so the team should start using it if it does not already. Because of this, we will talk a little bit more about GPG and keys.

GPG supports symmetrical ciphers, public key cryptography, and digital signatures. A symmetrical cipher uses the same key for encryption and decryption. Public key cryptography is where a key is split into two, and one half is posted for everybody to download (this is called public key), whereas another is kept secret and is called the private key. A digital signature serves to show that some document is signed by a certain person and that the document has not been altered after it has been signed. The key component for digital signature is a one-way hash function that maps an arbitrary large document into a fixed and the finite length hash. The most-known hash functions are Message Digest 5 (MD5) and Secure Hash Algorithm 1 (SHA-1). By encrypting that hash, you can produce a digital signature of the original document.

Symmetric Versus Asymmetric Keys and Key Authenticity

For the communication to remain confidential, encryption keys must be kept secret. This is especially true if a symmetric cipher is used as the same key that is used for encryption and decryption. In public key cryptography, a private key must be kept secret, whereas the public key is usually posted to a public key server for everyone to download.

Using symmetrical cipher has a few drawbacks:

- Initial key distribution

- Key compromise

- Authentication

To start exchanging encrypted messages with someone for the first time, you must securely provide the key to that person. Obviously, you cannot just send it in an email because anyone who can intercept that email can read the key[5]. To work around this, people tend to exchange keys over a telephone (that is, call the other person and tell her), organize face-to-face meetings, use telefax, or post. A telephone is the fastest method, but to establish any semblance of confidence, you must be able to positively recognize the voice of the other person on the phone. After you distribute the key, you must worry about a key compromise. If anyone loses the key, a new key must be distributed to everyone to maintain the security of your communication.

Assume now that you successfully exchanged your secret key among 50 participants. You receive an email from Bob and can decrypt it using the secret key. How confident are you that the message is actually sent by Bob? Decrypting the message confirms only that the correct key was used. But that someone can be anyone from the group of 50 people because all of them know the key! Symmetric encryption, by itself, cannot authenticate the sender. To accomplish authentication, the symmetric encryption must be augmented with some other methods.

A naïve way to ensure authentication is to exchange a unique key between each pair of participants. This, however, introduces problems of key management and scalability. In this scenario, Bob will have 49 different keys, one for each person he wants to exchange mails. The total number of keys that would be in use among 50 people is 1225 ($n*(n-1)/2$), which would not be easy to manage.

All of this does not mean that symmetric encryption does not have its place. It does because it is faster and requires less processing power than the public key cryptography. What is commonly done is that public key cryptography is used to share symmetric keys that are then used to encrypt the communication.

Public key cryptography has elegant solutions for issues that are problems in symmetric cryptography but is not without problems of its own. The biggest one is that generally you cannot be sure that a public key actually belongs to a person or an organization the key claims to belong to. The way to address this issue is either by a web of trust or using certification authorities (CA).

A web of trust is formed when people and organizations sign each other's keys. The underlying idea of a web of trust is that the trust is transitive (which is not true!). We will revisit this particular topic a bit later in this chapter. The way a web of trust is supposed to work is that Ada knows Bob and Charlie, so she signs their keys. If Charlie, who does not know Bob at all, now wants to send an encrypted message to Bob, he can verify who signed Bob's key. If Charlie finds Ada's signature in Bob's key, Charlie can be confident that Bob's key actually belongs to Bob. This is possible because Charlie knows Ada and trusts her.

---

[5] Interestingly, many reputable websites would do exactly that. If you click the Forget Your password link, they send your password in an unencrypted email.

Certificate authorities (CA) are an attempt to outsource the identity verification part to a trusted third party. Before obtaining a certificate, a person or an organization must prove its identity to the CA. If the CA is satisfied with the proof, it will issue a certificate confirming that Bob's key actually belongs to Bob. Some of the public certificate authorities are Verisign, CAcert, DigiCert, InstantSSL, GeoTrust, and many others. Some CAs are commercial organizations, and you are required to pay for the certificate (either a one-off or monthly/yearly fee), whereas others will issue you a certificate for free. You can also set up your own CA if you want.

In practice, the question of an encryption key's authenticity is addressed in a way that each IRT publishes its public key on its website. If teams are members of FIRST, or a regional group such as TF-CSIRT, contact details and public key details can be taken from the respective organization's website. These organizations endeavor to verify basic team information and keep it up to date.

Creating Encryption Policy

Your encryption policy must provide answers to the following questions:

- When will the encryption be used? Includes both in transport (for example, email) and storage.

- What encryption algorithms, software, or hardware will be used?

- How many keys will be produced? Will it be one for the entire team, one for each team member, or both?

- For what purposes would each key be used (for example, only signing, only encryption, or both)? Will the team key and personal keys be interchangeable?

- How will you establish legitimacy of the team's key? How will other people know that this key belongs to your IRT?

- If IRT's members will use their personal keys, how can you assure others that these people are indeed members of the IRT?

- What is the internal distribution of the team's key?

- How long will the key be valid?

- What is the procedure for revoking a key?

The rest of this section is devoted to elaborate on the preceding points and give general guidelines for how they can be addressed.

Encryption Usage

The following guidelines are generally accepted in the IR community:

- All emails sent by an IRT must be signed so that their authenticity can be verified.

- If you receive an encrypted email, you should respond with an encrypted email. You may break this rule if your answer is simple (for example, "Thanks" or "OK"), and you are certain that your response does not disclose the planned course of action or other information that might be useful to whoever can intercept the email.

- All emails containing nonpublic information should be sent encrypted.

- When an encrypted email exchange is started, keep on using it. If there are two threads on the same subject, one encrypted and the other not, there is a good chance that someone will cross-post mail from one thread to another (and leak confidential information) and that both threads will eventually end up unencrypted.

- Only the information owner (that is, one who initiated the information exchange) can decide whether further exchanges will require encryption.

There is no firm rule for email storage. One school says that all information should be stored in the way it is received, whereas another argues that it should be stored in decrypted form. If you use a database to store information about the cases, and if the database supports encryption (independent from the encryption used to protect emails in transit), decrypting emails before stringing them into a database should not be an issue. However, if you archive your emails in a flat file without any further protection (for example, no disk encryption), you should probably keep the emails as they are received.

The downside of keeping emails in the original form is that you also must keep all your old decryption keys so that you can read your email archive.

Encryption Algorithms and Software

GPG/PGP is the de facto standard in the IR community, so you are strongly recommended to use it. Some governments or government-related teams might not be allowed to use GPG because they are required to use an approved encryption system and software. Even in these cases, occasionally, the IRT might be granted an exception and use GPG when exchanging information with the rest of the IR community. The usual price for this exception is that the IRT key must be escrowed by the organization.

Team Key Versus Personal Keys

Virtually all the existing IRTs have a team key and each IRT member has a personal key tied (that is, signed by the IRT's team key) to the IRT. Some teams have a hierarchy of keys. They usually have one master key and one team key, and each team member has a personal key. The master key is used only to sign the current team key. The current team key is then used for all other purposes—sign outgoing mail, sign team members' keys, and so on.

There is no firm guidance on having personal keys tied to the IRT. This seems to be a question of personal preference.

Use of Keys

One of the more common setups is that the team key is used for the following:

- Signing individual team member's keys; that way, you are signaling who is a member of the IRT.

- Signing all outgoing emails so that recipients can verify that the information is genuine.

- Encrypting incoming email; if someone wants to send you something sensitive, that person should use your team's key to encrypt the information.

If the IRT decides to create a master key, the master key is used only to sign a current team key and nothing else. Some teams also allow that individual team members sign outgoing emails with their personal keys instead of the team's key.

The best practice is that all incoming emails should be encrypted with the team's key. That way, any member of the team can decrypt the message.

Legitimacy of the Team's Key

The first step is to publish your team's key on your website. Assuming that your website is not compromised, everyone should be able to obtain your key from there. The next step is to get your key signed by several other IRTs. The last step might be to obtain a certificate for it. Use of certificates is not widespread in the IR community, and many teams would simply ignore certificates.

Legitimacy of Personal Keys

How can you ensure that only real team members are recognized as such and prevent imposters from false impersonation? That can be done by signing team members' personal keys with the team key. Therefore, whoever has their personal key signed by the current team key is indeed a team member. This is especially important if the team's key is not used for signing outgoing mail but personal keys are used instead.

Internal Team's Key Distribution

Who needs to have the key? That follows from how it is used. If the key will be used only for decrypting incoming mail, maybe only people who are reading incoming traffic must have it and nobody else. If it will also be used for signing outgoing messages, all people who can be in the position to respond should have it. If only some outgoing messages will be signed, maybe only people who are entitled to release those messages must have the key and nobody else.

In practice, it is common that all team members have access to the team key (but not the master key if it exists!).

Lifetime of the Keys

Both the team and individual keys must be taken into account. It is considered good practice to change the key periodically. How often depends on how the key is used. The longer the key is valid, the more messages will be sent encrypted by it. If the key gets compromised, more messages can be (potentially) read by an attacker. Changing the key too often increases the burden on people who frequently communicate with you; they will have to fetch a new key every so often. The team must also think about archived messages. If they are kept encrypted at that time with the valid team's key, the team must keep copies of all expired keys. If old messages are constantly being re-encrypted with the new key, changing the key too often can increase the team's workload.

The preceding information also applies to the personal keys, if they are allowed and used. However, given that the individual's keys are used less frequently, their lifetime can be longer than the team's key.

Finally, if a master key is created and is used only to sign a current team key, the master key can have a long lifetime.

In practice, the team key is valid for a period of 2 to 4 years, whereas personal keys and the master key can have an indefinite lifetime.

Key Revocation

A key is usually revoked for two main reasons, apart from naturally expiring. One is that a team member has left the team, and another is that the key is compromised. In any case, the old key is declared invalid, and the new one is created.

When announcing a new key, the team should also give the reason why the old key is revoked. The most dramatic event is when the key is compromised. In that case, the team should give an estimate of when the compromise happened. If you cannot determine when the compromise happened, the time when the team learned of the compromise must be stated together with the fact that the key has been compromised for an unknown period of time. This is important so that other teams who used the compromised key to send the information can assess their potential exposure.

Digression on Trust

Many people tend not to have a correct notion of what trust is. Then again, some do but they use terms colloquially, so it is hard to distinguish. According to the Oxford English Dictionary (second edition 1989), trust is "Confidence in or reliance on some quality or attribute of a person or thing, or the truth of a statement." The question is, how can Ada start trusting Bob?

The only way Ada can start trusting Bob is to work with him and, over time, if Bob is constantly performing up to Ada's expectation and showing characteristics that she is looking for, she can start trusting him. The keywords here are "over time" and "expectations of the other party." Another important point is that this trusting relationship is being developed only between Ada and Bob because they are the ones who are cooperating. Let us now introduce Charlie, who trusts Ada and she trusts him. There is no reason why Charlie would trust Bob just because Ada trusts Bob. Charlie and Bob may be competitors, or there is some personal animosity between them, and they may look for ways to undermine each other rather than cooperate. Trust is not transitive. It must be earned, and that is a long process.

For the preceding reasons, the "web of trust" described in the context of public key cryptography is a misnomer. Trust cannot be developed that way. That "web of trust" can serve only to provide assurance that Bob's public key actually belongs to Bob. There is no trust in Bob, his abilities, integrity, or the way he will handle things, but only assurance in Bob's key authenticity.

It might sound like a philosophical discussion, but the distinction is important. Trust is the currency of IRTs, and everyone is minting their own coin. That is the only thing that cannot be given but must be earned. To gain trust, it takes a long time, but to lose it, only an instant. When lost, it will take an even longer time to regain it back. Even when the trust is regained again, the hint of doubt can still linger.

The other part of the picture is not whether your actions and intentions are good and honest but how they are perceived by others. Trust is about how others see and interpret your actions and not how you see them. Think hard before you do something that can make others lose their trust in you. In some cases, it may be a good idea to talk with other teams and ask for their opinion on your planned actions. How would they feel if you start doing things in a certain way? Would they still have the same trust in you?

The last thing on trust is the transition from trusting a person to trusting a team. Trust, being a human concept, first develops between individuals, like Ada trusting Bob. Bob and Charlie might be part of the same team, but Ada will have a tendency to have more trust in Bob than in Charlie. For Ada to start having confidence in the team, instead of only trusting Bob, she will have to work with other members of Bob's team. That is something that requires a conscious effort from all parties because the initial impulse would always be to work with people you worked with before. If other members of Bob's team show consistency in execution and a high level of integrity and professionalism, Ada will feel confident working with Bob's team and will have trust in the team rather than individuals. This is a long process that requires a lot of effort.

Engaging and Cooperation with Other Teams

On many occasions, the IRT must engage another team to resolve the incident. This policy describes under which circumstances an external team will be engaged. What information will be provided and how? Is it necessary to have a Nondisclosure Agreement (NDA) or any other kind of formal agreement with the other team? What must be covered by that document? How should you cooperate with teams for the first time if there is no time to establish a formal relationship? What if a competitive relationship between the teams and host organizations exists? How can that change, if at all, the rules of engagement? How can a competitive relationship influence information exchange? In practice, many of the issues raised have a simple solution.

What Information Will Be Shared

Always share the minimum necessary for the other side to react. Only relevant information should be shared.

Nondisclosure Agreement

Unless you are proactive, the reason why you would contact someone for the first time is that you have a problem and hope that the other team can help you solve it. In most instances, this means an urgency, and there is no time for a formal process to happen. You will ask the other team if they can help, and if the answer is positive, you will send them relevant information and hope for the best. Generally, no agreements of any kind are required when working with another IRT.

If you cooperate, or expect to cooperate, on a regular basis with another team, formalizing your relationship with the team would be the prudent next step. If you go down this route, consider whether that level of cooperation should also be established with more than that single team. In that case, you should consider drafting a multilateral NDA rather than an NDA between only two parties. This can save you a lot of paperwork if you would like to bring a third or fourth IRT into the fold. Without a multilateral NDA, all IRTs would have to sign bilateral NDAs with all other IRTs, which is a waste of effort.

Competitive Relationship Between Organizations

When security is concerned, there is no competition. We (the good folks) should be united against the bad folks. As far as security is concerned, we are all on the same side and should cooperate.

In practice, the reason why you would contact your competitor about a security incident is because you have a problem. It is usually that a computer from your organization is attacking their computer or vice versa. Cooperation is a matter of resolving an incident and is unrelated to the competitive relationship that might exist between the organizations.

Some organizations might voice an opinion that if we notify our competitors that we suffered a security breach, they, the competitors, may use that information to their advantage. It would be naïve to assume that all organizations always play fair but, in the majority of instances, both organizations are equally eager to resolve the incident and are equally exposed.

The bottom line is, competitive relationships between organizations must not be carried down to the IRT level. Information about incidents should be shared in the same manner as with any other IRT.

Summary

Forming any team is not easy, but forming an incident response team has its own additional challenges. Unlike most other teams, the IRT must have interactions with every part of the organization and is also highly visible outside the organization. It operates on a truly global scale that brings all sorts of legal and political issues that must be taken into account when forming a team.

References

Campbell, K., Gordon, L.A., Loeb, M.P., and L. Zhou (2003). "The Economic Cost of Publicly Announced Information Security Breaches: Empirical Evidence from the Stock Market," *Journal of Computer Security*, 11(2003), p. 431–448. Available at http://iospress.metapress.com/content/5nkxhffc775tuel9/. [Accessed September 23, 2010].

Computer Security Incident Handling Guide, Recommendations of the National Institute of Standards and Technology, NIST Special Publication 800-61 Revision 1. Tim Grance, Karen Kent, and Brian Kim, March 2008. http://csrc.nist.gov/publications/nistpubs/800-61-rev1/SP800-61rev1.pdf.

Council Directive 93/104/EC of 23 November 1993 concerning certain aspects of the organization of working time, Council of the European Union, 1993-Nov-23. http://eur-lex.europa.eu/LexUriServ/LexUriServ.do?uri=CONSLEG:1993L0104:20000801:EN:PDF.

CSI Computer Crime and Security Survey 2009, Robert Richardson, 2009. http://www.gocsi.com/forms/csi_survey.jhtml.

Data elements and interchange formats—Information interchange—Representation of dates and times, ISO 8601:2004, 2004-12-03. http://www.iso.org/iso/en/CatalogueDetailPage.CatalogueDetail?CSNUMBER=40874&ICS1=1&ICS2=140&ICS3=30.

Directive 2002/58/EC of the European Parliament and of the Council of 12 July 2002 concerning the processing of personal data and the protection of privacy in the electronic communications sector (Directive on privacy and electronic communications), European parliament and the council of the European Union. http://eur-lex.europa.eu/LexUriServ/LexUriServ.do?uri=CELEX:32002L0058:EN:HTML.

Directive 2003/88/EC of the European Parliament and of the Council of 4 November 2003 concerning certain aspects of the organisation of working time, Official Journal L 299, 18/11/2003, p. 0009–0019. http://eur-lex.europa.eu/LexUriServ/LexUriServ.do?uri=CELEX:32003L0088:EN:HTML.

Directive 2006/24/EC of the European Parliament and of the Council of 15 March 2006 on the retention of data generated or processed in connection with the provision of publicly available electronic communications services or of public communications networks and amending Directive 2002/58/EC, Official Journal L 105, 13/04/2006, p. 0054–0063. http://eur-lex.europa.eu/LexUriServ/LexUriServ.do?uri=OJ:L:2006:105:0054:0063:EN:PDF.

Forum of Incident Response and Security Teams. http://www.first.org/.

The GNU Privacy Guard. http://www.gnupg.org/.

Incident Cost Analysis and Modeling Project I-CAMP II, Committee on Institutional Cooperation and USENIX. Virginia Rezmierski, Adriana Carroll, and Jamie Hine, published 2000.

The International PGP Home Page. http://www.pgpi.com/.

ISO/IEC 27001:2005, Information technology—Security techniques—Information security management systems—Requirements, International Organization for Standardization, 2005. http://www.iso.org/iso/iso_catalogue/catalogue_tc/catalogue_detail.htm?csnumber=42103.

ISO/IEC 27002:2005, Information technology—Security techniques—Code of practice for information security management, International Organization for Standardization, 2005. http://www.iso.org/iso/iso_catalogue/catalogue_tc/catalogue_detail.htm?csnumber=50297.

ISO/IEC 27005:2008, Information technology—Security techniques—Information security risk management, International Organization for Standardization, 2008. http://www.iso.org/iso/iso_catalogue/catalogue_tc/catalogue_detail.htm?csnumber=42107.

ISO/IEC TR 18044:2004, Information technology—Security techniques—Information security incident management, International Organization for Standardization, 2004. http://www.iso.org/iso/iso_catalogue/catalogue_tc/catalogue_detail.htm?csnumber=35396.

ISO/PAS 22399:2007, Societal Security—Guidelines for Incident Preparedness and Operational Continuity Management, International Organization for Standardization, 2007. http://www.iso.org/iso/iso_catalogue/catalogue_tc/catalogue_detail.htm?csnumber=50295.

PGP Corporation. http://www.pgp.com/.

RFC 1321, *The MD5 Message-Digest Algorithm*, R. Rivest, 1992-April. http://www.ietf.org/rfc/rfc1321.txt.

Secure Hash Signature Standard (SHS), FIPS PUB 180-2, August 1, 2002. http://csrc.nist.gov/publications/fips/fips180-2/fips180-2.pdf.

UK Department of Trade and Industry Information Security Breaches Survey 2008, managed by PriceWaterhouseCoopers, April 22, 2008. http://www.pwc.co.uk/eng/publications/berr_information_security_breaches_survey_2008.html.

Chapter 3

Operating an IRT

After an IRT is established, your next concern is how to successfully operate your team. This chapter covers the following topics to help you improve the operation of your IRT:

- Team size and working hours
- New team member profile
- Advertising team's existence
- Acknowledging incoming messages
- Cooperation with internal groups
- Prepare for the incidents
- Measure of success

Team Size and Working Hours

One of the more common questions that organizations setting up their incident response team ask is, "How large should an IRT be?" Providing that budget is not a constraint, the team's size is a function of what services the IRT wants to provide, the size and the distribution of the constituency, and planned working hours. (That is, will the IRT operate only during office hours or around the clock?) In practice, if you are starting from scratch and the IRT's task is defined as "go and deal with the incidents," a small team should be sufficient for the start. The first 12 to 18 months of the IRT's operation can show whether you need more people on the team.

Many teams after their formation operate only during the office hours. (For example, if you are in western Europe, that would be Monday through Friday from 09:00 to 17:00.) For this kind of coverage a two-person team should suffice. Although office-hours coverage is fine for the start, the IRT should look into extending its working hours to be active around the clock.

The main reason for extending the working hours is that some services (for example, a public website) are available at all times. If someone compromises computers providing these services, the IRT must be able to respond swiftly and not two days later after the weekend is over. Miscreants do not work standard office hours, so the IRT must do the same.

One of the standard ways to extend working hours is to have someone who is on-call. This person can answer telephone calls and check incoming emails after hours and over the weekend. This setup can be augmented by cooperating with other teams. If, for example, the IT has someone who is on-site outside office hours, the IT person might be the one who will accept telephone calls, monitor emails, and alarm the IRT only when needed.

From a technical perspective, it is easy to have someone on-call. It is not necessary to have someone in the office because modern, smart mobile telephones can receive and send emails, surf the Internet, and you can even use them to talk. Smart telephones generally cannot do encryption, so you would need to devise a way to decrypt and encrypt messages. From a staffing perspective, if you want around-the-clock and weekend coverage, the number of the people in IRT would depend on whether the duties can be shared with other teams in the organization. If the duties can be shared, you might not need to increase the size of the IRT. If not, increasing the team size should be considered. A three-member team might be a good size given that one person might be on vacation and another might be sick, which would leave only one active person. Although two people can also provide around-the-clock coverage, it would be a stretch and might burn them out if they would operate that way for a prolonged period of time.

If the host organization is within the EU, it must pay attention to the European Working Time Directive (Council Directive 93/104/EC and subsequent amendments), which regulates that the working week must not be longer than 48 hours, which also includes overtime. On the other hand, people might opt-out from the directive and work as long as required. The host's human resources department must investigate this and set up proper guidelines.

Irrespective of what hours the IRT operates, that fact must be clearly stated and communicated to other teams and the constituency. Do not bury it somewhere deep in the documentation but state it prominently close to the place containing the team's contact details. Setting the right expectations is important.

When the IRT operates only during office working hours, the team must not forget that it is living in a round and multicultural world. Living in a round world means that the team must state its time zone. Do not assume that people will automatically know in which time zone the team operates based just on the city and the country. It is possible that the constituency, or larger part of it, is actually situated in a different time zone from the one in which the IRT physically operates.

A multicultural world means that people in one country have different customs from people in other countries. We do not necessarily have weekends or holidays on the same days. Take an example of an IRT that operates from Israel and a large part of its constituency is in Europe. Will it operate on Saturdays? What are its office hours? Will it work on December 25th? The people who report an incident to the team might not know these details in advance. It might be the first time they are reporting something to the team, and they do not know what to expect. The point is that all the information related to your working hours must be visibly and clearly stated on your team's website.

Digression on Date and Time

While on the topic of a multicultural world, we must mention date and time formats. You always must use an unambiguous format for the date and time. To that end, ISO 8601 is strongly recommended to be adopted by the IRT. In short, according to the ISO 8601, a date should be written in YYYY-MM-DD and time in hh:mm:ss format. ISO format is suitable when the data is automatically processed. Because not all people are familiar with the ISO 8601 standard, it is highly recommended to use the month's name (for example, October or Oct) instead of its number in all correspondence. That way, you can eliminate any possible ambiguity on a date. When sending data that is a result of some automated process or that will be processed, you should also add a note that all dates are in the ISO format so that recipients know how to interpret them.

As far as the time is concerned, do not forget to include the time zone. This is especially important if recipients are in different time zones. You can either use the time zone's name (for example, "GMT" or "Greenwich Mean Time") or the offset from the GMT (for example, GMT + 0530—GMT plus 5 hours and 30 minutes). The preference should be to include the offset rather than the time zone's name because the names can be ambiguous. For example, EST can mean either Eastern Summer Time or Eastern Standard Time. Eastern Summer Time is used in Australia during the summer, and its offset from GMT is 11 hours (GMT + 1100). On the other hand, Eastern Standard Time can be in either Australia or North America. The Eastern Standard Time in Australia is used during the winter and is 10 hours ahead of GMT (GMT + 1000), whereas the same Eastern Standard Time in North America has an offset of −5 hours from GMT (GMT − 0500).

One good website related to time zones is time and date.com, owned and operated by Time and Date AS. It is at http://www.timeanddate.com and is useful when dealing with multiple time zones.

New Team Member Profile

There was a time when requirements for becoming a member of the Cisco PSIRT team included, apart from sound security acumen and knowledge, things such as "works 24 hours a day, leaps over tall buildings, and is capable of stopping a running train." Shirts with the letter "S" were given when you joined the team, but we had to bring our own cape. That was the humorous side of the requirements, but reality, as everyone knows, is much stranger than fiction.

Computer security is not just a job; it is a way of life and a special state of mind. When most people see a new device or an application, they think: "Nice features. How can I use them?" Security-inclined people think: "How can protection be circumvented, and how can someone misuse a feature?" That is what immediately separate security-oriented people from others. Working in the computer security arena requires dedication, an open mind, and knowledge. One comforting thing for people who would like to work in an IRT but are afraid they would not be given the chance because they lack knowledge and experience is that these things are important but are not paramount. You can learn facts, but you cannot "learn" lateral thinking and security acumen.

When hiring, the IRT should look at the way a candidate thinks about problems, the way the problem is approached, and how quickly new information is used to reevaluate it. Often a candidate might be asked some trick questions that are completely unrelated to security, or even computers, just to assess how the candidate thinks. If candidates have the right qualities, they can learn the details afterward. It is always much easier to memorize simple facts such as "/etc/shadow file contains passwords" than to understand reasons why passwords have been moved from /etc/password and placed in this other file.

Obviously, having the knowledge is good and, all things being equal, candidates with more knowledge and experience will probably have an advantage over inexperienced ones. Therefore, for all prospective IRT members, keep on learning and be curious.

Apart from security acumen, a good candidate must also posses the following skills:

- Good technical skills. Understand operating systems, networks, cryptography, a few programming languages (for example, Perl, C, and Java), and how all these elements interoperate.

- Have good interpersonal skills.

- Do not panic easily.

- Form a mental image of an incident based on sketchy information and make decisions.

Strong Technical Skills

Good understanding does not mean knowing all the details, but it does mean knowing salient details, why things are set up that way, and where to look for full details. Here are two examples of what would be a minimum of knowledge on two topics:

- **Microsoft Windows configuration parameters:** Microsoft Windows stores configuration details in the Registry, which is divided into hives. Each Registry hive is further divided into keys, subkeys, and values. A tool Reg.exe is used to edit the Registry. Further details are on the Microsoft website.

- **Border Gateway Protocol (BGP):** Transfers routing information in the Internet. The routing information is used by individual routers to make decision where to route a particular packet given its destination. More information about BGP can be found on the Internet Engineering Task Force (IETF) and Cisco websites.

In both examples, it is sufficient to know the basic principles about how things are related and what their function is in the overall scheme. Knowing where to look for more information, or who to ask, is also required. Good team members must be able to learn new things fast, and "fast" means in a matter of a few hours. Understanding malware written in a programming language that you never have seen before should slow you down only for how long it takes to locate and download a reference manual for that language.

Effective Interpersonal Skills

Handling incidents requires good interpersonal skills. Electronic mail is used a lot in the communication with other teams, but it is not known for its capability to transfer subtleties. People can interpret the same sentence differently depending on the way it is said and the tone that was used, but none of that can be conveyed by email. Often people who exchange emails are using a common language (English, most of the time) that is not the native tongue for either of them. Adding cultural differences into the mix can make the communication challenges even more demanding. To improve the understanding of the case, you should always consider picking up the telephone and calling the other party.

There are, however, some potential drawbacks when talking to a member of the other IRT. When non-native speakers are involved, there may be disparity on how well the other party mastered the spoken versus written language. Some people might have an excellent command of a written language but a mediocre, if not bad, command of the spoken language. That can happen if the person does not have a sufficient opportunity to practice talking and listening to a foreign language but spends a lot of time reading it. Even if a person is good at speaking a foreign language, it is still a question of the accent. That can occasionally cause problems even for native speakers when one, or both, sides have a heavy local accent. As you can see, there are ample opportunities for misunderstanding, so the members of an IRT must be able to handle the situation well.

One situation that can arise when handling a live incident is that a person reporting the incident says offensive things or becomes abusive. In most cases, when that happens, that kind of behavior is not normal for the reporter but is the consequence of the attack. The attacked person might feel that he is not understood and that the IRT member is taking the situation too lightly, so the reporter might become agitated. The IRT member must be able to recognize when such a behavior is the result of panic and when it is not and adjust the approach accordingly.

Does Not Panic Easily

Occasionally a team needs to handle an ongoing incident. The party from the other side is being attacked right now, its business is disrupted, and it is losing money or sensitive information is being siphoned off. It is understandable if that person is not calm but agitated and panicked. For IRT members, it is important to know how to handle that situation. First, the team members must not be easily agitated herself but have a steady temper. They also must work to calm the person on the phone to get the information on what is happening.

Forms an Incident's Image

When handling live incidents, the IRT member must be able to quickly form a picture of what is going on. To assess the situation, decide on possible ways to deal with the situation and recommend actions, which must be done in real time with only partial information. Sometimes the information is partial because the person reporting the incident forgot to provide it, and sometimes because she genuinely does not know it.

Apart from creating a picture, the IRT member must be able to make decisions autonomously and confidently. Someone who is indecisive cannot provide effective help during an ongoing incident.

Advertising the IRT's Existence

It is not sufficient only to have a team; other people must know about it. The team's existence must be announced internally within the constituency and externally to other teams. Only when people know about the team will they ask the IRT for help. One of the more obvious things is to set up a website that explains what the team does and how it can be reached. But that should not be the end of the effort. A website is passive. The team must invest energy and actively introduce itself. That advertising can take many forms and not be limited to the following:

- Attend and present at conferences and meetings.

- Send letters to appropriate people within and outside the constituency.

- Print posters and place them at visible places within the organization.

- Print and give away mugs, pens, stationery, or similar giveaway items.

- Include information about the team in new hire documentation packets, sales material, or a service offering prospectus.

- Meet with key people within and outside the constituency, and talk to them about the team and its purpose.

- Print an advertisement in a magazine or newspaper. Give interviews.

- Broadcast an advertisement on the radio or TV.

- Publish research papers or books.

All these actions can announce the team's existence, its goals and missions, and publicize its achievements. Another goal, when possible, is to seek feedback on the team. How it is fulfilling its mission and how to improve. Nobody is that good that there is no room for improvement.

Acknowledging Incoming Messages

Receiving an email about a compromised device is usually how work on a new incident starts. The first step in this process is for the IRT to acknowledge receiving this initial notification. The acknowledgment must fulfill several goals:

- Ensure the sender that the report is received and given attention.

- Communicate the incident tracking number back to the sender (if assigned).

- Set the expectations on what will happen next.

- Provide information about the IRT and how it can be contacted.

- The acknowledgment reflects team image, so it must look professional and be courteous.

Giving Attention to the Report

Some teams might opt for an automatic response to the sender, but that, albeit providing a quick response, might be viewed as too impersonal. This autoresponse mechanism is easy to set up, so many groups and organizations (not necessarily related to handling security incidents) use it. Unfortunately, a majority of these groups and organizations never follow up on these reports—or it appears that way, so most of the people now mistrust these automated responses. Mistrust in a sense that the sender does not have confidence that his report will ever be worked on. Some people mistrust these automated responses so much that they do not even consider them as a real acknowledgment.

Most people prefer communicating with another human being than an impersonal machine. Having someone who can compose a reply is much better, even if the confirmation is not as instantaneous as it would have been if it were automatic. It is perfectly fine to have a template answer that will be used to acknowledge the receipt of a report, but it is also acceptable to modify it for the added "human touch."

Following are some examples of varying the template text:

- Use the sender's name in the response.

- Ask for additional details.

- Add seasonal greetings (for example, "Happy New Year") but only if you know the sender. Not all people celebrate the same holidays, and some might get offended if they are wished well for a "wrong" (in their eyes) holiday or occasion.

Incident Tracking Number

If the report represents an incident, it must be assigned a tracking number. That number must be told to the sender so that she can use it in subsequent emails. That way, both parties will always know which incident they are talking about. When exchanging encrypted email, the Subject line should contain only the incident number and nothing else. That way, it gives away the minimum details to whoever intercepts the message.

Setting the Expectations

You must set the right expectations on what will happen next and how long it might take. If the report is not an incident, state so clearly with the explanation on what to do if the sender does not agree with the assessment. If the report is an incident, state whether it is being handled right now, and if not, when it might be taken into the process.

Making sure that the other party knows exactly what is happening now, what will follow, why, and when is important to prevent misunderstandings. It is always better to include more information than to leave the other party guessing what is going on, because most of the time, these guesses will be wrong. In this context, more information means where you are in the process of handing that incident and not more information as in personal information from other compromised sites.

Information About the IRT

Where can more information about the IRT be found and how can it be contacted? This is usually only a pointer to the IRT's website that contains all the details. There will always be people for whom this is the first time they communicate with the IRT. They obtained your email address from someone but they do not know what the IR team does and how. Adding a pointer to where people can learn more about the team is easy and can help first-time reporters a lot.

Looking Professional and Courteous

To make your responses more professional, you can prepare some template text in advance so that whoever will be composing the actual response can cut and paste parts of the template. The template adds to the uniformity of the acknowledgments that, in turn, helps people who are reading them as they get to know what information will be in the acknowledgment and where. This does not mean that people will now send a prepacked response instead of leaving that to auto-responder software. The template is there so that all relevant elements are included in the acknowledgment, and each team member can add their own touch to the response.

Sample Acknowledgment

An example of an acknowledgment can look like this:

Subject: Your report [IRT-1845249561249]

Reply-to: irt@example.org

Dear Miyamoto-san,

We received your report, and it is assigned tracking number IRT-1845249561249. Please keep this number in the subject line of all subsequent emails related to this incident.

This incident will be taken by one of our incident managers within the next 48 hours. You should receive a further email from the incident owner around that time. In the case that you are not contacted within 4 working days after you receive this email, please contact us again so that we can investigate the problem.

Our contact details, as our incident handling policy and other information about the IRT, can be found at http://www.example.org/security.

Regards,

Adela

——-

IRT http://www.example.org/security

Emergency telephone: (+1) 234 5678 9012

Cooperation with Internal Groups

In the same way the IRT cannot operate in isolation from the other IRTs, it also cannot operate without support and cooperation from various internal groups and departments. Depending on the particular case, not all departments or functions might be present in the host organization, but if they are, the IRT should consider liaising with them. The groups and departments are as follows:

- Physical security

- Legal department

- Press relation

- Internal IT security

- Executives

- Product security teams

- Internal IT and network operation center (NOC)

Physical Security

Without good old-fashioned physical security, many state-of-the-art security mechanisms would not properly work. There are examples where hardware keyloggers have been installed on computers. That was possible only if someone had physical access to computers. Equipment theft is also possible only if someone can physically grab the equipment.

This group usually operates, or has access to, Closed Circuit TV (CCTV) cameras, if they are installed on the premises. Therefore, their cooperation is invaluable in cases where identity of a person must be confirmed.

Occasionally, it is these people who have power to arrest and detain. So, if the IRT is sure that they identified the culprit within the organization, someone from the physical security group would make an arrest.

Legal Department

Many of us have made some joking remarks on lawyers' accounts, but joking aside, they exist to protect the organization and to protect you. They can be an invaluable asset. The IRT must work to identify whom, from the legal side, would support the team in its job. The best results can be achieved if someone, or a few people, are given an extra task to support the IRT on a long-term basis.

You must expect to invest a considerable effort at the beginning while the legal team learns about the security world and the IRT learns about the legal challenges. Only after both sides understand each other's positions can real cooperation begin.

The IRT should bring all new or different incidents to the attention of the legal team. In the majority of cases, the legal team might decide that the new case falls under one of the previously encountered issues. It is a remaining few that will prompt the legal team to look deeper into the matter to see how the organization can better protect itself from the legal perspective. These improvements might range from the way the IRT approaches similar incidents to modified contracts that the organization will use in the future.

It is also a good idea that lawyers from different organizations reach out to each other and start a dialogue. This area is relatively young, and there are many interesting challenges ahead. It is much easier if they are approached collectively than individually. One such attempt is underway as a part of the Vendor Special Interest Group forum under FIRST. Interested parties can visit http://www.first.org/vendor-sig/index.html and contact moderators.

Press Relations

Sooner or later, the IRT might be involved in a big, or interesting, case, and the press might approach the team to give a statement. Talking to the press can be tricky. Usually the journalists would like to receive as much information as possible, whereas the IRT might not want to disclose all the information, at least not at that particular moment.

The easiest way to handle the press is to have a dedicated PR person assigned to the team to work closely with it. Failing that, the next option is to have someone from the IRT receive PR training and act as the team's spokesperson. The last, and the least desirable option, is to have somebody, without any training, step in front of the journalists. Whatever your case happens to be, following are a few simple tips on what to do when talking to the press:

- There is no such thing as "off the record." Whatever you say can end up being printed. If something is not to be mentioned at the time, do not mention it under any circumstances.

- Be prepared. If possible, ask for questions in advance and prepare the answers.

- Ask to review the final article before it will be published.

- Do not lie. Sooner or later, people will find the truth, and then your credibility is gone—not only your personal credibility, but also the credibility of your team and the organization.

- Do not speculate. Know the facts and stick to them. It is better to say that something is not known than to speculate.

- Know what can be said. Always keep within safe limits. When necessary, a "no comments" phrase can be handy to use.

- Have a message to pass to journalists.

- Do not always answer a question that was asked but one that you would like to be asked (thank Alan Greenspan for this one). If used judiciously, this can help with getting your points to journalists.

Listed like that, it does not sound like much, but it might not be easy to accomplish every time.

If your team is lucky to have a dedicated PR person, she can help you with promoting your team. The PR person can also proactively work with journalists and help them understand what the IRT is doing, why, and how. This all can help you greatly in the time of crisis because informed journalists can present the facts in a more accurate light.

If you judge that an incident might generate inquiries from the press, you should prepare a holding statement that can be used if a journalist contacts the organization and asks for a statement. An example of such an event might be an incident that affects many other companies or has especially significant and severe consequences for your organization.

In virtually all cases, there is not much benefit from proactively contacting the press and offering information about an incident. If an incident occurs, the organization has the IRT that can handle the situation. The business continues as usual. The exception to this rule might be a situation in which someone else will publicize the situation, and you want your version of the events to be heard first.

Internal IT Security

Some organizations might have a separate group that handles only internal security cases, cases pertaining to the host organization. This setup can occur when, for business reasons, all customers' incidents are handled by one team and internal cases by another.

In that case, the internal IT security group is a natural an ally of the IRT. Having a close relationship can be mutually beneficial. Both teams can organize regular meetings to exchange information on what kind of attacks they are seeing and observe trends. The group handling customers' incidents should provide information only on types of attacks but not who has been attacked. In addition to the regular information exchange, both teams should enable members from one team to rotate into another team and spend some time working with the other group.

Despite all this synergy between the teams, some functions will be duplicated. If business reasons dictate the existence of two teams, duplication is natural.

Executives

It was mentioned previously that the IRT should have an executive sponsor. Apart from having a sponsor, the IRT must have the means to reach other executives. There must be an arrangement for the IRT to brief the executives on a regular basis and when emergencies occur.

Regular briefings are important so that the executives can learn about the organization's exposure to the newest security threats. They can also learn about the IRT's challenges to address the threats and make appropriate decisions. This communication is even more important during the crisis. Additionally, because of the exposure the team will get, the executives will know whom to talk to when they need more information. This way, executives will not waste time asking around and receiving nonauthoritative or plainly wrong information. For executives, it is vital to be informed whether their part of the organization is affected by the incident and, if it is, how and to what extent.

Direct communication with the executives is important for the IRT because it provides a visibility opportunity for the team. The security of the organization and the IRT will gain in stature in the eyes of the executives. Visibility and consistent good performance will transform the IRT into a trusted adviser to the executives on matters related to information security.

A consistent and constant information flow from the IRT to the executives is important. For executives to rely on the team's messages, they must follow a fixed pattern. Even if the message is "nothing to report," it must be delivered when expected. In a crisis, the messaging period will change and will be delivered when required instead of waiting for the next scheduled time slot. It is not necessary that the message is always delivered in person. Often an email or voice message will suffice.

The format of the message must be suitable for the purpose. Executives are busy people with little time to waste, so the communication must be specifically tailored to fit the purpose. That encompasses not only the graphical layout but also the file format and media. Big Microsoft Word files are not useful if received on a Blackberry. Voice mail can be a more noticeable event than receiving yet another email. On the other hand, it is easier to reread a mail message multiple times than listen to the same voice mail, especially if the interesting part of the message is close to its end. The teams must know what it wants to accomplish and tailor the messaging accordingly.

Here are few tips when communicating with the executives:

- **Frequency:** Not more often that every two weeks but not less than once a month for regular updates. During a crisis, the first message should be sent as soon as the severity of an incident reaches a certain criteria. (For example, the number of compromised hosts, certain key hosts, or what services are compromised.) After that point, the frequency should be a function of the incident, and reporting can be done from every hour to once a day.

- **Content:** Keep it short and simple. Provide pointers to where all details are being kept. Order information chronologically so that the most recent information is presented first. Background information can be added at the end. Do not forget to include the impact to the organization—why this communication is important to the executives. The next steps and the time of the next communication also must be presented, together with actions that executives must undertake.

When sending both an email and a voice message, they should not be identical. The email can contain more background information, whereas the voice message should focus only on the most recent developments.

■ **Format:** Between two slides to four slides for regular face-to-face meetings. For all other regular updates, text email (no Microsoft Word or Adobe PDF documents) together with a voice message should be used. Text email is preferred over all other formats because it can be quickly downloaded even over a slow connection (for example, a 2400-baud modem line in a hotel) and easily read on any device.

A web page must be created where executives can find all the information. That must be a single top-level page that gives an overall view of all current events. This top-level page must then contain links for each individual incident and to all other communications to the executives.

■ **Length:** Optimally, approximately 2 and not longer than 3 minutes for a voice mail and a one-page email (approximately 200 words to 300 words). Everything else should be given as additional information on a web page.

Here are examples of a voice message and an accompanying email that provide an update on an ongoing incident. We will assume that the update is provided once daily. The voice mail is given first:

This is Joe Smith with an update regarding the incident that occurred on January 30, 2009. This voice mail is sent to the emergency executive council. The full list of the recipients is given at the end of this message. All information in this message is confidential.

On January 30th, unknown attackers used an unpatched vulnerability to gain access to servers in accounting and engineering. The unauthorized access was discovered when attackers were transferring files to an external server. There is no PR coverage of the incident.

The status on February 3rd is that 60% of all servers in the organization have been patched. All servers in accounting are patched and are all back online. 80% of servers in engineering are patched. The help desk is the most exposed part of the organization, with only 20% of servers patched. Our IRT report web page contains full details of the patching progress.

In addition to patching, our intrusion prevention systems are updated with the new signature, and all firewalls are configured to make exploitation of the vulnerability harder.

We expect to patch all servers in the organization by February 10th. Determining the extent of leaked personal information will be finished by February 5th. After the scope of the leak is determined, the Legal and HR department will be engaged to asses our legal exposure.

No actions are required from the executive council at this time.

The next regular update is on February 4th at 14:00.

This message is sent to: name_1, name_2, ...

Regards,

Joe Smith

The accompanying email can look like this:

From: IRT@example.com

Subject: Status on the security compromise on 2009-Feb-03

—— CONFIDENTIAL – DO NOT DISTRIBUTE ——

Hello,

This is Joe Smith with an update about the incident that occurred on January 30, 2009. This email is sent to the emergency executive council.

Background

On January 30th, unknown attackers used an unpatched vulnerability to gain access to servers in accounting and engineering. The unauthorized access was discovered when attackers were transferring files to an external server. There is no PR coverage of the incident.

All details related to this incident can be found at http://www.example.com/IRT/incident web page.

Current status

Patching is in progress across all the organization. The following table provides status per individual parts of the organizations:

Accounting: 100%

Engineering: 80%

Manufacturing: 40%

Web-farm and mail servers: 70%

Help desk: 20%

Overall: 62%

In addition to patching, our intrusion prevention systems are updated with the new signature, and all firewalls are configured to make exploitation of the vulnerability harder.

The next update will be sent on Feb 04 at 14:00.

Next milestones

Feb 05—Determine the scope of personal information leak.

Feb 06—Engage Legal and HR to determine legal exposure due to personal information leak.

Feb 10—100% of servers to be patched.

Pending executive actions

No actions were required from the executive council at this time.

Regards,

Joe Smith

—— CONFIDENTIAL – DO NOT DISTRIBUTE ——

Product Security Team

If the host organization is a vendor that is responsible for developing and maintenance of a product or service, it should have a dedicated team that deals with security vulnerabilities in the products. Similarly, like with the situation with IT, both teams, product security and IRT, can benefit from having close ties. The product security team can provide information on different vulnerabilities so that the IRT can start looking at whether it is being exploited. Information on vulnerabilities can also be used to reevaluate some old data. What was previously seen as only noise or random attempts might suddenly be seen as focused efforts to exploit a particular vulnerability.

The product security team can benefit from receiving information on new attacks, analyzing how the attacks affect its products, and passing the knowledge to the group responsible for maintenance and product design.

Even if the organization is not a vendor, the team should establish ties with vendors' product security teams. At least, the IRT must know how to contact them. Vendors always appreciate when they receive notification on a new vulnerability or other suspicious behavior of their products.

Internal IT and NOC

Depending on the organization's size and complexity, you may have a separate IT group that maintains and monitors the internal network. If you are an Internet service provider (ISP), you probably would have a separate network operation center (NOC) that maintains a network used by your customers. These two groups are your partners. They can provide the IRT with the current information on what is happening in the network (internal or external). They can also provide early warnings about new attacks while they are being tested[1]. NOC, in particular, can add network-centric view on attacks and contribute methods how to combat attacks using network infrastructure.

Be Prepared!

An IRT, by its nature, deals with emergencies and exceptions. As such, it is hard to be prepared for something that cannot be foreseen. Although nobody can be prepared for

---

[1] Occasionally, you can capture early samples of new exploits while they are tested by miscreants before deploying them on a large scale.

the exact incarnation of the next worm—because we do not know what it will look like—you can be prepared for a general threat of worms. The new worm is expected to have some general characteristics common with previously seen worms. It is known how previous worms affected the organization, so the IRT can prepare to handle future outbreaks similar to the previous ones. Following are some steps that can be taken to prepare to handle incidents:

- Know current attacks and techniques.

- Know the system the IRT is responsible for.

- Identify critical resources.

- Formulate response strategy.

- Create a list of scenarios and practice handling them.

Know Current Attacks and Techniques

It is imperative for the IRT to possess an intimate knowledge of current attack techniques and attacks themselves. Without that knowledge, the IRT would not know how to distinguish an attack from some legitimate activity. Obviously, the knowledge must not be limited only to the attacking side. It must also cover the defense. How can you protect your organization from various attacks and what are the potential drawbacks of different methods? This also encompasses features and capabilities of installed equipment. And last, but not least, know the network's topology and characteristics.

The next question is, How should you gather that knowledge? Unfortunately, there is no easy way to accomplish that. It must be done the hard way. Reading public lists like Bugtraq, full-disclosure, and others is standard for every team. Attending conferences and learning new issues is also important. Analyzing what is going on in the team's constituency is obligatory. Monitoring, as much as possible, underground is necessary. Setting up honeypots and honeynets and analyzing the activity is also an option. But, above all, talk to your peers and exchange experiences. That is something that cannot be substituted with anything else. All evidence points to the fact that miscreants do exchange information and that they do it rather efficiently. Good guys, on the other hand, tend to lag behind in sharing the information. Chapter 6, "Getting to Know Your Peers: Teams and Organizations Around the World," talks more about some of the main forums that IRTs can use to interact with peers.

It is not necessary for each IRT member to monitor all the sources. There are simply so many potential sources to collect the information that it is almost impossible for a single person to track them all. One workaround is to contract out this task to an external company or, if it is done internally, share the task among team members so that not all of them are monitoring the same sources.

When monitoring sources is contracted out, you need to make sure that the received information is relevant to the IRT. For example, if your constituency is predominately using the Solaris operating system, the information on vulnerabilities in Microsoft

Windows is not that useful to you. The positive side of contracting out this task is that you are freeing your resources. The potential negative side is that you might need to renegotiate your contract if you want to change the scope of the information you are receiving.

If the information collection is done internally, you can include other groups or individuals to help you with that task, even if they are not part of the IRT. This help can be either formal or informal. If your organization has a group that monitors external information sources, you can make a formal arrangement with them to receive only the information that might interest the IRT. If you do not have such a group in your organization, you might find security-conscious individuals who are monitoring some of the sources that might also interest the IRT. If there are such individuals, you can ask them to forward all potentially interesting information to the IRT. This would be an informal arrangement that, in some cases, can be reliable and function quite well. If you have such arrangement, do make sure to nurture that relationship. Commend these people for what they are doing and try to make them feel appreciated. You can give them some small awards or take them out for a dinner. People like to see that their work is appreciated, so an occasional meal together will pay for itself many times over by the work these other people will do.

If your IRT decides to operate a honeypot or honeynet, you must make sure that you will have sufficient resources to do so. A honeypot is a nonproduction service exposed to the Internet with the purpose of being (mis)used by an attacker. The IRT can then capture malware and gain firsthand knowledge about how it infects devices and propagates. The service can be emulated with special software or it can be a real service. A honeynet is a network of honeypots. One way to arrange a honeynet is to assign an unused (either by your organization or in general) portion of IP addresses to a group of computers and monitor all traffic going in and out of that network. Computers can be either real hardware or virtual. If they are virtual computers, you should know that some malware can detect whether it is executed on a virtual platform and, if it is, the malware will not behave maliciously.

Although installing a honeypot and honeynet is relatively quick, monitoring and analyzing what is going on requires a considerable effort. You also must make sure that your honeypot is not used to attack someone else. Overall, honeypots can be valuable sources of information, but they also require significant effort to properly use them.

Know the System IRT Is Responsible For

The IRT must know what it is protecting, the location of the boundaries of the systems for which it is responsible, and the functions of different parts of the system. After defining boundaries, the next step is to identify the groups (or people) that can be contacted when the IRT must cross the boundaries. All this is only the start. These steps just define the area of the IRT's responsibility. The next task is to determine what is "normal" within that area. This is important because the incident is something that is not expected. It is an activity that is not standard. Most of the malware would initiate actions that are not usual for an average user (for example, starts mass mailing or connects to an IRC channel). If the

IRT knows what is normal for the given system, it will be easier to spot deviations and start investigating them. This is also known as determining the baseline. Depending on the organization, some of the tasks to determine the baseline can be done by IT or some other department and not the IRT. Irrespective of who is doing it, the IRT must be able to receive and use that information to spot anomalies.

The baseline means different things for different aspects of the overall system. On the highest level, it can consist of the following things:

- Number of remote users

- Number of internal users

- Total consumed network bandwidth, inbound and outbound, at all links (for example, between branch offices, toward the Internet)

- Traffic breakdown per protocol and application (TCP, UDP, mail, web, backup, and so on) and bandwidth utilization per protocol

Each of the categories can then be further refined and a more detailed picture can be formed. For remote users, remote IP addresses can be recorded. A traffic model of a user can be formed by recording how much traffic (packets) is generated inbound and outbound and what protocols and applications have generated it. For some protocols, what types of packets are being generated can even be recorded. If we take TCP as an example, the ratio of SYN packets versus ACK packets can be recorded. How many fragmented packets are in the mix? That information can then be used to identify the presence of anomalous traffic because different types of packets are used by different attack programs. Another type of information that can be recorded is the direction of the traffic. That is important because the site can be the target or source of an attack.

Information used to build the baseline should come from multiple sources to build a better picture. Traffic snapshots (or full captures for small sites), Netflow data, syslog logs, logs from intrusion prevention/detection systems, and application logs of all of these sources should be used to build the baseline.

Collecting data to form the baseline can be illuminating. On occasions that can give an interesting picture and reveal all sorts of things that are being done without the knowledge of appropriate groups. It does not always have to be in the negative sense. It is common to find some servers still offering services and being used, even though they were officially decommissioned several years ago. Various cases of network or system misconfigurations can also be detected (for example, traffic being routed down the suboptimal path). Unofficial web servers and wireless access points are also likely to be discovered during the process.

Taking only a single snapshot might not be sufficient to establish a credible baseline. Traffic and usage patterns change over time. They are different depending on the hour within a day, a day in a week, and month in a year. During lunch time, it is expected to see less traffic than in the middle of the morning. Around holidays, traffic will be again lower than during the normal working days. Adding or removing a significant number of computers will affect the baseline, too. The message is that information should be constantly updated with the latest measurements.

The baseline does not need to be precise to the byte and must not be used rigidly. If, for example, 40 percent of incoming traffic on the main Internet link is TCP, the times when that ratio increases to 45 percent do not need to be immediately considered as a sign of an attack. But if it suddenly jumps to 60 percent or more, it is probably suspicious. There will always be some variation in each of the baseline components, and the IRT must be aware of what the expected variation is. That can be determined only with prolonged and continuous inspection.

Identify Critical Resources

The next step in the process is to identify critical resources. What resources are critical for the business and in what way? What will happen if a resource is unavailable? If the company website is used only to present what the organization is about, it being unavailable might not have severe consequences. If the website is also used for ordering, you need to keep the period of not being available as short as possible. The billing system might be more critical than email infrastructure, and so on.

This part of the process must be done with help from different groups and departments within the organization. Each of them should identify what resources are critical for their business. All that information then must be taken to a higher level of management and looked at from the global organization's perspective. Although something might be critical for a given department, it might not play a significant role from the overall business perspective. The criticality of services should be reviewed periodically and after significant change in the business model is introduced.

Formulate Response Strategy

After completing the inventory of critical resources, an appropriate response strategy can be formulated. This strategy is supposed to answer questions such as: If a service, or server, is compromised, what can and should be done? Here are few examples that illustrate this point:

■ If a company's website is defaced or compromised, what needs to be done? If the website is used only for general information, it can be simply rebuilt, and no effort will be spent trying to identify how the compromise happened or who did it.

■ If a host used for collecting billing information is compromised and the attacker is siphoning credit card information from it, can you simply shut off the computer to prevent further damages? Although that can prevent data theft, it might also prevent collecting billing information, and the organization will lose some money as a consequence.

■ What level of compromise needs to happen before a decision to attempt to identify a culprit for possible prosecution will be made versus just shutting him out? This can possibly mean that the attacker will be left to (mis)use the compromised system for some time while the investigation is going on. What is the point when the business might seriously suffer as the consequence of the compromise and the investigation has to be stopped?

Answers to some of the questions can also lead to rethink the way the system is organized or services are offered. In the case of a website, maybe it can be made static and burned on a DVD so that the possibility of defacement is reduced if not eliminated. Maybe some critical services can be split across multiple computers, so if one is compromised, it can be shut down without affecting the other service.

Why is this important? When the attack is ongoing, there might not be sufficient time to think about what the various actions of the attacker and defenders can cause to the organization. At that time, the IRT must react as quickly as possible to minimize the impact to the organization. Knowing how different computers and services depend on each other and how important they are to the organization enable the team to respond quickly and accurately while minimizing the impact and disruptions to the business.

Create a List of Scenarios

Instead of waiting for incidents to happen and then learning how to respond, the IRT should have regular practice drills. Some most common scenarios should be created, and the team must practice how to respond to them. This is especially important after new members join the team. Even if they are experienced in incident handling, each organization will have some processes slightly different, and practice drills are the right time and place to learn them. The main purpose of these exercises is that people gain practice and confidence in handling incidents. They also serve to test how effective the current response might be given changes in the network (added new devices or software features) and to accordingly modify the way to respond. These exercises do not need to be limited only to IRT but can involve other parts of the organization. In such joint exercises, all involved participants must know when the exercise is active. This is to prevent confusion so that people will not panic or take wrong actions thinking that the real compromise is happening.

What can these scenarios look like? For a start, they must cover the main aspects of all handled incidents. If these incidents happened once, there is the possibility that they will happen again. Here are some suggestions of what can be covered:

■ Virus or worm outbreaks

■ External and internal routing hijacked

■ DNS-related attacks (for example, the organization DNS entry gets changed and points to a bogus site)

■ Computer compromise

- Network sniffer installed on several computers

- Website defacement or compromise

- Phishing attacks

- DoS attacks

- Emergency software upgrade

These may be the most common scenarios that one organization might encounter. Depending on the organization's role and technical capabilities, some additional scenarios can be created. Also, some of the scenarios might not be applicable to the team because of job separation (for example, software upgrade is done by the IT department).

These practice drills can be only a paper exercise, or they can be conducted on an isolated network segment. Instead of using physical devices, it also might be possible to either simulate them or to use virtual devices (for example, virtual computers in VMware). What method and technology will be used depends on the goals and capabilities.

Devices we can simulate are computers, routers, and networks of devices. In these simulations, devices can be either targets of simulated attacks or used to observe how malicious software behaves. Some of the software for creating virtual computers are VMware, Parallels, Xen, and QEMU. A more comprehensive list of different software is posted at the Wikipedia web page at http://en.wikipedia.org/wiki/ Comparison_of_platform_virtual_machines. Some of the software for creating virtual computers can also be used to connect virtual computers creating virtual networks. Dynamips, Dynagen, and Simics are some of the software that can be used for simulating routers and network of routers.

A paper exercise is good for formulating the initial response on an attack that has not been encountered yet and to modify an existing response after the system changed because the equipment changed or software was upgraded. Testing the response, on the other hand, is best done on the actual equipment. At that time, all the previously invested work to determine the baseline and what is the normal state for the network pays off. Having this information, the team can send (or simulate) the right amount and the mix of traffic and then superimpose attacking traffic on top of it. In some instances, that might not be relevant, but in others, such as DoS attacks, it can be relevant. The instances when the baseline is not that important are in the presence of single-packet attacks. In that case, it is sufficient to send only a single packet to compromise or reset a device or a process on the device. You need to use real devices for the verification to make sure that the simulator reflects the real device's behavior. It can take some time for the simulator to be updated with the newest features present on the devices.

Use simulators and emulators to practice the response once when you are sure that it actually reflects how the real device will behave and when it is known what the response is. After the response is established and practiced, new elements should be added to it.

Some unexpected or unusual elements should be introduced. They can be various things, such as the following:

■   The telephone network is down; at the same time, team members cannot use fixed telephony or mobile phones to communicate.

■   It is impossible to physically reach the affected device (for example, a computer is locked in a room and the room key is lost).

■   A new device is introduced into the network without anyone's knowledge (for example, a load-balancing device inserted in front of the web farm) or the network topology is changed.

Introducing these elements should prevent people from trying to fit the problem into the solution instead of the other way around. Each new case should be like the first one and should be handled with a mind open to any eventuality.

The last things to practice are, seemingly, impossible scenarios. You must accept that, occasionally, the research community does come up with a revolutionary new attack technique, and things that were considered impossible suddenly become routine. Here are a few examples:

■   A scenario that contains a logical paradox. That would be the trick case to verify that the handler can notice the paradox. An example might be to invent a device under attack that is not connected to the network or withhold information about an intermediate device.

■   A feature suddenly stops working (for example, packet filters do not block packets; rate limiters do not limit packet rate).

■   Significant improvement in attack techniques (for example, a complete compromise of MD5 and SHA-1 hash functions, an AES crypto system is broken, and the number factoring becomes trivial).

For some of these scenarios, there may be no valid, or possible, responses, so their value lies in forcing people to think out of the the-box. Some of the scenarios might one day become reality—a collision in MD5, a number factoring using quantum computers—so thinking about them today might give the organization an edge.

Measure of Success

How can you measure whether the IRT is successful? Executives always like to know whether the budget given to the IRT is well spent and whether the organization is more secure now than it was before. There is no universal answer to these questions. Instead of trying to provide partial answers, it is better to describe a framework on how to create metrics that will be used to measure the team's success.

At the start, it must be said that, by itself, counting the number of incidents the team has handled in a given time period is not a good measure of how the team is doing. It can certainly be a component of the measure, but that number by itself is not informative, and there are good reasons why. After the team starts operating, it will initially see only a few incidents. Quickly that number will start to rise rapidly, and the more the team is working on them, the more incidents will come to light—and the number of incidents will just keep on growing. From that perspective, it might appear that the team is not doing things right because before it started working, there were only a few incidents, and now they never stop. In reality, the reason for seeing an increased number of incidents is because the IRT is actively looking for them while before nobody took notice of them, even when the signs were obvious.

The way to approach creating the metrics to measure the team's success is to start from who is the team's constituency and what is the team's goal, and what it tries to do for the constituency. That will provide the starting point of defining what can be measured. Additionally, you can try to measure changes in the risk the organization faces from a compromise. Part of that risk assessment is the speed of recovery and limiting the damage after the incident. The final part of the metrics is the team's influence and standing with the community. A good guide on how to define what to measure, how, and why is the ISO 27004 standard. Let's now look at some examples of how metrics for measuring the team's success can be defined.

One of the goals for most of the IRTs is to increase security awareness within the constituency. This goal can be aligned with specific policies such as "All users will receive basic security training" or "All users' passwords will be longer than six characters." Data on a number of users receiving security training and the results of checking users' password can be easily obtained, so you can calculate where you are in meeting the policy goals. This then directly feeds into one of the measures of the team's success.

Assessing changes in the risk the organization faces from computer attacks is harder to accomplish. You cannot directly measure the attacker's willingness to attack your organization, but you can use the fact that attackers are mostly opportunistic creatures to your advantage. If you are a hard target, attackers will go after others who are easier targets. What you can measure here is what is happening to your organization relative to your peers and the industry. Reliable data on attacks is hard to come by. CSI and BERR surveys (mentioned in Chapter 1) can serve as guides, but the numbers must be taken with caution. Attacks do not have to be targeted; you can also compare the number and severity of virus outbreaks within the organization versus the industry. One example that illustrates this very well was an outbreak of a particular worm a few years ago. Most of the other organizations were infected, but Cisco was not because of the measures the Cisco InfoSec team implemented.

Being a leader in the field is also a sign of the team's success. This can be measured by looking at the number of talks the team was invited to give, the number of interviews the IRT members gave, and how many of the team's ideas were incorporated into best practices and international standards.

Summary

Running a successful IRT involves many aspects. The team must have the right people and do the right thing. Not only must you pay attention to major things, but you also must not lose sight of the small details. Although all these details might look overwhelming, with dedication from the entire team, they can be achieved, and you will have a successful and respected IRT.

References

Comparison of platform virtual machines, Wikipedia. January 19, 2009. http://en.wikipedia.org/wiki/Comparison_of_platform_virtual_machines.

Computer Security Incident Handling Guide, Recommendations of the National Institute of Standards and Technology, NIST Special Publication 800-61 Revision 1. Tim Grance, Karen Kent, and Brian Kim, March 2008. http://csrc.nist.gov/publications/nistpubs/800-61-rev1/SP800-61rev1.pdf.

Council Directive 93/104/EC of November 23, 1993 concerning certain aspects of the organization of working time, Council of the European Union, November 23, 1993. http://eur-lex.europa.eu/ LexUriServ/LexUriServ.do?uri=CONSLEG:1993L0104: 20000801:EN:PDF.

Data elements and interchange formats—Information interchange—Representation of dates and times, ISO 8601:2004, 2004-12-03.

Directive 2003/88/EC of the European Parliament and of the Council of 4 November 2003 concerning certain aspects of the organization of working time, Official Journal L 299, 18/11/2003, p. 0009—0019. http://eur-lex.europa.eu/LexUriServ/ LexUriServ.do?uri=CELEX:32003L0088:EN:HTML.

Dynagen, http://dynagen.org/.

Dynamips, http://www.ipflow.utc.fr/index.php/Cisco_7200_Simulator.

Forum of Incident and Response Security Teams, http://www.first.org/.

The GNU Privacy Guard, http://www.gnupg.org/.

The International PGP Home Page, http://www.pgpi.com/.

ISO (2009), Information security management measurements, ISO/IEC 27004:2009. http://www.iso.org/iso/en/CatalogueDetailPage.CatalogueDetail?CSNUMBER= 40874&ICS1=1&ICS2=140&ICS3=30.

PGP Corporation, http://www.pgp.com/.

Virtutech Simics, Simics, http://www.virtutech.com/.

Chapter 4

Dealing with an Attack

Computer and network security incidents do happen. They occur every minute of every day somewhere in the world. Many go unnoticed. Others might be caught through automated monitoring solutions, direct contact, or even pure luck. You might find yourself responding to any of the following kinds of incidents:

- Direct network intrusion

- Brute force authentication attack

- Denial-of-service attack

- Lost employee laptop

- Lost backup tapes

- Exposed confidential or proprietary information

- Extortion

- Attacks through portable media such as USB thumb drives

- Spyware

- Keyloggers

- Wireless sniffing

No matter the vector, you must be ready to respond. When responding to an incident, you need to be prompt and take swift action without panicking, overreacting, or taking unnecessary risks.

Let's visit a house fire scenario for comparison. A fire truck is dispatched moments after the alarm is received to respond to the fire quickly. The emergency vehicles are maintained and kept full of fuel and other supplies. When in route, the firefighters do not go so fast or take unnecessary risks that they would wreck and take a chance on not being able to respond.

When the firefighters arrive on the scene, everyone knows their role. Each person has a task. These tasks might include someone to hook up hoses to fire hydrants, someone to pull hoses from the truck to the hydrant, someone to hook fire hoses to the truck for the firefighting team, someone to block traffic so that hoses do not get run over, and someone to move spectators out of harm's way, among other duties. They rely on their training not only in the active handling of the emergency, but also with other details, such as where to park the truck to minimize obstruction if other vehicles need to get close to the scene, having a quick escape if necessary, and not putting the truck in danger. Firefighters avoid wasting time or energy getting excited about a fire without actually performing an action that would lead toward the resolution.

Similarly, when an incident occurs, your response needs to be just as smooth, well planned, and practiced. This chapter is devoted to helping guide you through what is required. What will be covered here are different components on incident handling, or a set of actions, required for incident handling. These components are presented in an order relatively common when dealing with incidents. However, this is not the "best order" or "desired order." Each incident must be treated in its own right, so the order of actions can be different.

At a high level, the components include the following:

- Assigning an incident owner.

- Determining the need to involve law enforcement.

- Assessing the incident's severity.

- Assessing the scope.

- Solving the problem. The solution might vary depending on the incident, so it can range from just stopping the attack and restoring the system to prosecuting the attacker.

- Determining the need to involve other teams.

- Determining the need to involve press relations.

- Undertaking post-mortem analysis.

Assigning an Incident Owner

First and foremost, an owner of the incident must be identified. The owner of the incident is the incident handler, or handler for short, who is responsible for coordinating, leading, and making decisions in the resolution of the incident. The incident handler should be responsible for the entire incident. This does not mean that they have to perform super-human acts or make every decision, but they must be responsible for making sure that all aspects of the incident are addressed properly by the appropriate resources.

To save precious time during an incident, the handler must be identified quickly and efficiently. Time spent identifying who will take the lead is time spent not actually dealing with the incident, so you must minimize that amount of time.

You can accomplish this in several ways. One possibility is to have a duty roster identified ahead of time. This roster simply states that on this day at this time, a named individual is on-duty and has the responsibility to respond. Rotation of that duty can occur at whatever frequency works best for your organization or team. For some organizations, it might be a weekly rotation. Others might use a daily rotation. The key is to choose a method and identify a duty person.

Another possibility for determining a handler might be based on the level of responsibility. You can determine this by a mandate, such as the first person on the scene from a responsible team or by a seniority level within the organization. If you choose this latter method, make sure those individuals who might find themselves in the position of coordinator are well suited and ready to manage a crisis.

After you identify the handler, it is critical for the handler to step up and take charge of the situation. I have engaged with many customers who have been attempting to deal with an attack. It is enlightening to join their conference bridges to see the lack of coordination. Often they are either unsure where to start or have started dealing with the many aspects of the incident and are hard to pull back together to approach the problem in a more organized manner.

You might also want to define a backup incident handler. Ultimately, we are all human and need to take time for breaks, to eat, and to get some sleep. In large incidents, it is useful to have a backup incident handler who can help lead if the primary incident handler gets pulled away or gets stuck dealing with a specific portion of the incident. Having a backup incident handler present also can provide valuable experience for other members of your IRT, especially for the less-experienced members.

Law Enforcement Involvement

Early on in an incident, you need to know whether law enforcement (LE) is already involved or whether it is likely for them to be involved. Engaging with law enforcement can change how your team will report the case or handle it. The consequences of improperly handling the case can result in having evidence tainted and made inadmissible in a court. Inadmissible evidence makes prosecution of the crime more difficult.

The IRT must be aware of the appropriate procedure of how to handle incidents when law enforcement is involved. Depending on the jurisdictions involved, procedures can vary. Evidentiary procedures and forensics is not covered in this book, but remember to take good notes about the incident. These notes should preferably be recorded in a book with numbered pages where individual pages cannot be inserted or removed easily. The notes themselves should be as complete as possible with dates, time stamps, and observations recorded. This will help you later when you have to write up an incident report or possibly need to jog your memory for legal testimony.

If you are a third-party response team, such as the Cisco PSIRT team, inquiring about involving law enforcement is a question that the customer often has not even considered. Some people respond back with a question for the IRT about whether law enforcement should be involved. If the IRT is not absolutely certain that law enforcement must be involved, the safest approach is to present options and allow the reporter to decide. As the victim, they will likely be the ones that have to press charges, collect evidence, provide testimony, and document damages.

For the IRTs that are part of the attacked organization, it is easier to make this decision. There might be instances in which reporting is mandatory, as in situations involving life and death, kidnapping, or child pornography. The list must be prepared by the legal expert, and the IRT must be familiar with it. For all other cases, the team should consult its management and legal experts.

What is important to note is that law enforcement should not necessarily be involved the moment the incident is discovered, unless the incident is time-critical. After an incident is discovered, there is nothing to report other than "an attack is in progress." A decision to involve law enforcement must be made as early as possible because it affects how the incident is handled. The actual reporting to law enforcement can happen later.

Legal Issues

In handling any incident, you need to be aware of the possible legal requirements and implications. Although this is not a specific step in handling an incident, this is an important issue. The legal environment in which the IRT operates has a great influence on how incidents are handled.

Chapter 1, "Why Care About Incident Response?," gives a few examples of legal requirements that help define a need for an IRT. An IRT needs to be familiar with those same requirements to understand your obligations. For example, under the State of California law SB 1386, your organization might be required to report the incident if personal information has been stolen. Other governments are enacting or are considering enacting similar laws for computer crime and data loss.

Additionally, the IRT needs to be aware of other laws that might apply. For example, in the United States, there is a distinction between legal and illegal gambling. If U.S.-based IRT finds itself in a position to help a gambling website handling an attack, the IRT might need to know what kind of gambling is conducted. If it is legal gambling, everything is fine. If illegal gambling is involved, the IRT might be breaking a law by helping the gambling site. Other governments might have laws that can create similar situations in which the IRT might inadvertently break the law by helping someone under attack. Therefore, it is worthwhile to consult a lawyer who is familiar with any local, state, federal, or international laws that apply to the IRT.

Assessing the Incident's Severity

After identifying the incident handler, you now need to understand the problem and its severity. The main purpose of this step is to assess the impact of the incident on your organization. Knowing the impact can determine the urgency and priority with which the incident will be handled. Your team might be handling several incidents at the same time, so assessing the severity of the new incident is important.

As you begin assessing the incident, you might not have sufficient information to make any decision on how to react. You might know only what the incident reporter thinks is the problem, and that might not be the real problem. The reporter might not know the scope and the severity of the incident. Keep in mind that the reporter is telling you only what she sees. What are the immediate consequences to her are not necessarily the actual extent of the incident.

As you gather information, you will not only start to understand the problem, but it will also help you in planning your solution. When collecting information about the incident, start from small and then gradually widen out. In other words, you start with what the reporter is experiencing and then try to find out how other parts of the organization might be affected.

Following are documents that can help you during this stage:

- **Network topology:** Helps trace which devices connect to which other devices. Some attacks use vulnerabilities that can be exploited only if devices are directly connected (for example, wireless networks and certain nonroutable protocols such as Address Resolution Protocol [ARP]).

- **Logical network topology:** With logical abstracts such as a Virtual Local Area Network (VLAN), a group of devices can be viewed as a single administration entity even though they are not physically connected to each other. This also extends to items such as domains in Microsoft Windows networks.

- **Function (purpose, role) of major devices:** The applications running on a computer that are important for the organization and what other parts of the network depend on a certain device. If a database is running on a computer, what is that database used for? If it is a router, what parts of the organization does it connect to?

- **Organization's directory:** It is likely that you need to involve other people from the organization, either to gather more information or to inform about the incident.

Not having these documents in advance means that you must ask more probing questions. Absence of the documents can slow you down, but their possession is not crucial for incident handling.

What questions you might ask? It is hard to give a definitive list because each case is different in some aspects from the previous and future ones. Following are some of the questions that you can use to start assessing the situation:

- What do you see? How does this differ from the usual behavior? What is the usual behavior?

    These questions should help you determine what the immediate observable symptoms are. Be careful not to make your conclusions too quickly at this stage. Observed symptoms can be shared by multiple causes or might not have an obvious connection to the actual cause.

- Is this something that is happening to the reporter or that reporter (or reporter's device) is doing to others?

This is an attempt to determine whether the event is inbound or outbound. In other words, is it "Someone is doing something to my computer" or "My computer is sending something to others." In most cases, the reporter will report symptoms as if something is happening to her device. Deeper technical analysis is required to determine the exact direction of the event.

- When are the symptoms noticed? Has anything changed before the symptoms occurred? Are the symptoms still occurring or have they stopped? When did they stop? Did anything change before they stopped?

The purpose of these questions is to place events into a certain time frame, either absolute time (for example, 9:30 this morning) or relative to some other events (for example, after upgrading my web browser). Knowing the time when things happened will help you reconstruct the chronology of the incident and hopefully determine the speed at which the incident was progressing.

- Do you know the network topology? How is your device connected to the rest of the network? What is the path toward the edge of the network? Who knows this information?

Here we are trying to get a picture of the network's topology. If you or the reporter does not know how the topology looks, you must find someone who does. Knowing the topology can help understand symptoms. It can also aid in determining the root cause of the incident, assessing the scope, and the business impact of the incident.

- What are the business functions affected for the reporter? How important are they for the organization (as far as the reporter might judge)?

The reporter says that she cannot receive emails and access the company main database. The actual question is, "What is the business impact to the organization?" The business impact will not provide any technical details to the incident but will determine the urgency with which the incident must be handled. The inability of the reporter to read her private emails would not rank as a high-priority event. Similarly, not being able to verify a price for a private purchase of an item is not a big problem. However, if nobody else, including the company sales department, can access the database with prices, the severity of the incident increases dramatically. Again, be aware that the reporter might not know the extent and the full consequences of the incident. The reporter can tell you only what she sees.

After these several generic questions, it is difficult to foresee what further questions need to be asked. The ones suggested in the preceding text should be sufficient to enable you to assign an initial severity to the incident. Although you don't need to ask all the questions listed, you must address all the aspects of the incident. You must establish what is happening, when it started and stopped, possible triggers, and what is perceived as the business impact. Although this might seem like a long way to establish the possible business impact, you must be aware that the reporter sees only one fragment of the entire picture. With rare exceptions, the reporter is not aware of the full impact of the incident.

The incident's severity will determine the timing of deeper technical analyses. You should continue with the deep technical analyses if the current incident is the most severe in your queue. If more severe incidents are in the queue, the new one can be either reassigned to someone else who can deal with it immediately or it will have to wait.

The questions you ask will also differ if your IRT belongs to the organization. If the IRT belongs to the organization, you would probably have access to all required documentation, whereas if it doesn't belong to the organization, you need to ask more questions to determine the topology and interdependencies in the system.

An internal IRT also has the advantage of being able to determine whether the event should be classified as an incident, whereas an external IRT would need to rely on the reporter's judgment. Different organizations can classify the same event differently. For one organization, an unsuccessful attempt to access a server might be considered as an attempt of intrusion, whereas the other organization might ignore it completely. The guidelines for what constitute a security incident should be an integral part of your overall company security policy.

As you gather information, you will want to work quickly and efficiently to understand the problem and the scenario. It is wise to take good notes at this stage so that you don't miss an important detail. As you review those notes, they can help you ask additional questions that you might need answered.

Assessing the Scope

The initial assessment of the incident's severity provides you with the urgency. In other words, how fast must you start dealing with that incident? That step does not necessarily give you the full scope of the incident, so that is what should happen next. For our purposes, the incident's scope includes other parts of the organization affected either directly or indirectly by the incident. As you are assessing the scope, new information can change the incident's severity. The change can go either way, making the incident more or less severe.

Depending on whether your team is internal to the organization, this part of the process can be done without involving the original reporter. If you are an internal IR team, you might already have the network topology (physical and logical), so you can investigate the situation in the related parts of the network. The external IR team must involve someone from the affected organization who can provide this information.

During this stage you will look for any signs of the reported symptoms throughout the network. You will also look for signs of possible causes of the symptoms. If the reported symptom is a high central processor unit (CPU) utilization, you can look for a high amount of traffic directed to the device as a potential cause. Eventually, as you gather new information, you can understand what is causing the problem. When you understand the underlying cause, you can move to resolving the incident.

The main "tools" you will use during the process of assessing the incident's scope are your analytic skills and your imagination. You must be able to translate the symptoms into potential causes but also stay open to look for other, not immediately apparent, triggers for the observed symptoms. This openness is important because new attacks and techniques are developed on a daily basis, and you might be the one experiencing them first.

Ask the questions that no one else is asking. Let your curiosity lead to questions to ask. Some questions can seem simple or obvious; others can seem completely unrelated, only to be shown otherwise.

"My web server is under attack from a TCP SYN attack!"

If you were to hear this, you would possibly safely assume that the reporter has done his homework and figured out the kind of attack. The detail-oriented technician in you often makes you want to start proposing solutions. You could seek to block specific IP addresses or ranges; you could attempt to rate limit connections to your server; or you could... and the list goes on. Instead you might ask:

"What makes you believe this is a TCP SYN attack?"

Try to understand what the reporter sees and what data he uses on which to base the conclusion. It could be a valid conclusion if the only information analyzed seems to lead to that conclusion.

Before jumping to the same conclusion yourself, look, listen, and examine what is different. Do not always jump to the obvious conclusion. Take the complete picture into account:

"Where is this server located?"

"Where is the traffic coming in from?"

This can be important from a mitigation standpoint. What aspects of the physical or logical environment might be enabling the problem? What is the source of the offensive traffic? Why are you seeing it? Are you seeing all of it?

"What sites are hosted on this web server?"

How could this matter? It is a TCP SYN attack, remember? The answer to that question might simply be "the corporate website," or it could be a multihomed server where one of the websites hosted there is a target of political hacktivism. It could be that one of the sites hosted there does scientific research on cute bunny rabbits. It could be that the site has a name similar to another organization that has just fallen into disfavor.

In one case I worked on, when this question was asked, the solution involved the hosting provider moving the targeted website to a link where the traffic and mitigations for the attack could be isolated, while leaving the other websites and normal traffic to them undisturbed.

Understanding the possible motivations for the incident can help you respond with innovative solutions. Staying up to date on recent news can offer insight into the kind of attack and what the attackers might be after.

We have seen attacks where hactivists try to take down sites for political reasons surrounding recent events or tensions. We have seen attacks after natural disasters where criminals attempt to defraud those who want to donate to the relief effort. Other examples have included extortion, where the attackers have flooded betting sites with heavy traffic during popular sporting events preventing them from accepting online bets over the Internet. Some level of awareness of current events can be beneficial in understanding what is being attacked and why.

Although understanding motivation for attacks cannot provide an easy answer on what is happening to your network now, it can give you some ideas of the technical aspects of the incident. For example, if the majority of the tools used for DoS attacks are using TCP SYN packets, most likely your network will be attacked by the same kind of packets. That is not a certainty but only a probability. You might want to look for an increased influx of TCP SYN packets first to speed up the analysis. Be aware that, even if you find what you expect, that might not be all. Miscreants might be simultaneously using a variety of tools and techniques to attack you, so be prepared to look for other possible causes.

Remote Diagnosis and Telephone Conversation

More often than not, you will be in a position to diagnose the incident over a telephone, so you need to know how to conduct an efficient telephone conversation. It might sound silly that you need to learn how to talk on a telephone because you have been talking for many years. The truth is that people rely heavily[1] on nonverbal signals during the communication, and none of them, apart from the tone of voice, is present during a telephone conversation.

The following are useful hints on how to conduct an efficient telephone conversation for incident handling purposes. The way this conversation usually starts is like this:

"Hello, this is Sam from the IRT. How can I help you?"

"I am under attack! My web server is currently down! I cannot get out of the network to send email for help or locate documentation on how I can combat this! This attack has my eCommerce site down, and we are currently losing $100,000 an hour! Can you help me?"

Hint #1: Do Not Panic

You need to stay calm. As the incident handler, your calm approach and confidence will help you maintain control of the situation. If both parties are not calm and rational, you will accomplish little. Panic just prolongs the time to resolution. Always use a calm tone

---

[1] The estimates of the portion of nonverbal elements in a communication range from 60 percent to 65 percent.

of voice and sound understanding but not patronizing. Do not try to downplay the problem because the caller might interpret this as if you are not interested and that you do not understand the problem. Similarly, do not exacerbate things because that will certainly make the caller even more afraid and panicked.

Hint #2: Take Notes

As the caller describes the problem, the incident handler should not forget to take good notes. This is how you start to piece the big picture together as you work toward a solution.

You should also draw diagrams, flow charts, or anything else that can help to understand the complete picture of the problem to be solved. Even if you have network topology plans, it can pay off to ask the caller for this information. It is not uncommon that changes have been made to the network without proper documentation.

Hint #3: Listen

Often a caller just wants to blurt out everything that is wrong because he needs help immediately. After allowing the reporter to express the problem, he might be ready to listen. Even if you are certain that you know exactly what the caller will tell you, try not to interrupt him. From the caller's perspective, it is important to tell you what he has. Obviously, do not let the conversation run into an endless speech.

> "Okay. I understand that you are under attack. I will see what I can do to help you. Before I do that, can I get your name and telephone and mobile numbers if we get disconnected?"
>
> "My name is Alan. My number is xxx-xxx-xxxx and my mobile phone number is yyy-yyy-yyyy."
>
> "What organization or department did you say you were from again?"
>
> "Example.com. alan@example.com"
>
> "Okay, thanks Alan."

Hint #4: Ask Simple Questions

For those who have worked in the field of technical support, they can attest to how difficult it can be to diagnose a problem over the telephone. Often the person at the other end either does not understand what he is seeing or does not know how to solve the problem. If you need to diagnose something over the phone, remember to ask lots of simple questions. Complex questions can be misunderstood:

> "Alan, what is the IP address of your web server?"
>
> "What version of software is it running?"
>
> "What operating system is it running?"
>
> "Where are the attacks coming from?"

The simpler the expected answer is, the more likely that you will get it and the answer will be accurate.

Ask questions that do not allow for interpretation or opinion to be expressed. Be careful in asking the remote end for a diagnosis. They know what they believe to be seeing, but they could have missed something.

Hint #5: Rephrase Your Questions

Sometimes you might have to modify your questions. For example, asking "Are you seeing more hostname lookups than usual?" might not be understood. The caller might not know what a hostname lookup is or, if she knows what it is, she might not have access to log files to answer it. In such cases, you should either pose questions in a way that the caller can understand them or break the questions into smaller pieces.

Hint #6: Do Not Use Jargon

Try to use standard terminology as much as possible. Almost every group develops a specific jargon that is habitually used in conversations within that group. The only common thing between different jargons is that they are not used outside the group that invented them.

Do not be lax with terms. Do not use "box" to describe every device and "thingy" for all software. At the same time, it is not required to be too pedantic, so you can safely use terms like "packet," "frame," and "datagram" as synonyms.

Having said this, if the caller insists on using jargon, be flexible and accept that. On occasions, the caller might not know much about technology, so he uses the only expressions he knows. For example, the caller might have heard that her IT people connected her computer to "GW" but without actually knowing what that is. By trying to explain that "GW" probably stands for "gateway," and that it might be a router or a switch, will just confuse her. Make a note about this, but use "GW" when talking to the caller.

Hint #7: Admit Things You Do Not Know

There may be times when you are not familiar with some of the equipment involved. If that is the case, admit that up front to yourself (and the caller) and seek to pull in a resource who understands the details of the problem better than you.

Related to this, do not seek help from others too quickly. Specialists are precious resources and must be used judiciously. These people are always in high demand, and it is not fair to others to tie a specialist to your case and have him just in case he might be needed. Depending on circumstances, it might be sufficient for you to collect as much information you think is required and send it to a specialist for a later analysis rather than having him sit for five hours on a call for nothing.

Hint #8: Control the Conversation

It is not uncommon that, after the conversation starts, more and more people become involved and join the call. Pretty soon you can end up with anywhere from 10 to 50 people on the call. The next thing that will happen is that people will start side conversation and chaos follows.

Sometimes, higher management can be the worst offender in this respect. When dealing with severe incidents, someone from higher management might join the call every so often and ask for an update. Although it is great that this person shows interest in the case, it is not productive repeating the current status every 20 minutes for all participants on the call. In such instances it is beneficial to designate one person to act as a liaison to higher management. This liaison would then brief higher management at any time but offline so that the main call can proceed uninterrupted.

You must be able to control the conversation. Do not be afraid to ask people to leave if they cannot contribute to the case. If appropriate, ask a group of people to dial to another teleconference bridge and continue the discussion there. When they finish, one of them can dial in to the main call and report findings.

Controlling the conversation does not mean that you must talk all the time. Be ready to allow experts to ask their questions and let them be heard, but you must retain the overall control of the call.

Solving the Problem

Solving the problem, an incident in our case, is composed of two components. One is to understand what must be solved (the problem itself) and another is how to address it. Given that these two components are tightly linked, this section covers both.

After you understand the problem you are trying to solve, you can start formulating solutions. Part of any triage process is to prioritize each problem to be addressed. Each resolution can have various resource requirements, differing levels of effectiveness, and varying levels of impact. First determine what the reaction will be for each problem, and seek to contain it to prevent the situation from worsening. When the problem is contained, further resolution can then take place, with an end goal of restoration of the service. Let's look at this a bit closer.

Determining the Reaction

After you have more details about the problem, you can reach a point in which some decisions and actions can be initiated. But first you need to establish what needs to be achieved by a corrective action. What are the critical resources? Is there some service that must be kept running? Is it more important to protect the information or to keep the connectivity or service running? Consider an example where a website is compromised and the attacker is gathering credit card information and copying it to a remote location. If the server is disconnected from the network, the attacker cannot copy any further data.

On the negative side, customers cannot place their orders, and the organization will possibly lose revenue or customers. What is more important for the organization? What is its preference? Are there any legal consequences of choosing one action or the other? Answers to these questions must be considered before a decision to choose a particular action is reached.

Depending on whether the IRT belongs to the organization, reaching the decision on the reaction may be easier. For the teams that belong to the organization that is handling the incident, some decisions might be made in advance. Critical services can be identified and priorities, from the business and legal perspective, assigned to them. In this situation, the decision-making process can be as simple as looking into a document and finding the right section.

If the IRT is not directly part of the same organization, these decisions might need to be made by the person who reports the attack and not by the IRT. There are two good reasons for this. The first one is that the IRT does not know the organization or its business. The second reason is that advising a particular course of action can carry a legal liability for the IRT (and its parent organization). If, for example, the IRT advises that a computer should be disconnected, that might terminate a service that the attacked site is contractually obliged to provide. That unavailability of service can be seen as a breach of contract, so the attacked site may be sued. Because the attacked site was acting on the incident manager's advice and disconnected the computer, the attacked site might then sue the IRT's parent organization for the wrong advice.

For these reasons, if in doubt, the incident handler should present options and possible first-level consequences and then leave to the reporter to decide. In this example, in which the IRT is not the part of the attacked organization, the comment to Alan might be as follows:

> "Disconnecting the server will, of course, stop data from being copied outside the company. However, some of the programs that the attackers are using are written in a way to cause further damage if they detect that connectivity is broken. They even might start erasing your data or system files. Keeping the service running and connectivity intact could allow more data to be copied and thus result in more of your customers being compromised. Allowing this to continue might enable us to collect more data and establish where the attack came from and where it leads forward. What is your priority?"

If Alan is not the right person to make a decision, the incident manager must ask for a decision maker. It is also important to write down the decision and confirm it in writing at the earliest convenient opportunity. The main reason is to have a trace of what was done and why. Some national teams have a policy whereby they will not even accept an incident report over a telephone. If someone wants to report an incident, it must be done through an email so that it can be documented. Having a trace of decisions is important so that the process of solving the incident can be emulated (or repeated) when needed again. Another reason for confirming decisions is in a case of a dispute. If something goes terribly wrong, it will be easier to recall what decisions have been made, why, and by whom.

When the preferred resolution is understood, the incident handler can either start executing mitigation actions or begin making recommendations on how to react. Up to this point, the handler's role was to collect information from which informed and rational decisions can be made. The incident handler can now lead toward the resolution providing direction and confidence in the solution. This does not mean stop listening to the reporter or stop reevaluating the situation to make sure that it has not changed. On the contrary, the situation must be reviewed after each step. If the desired resolution state is not being reached, further investigation might be required before returning to formulate and implement further strategies.

Containing the Problem

When the reaction plan is formulated, it usually consists of two steps. The first one is to contain the problem and the second is to remove the cause. These two steps might be repeated multiple times until the problem is fully addressed. Containing the problem enables the rest of the organization to continue its business and provides maneuvering space to address the problem.

Containing the problem can mean disconnecting an attacking host from the network by breaking its network connectivity or powering down an infected machine. It can also mean enabling access-lists or inserting firewalls or other filtering technologies to prevent malicious traffic from reaching vulnerable hosts.

I once was helping a customer during one of the well-known worm attacks. As its network was struggling to keep up with the enormous traffic load from the scanning activity of the worm, a few key network devices kept crashing. Their focus was on trying to get those key devices back online and stable; meanwhile, the worm kept scanning and spreading, which worsened the problem from a network load standpoint and possibly increased the number of infected machines that needed to be addressed afterward. What proved to be the correct approach in this case was not to concentrate on the key devices but to disconnect the infected parts of the networks. That did not remove the infection from the network but prevented the worm from spreading to the uninfected parts of the network and enabled service restoration.

Do not rule out any mechanism that can be employed to also mitigate an attack or buy you valuable time by slowing down an attack.

Network Segmentation

The ultimate method for containment of an incident is the ability to achieve network segmentation. Just as a ship's water-tight compartment can hold all the water back from spreading to other areas, the same can be accomplished in a network.

Many technologies exist today that can help accomplish network segmentation. One well-known technology is the use of Virtual Local Area Networks (VLAN), which provide for traffic segmentation. VLANs likely cannot achieve complete isolation for hosts because most networks will have devices that connect VLANs together or devices that can move from VLAN to VLAN, such as a laptop. However, VLANs might offer the capability depending on the architecture of the network and users on that network to insulate a set of hosts or to possibly slow the spread of an infection.

Other possibilities are at Layer 3 in the OSI model. The use of access-lists (ACL) and routing tricks can possibly prevent remote attacks from succeeding, depending on the protocols. For example, an access-list might be used to block all Secure Shell (SSH) traffic directed to internal hosts from outside networks. That should stop common SSH brute force login attacks.

An example where routing is used to mitigate the attack might involve injecting a route so that malicious or unwanted traffic no longer reaches vulnerable hosts. This technique is usually referred to as black holing, as in "the traffic is sent to a black hole and cannot escape from there."

Other possibilities might exist at higher layers in the OSI model. An example of this would be application filtering. If your organization uses HTTP proxies, they can be configured to block access to certain malicious sites.

Finally, there are more draconian possibilities for segmenting a network. I have worked with customers who completely disconnected their Internet connection until they had adequate protection in place.

Resolving the Problem and Restoring the Services

Now that the assessment of the problem has occurred and containment has been achieved, the resolution can begin. The resolution is dependent on the incident. The resolution can be a combination of technical solutions, architectural changes, or process changes in which the end goal is to restore functionality and bring the situation back to normal.

Technical solutions are first to be implemented because they tend to be the quickest ones. They can be in the form of a software patch or an update, device configuration, purchase of a new service or a device, or any combinations thereof. Architectural or process changes take much longer to formulate and implement. It is never a good idea to re-architect your network during an incident because you might make serious mistakes in the heat of the moment. Any decision for such big changes should be guided by the results of the post-mortem analysis.

Given this different time scale, this step has two endpoints. The first one is when technical solutions are applied and the service is restored. In other words, this particular incident has been fended off. The second endpoint is when process or architectural changes were implemented. That should provide the resilience from the future attacks of the same class. Here you must define what "the same class" is. If you have dealt with a virus, your solution might not necessarily prevent you from being infected by any future virus. But your solution should be good enough to prevent any future virus that uses the same attack vector to infect you. An example could be a Microsoft Word macro virus. Your solution might not provide protection from a virus that exploits vulnerability in Explorer, but you should be immune to any future Word macro virus.

Monitoring for Recurrence

After the incident has been resolved and service has been restored, you need to take steps to monitor for any reoccurrence. If the attack were to be modified slightly, you would want to make sure that any mitigations or resolutions actually work. If you are not continuing to monitor closely, you might find yourself responding to a similar incident within a short period of time.

Monitoring should occur at ingress and egress points in the network, at key locations within the network (especially choke points if they exist) and on the target host. You can use various technologies for this, including firewalls and access lists, intrusion detection and prevention, Netflow monitoring, network sniffers, network management devices, and application logging. Although it is true that with most technologies you might catch only what you are looking for and not notice other anomalies, if you are not monitoring at all, you will never catch what you are looking for.

Involving Other Incident Response Teams

Chapter 6, "Getting to Know Your Peers: Teams and Organizations Around the World," talks about getting to know your peers. You might find in some incidents that you know someone who can assist you. Maybe that person or team has knowledge, experience, or expertise that they are willing to share. Maybe they are upstream from a network-based attack and can help mitigate the issue from their end. Maybe they can assist with a forensics investigation locally so that travel or additional expense is minimized. Maybe they can also investigate the incident on their end and get law enforcement agencies involved that you would have trouble engaging directly.

Generally, ask for outside help when you cannot move the case yourself any further. One common scenario when this happens is during DoS attacks. Although you can deploy various techniques to drop packets on your edge, they will still keep coming. The incoming packets will not cause much damage, if any, to your network but they will not stop either, and these packets will consume a bandwidth you are paying for. In such cases you could reach out to your ISP and ask it to block those packets on its edge to free the bandwidth. Similarly, if someone from a remote site managed to get its way into your network, you can reach out to your counterparts at the remote site to ask for help to identify who that attacker is.

Involving Public Relations

In some cases, an organization might be required to publicly report about an incident, or the incident can find its way into the press. No one wants to make front page news that they were hacked or lost a laptop with sensitive information or any other potentially embarrassing news.

For this reason, you might want to engage the resources of your public relations or media relations department (if you have one). If you are helping a third party in a support role, they might want to engage their PR department. If other teams or law enforcement are involved, their PR staff might want to know what is going on as well. The goal is to have someone aware of the incident, someone who can publicly answer any questions that may arise. Sometimes those answers might simply be "No comment"; other times, the answer may be more detailed. What you do not want to happen is for misinformation or speculation to become a distraction for the organization and especially for the IRT.

Additionally, besides just dealing with media inquiries, PR staff can help play a critical role in the dissemination of information. They can help not only with the mechanics of internal and external messaging, but also have skills in developing clear, concise statements that are less likely to be misunderstood.

In drawing up statements, including those intended for the press, be sure to maintain your credibility. Unless preempted by the events, you should make your own organizational decisions about the timing and how much information you want to divulge. Whatever you say should be an honest and truthful statement.

Post-Mortem Analysis

If your parents were like mine, they probably said to you at least once, "So, did you learn anything?" Basically they were asking you to evaluate what had happened to you, and what you would do to make sure that you were not in that situation again in the future. Additionally, should you find yourself in the same situation again in the future, what would you do differently? This is what a post-mortem analysis is about.

The idea is to gather data and to interview those involved. Honest, straightforward answers should be encouraged. Even highly critical and nonconstructive feedback can be constructive if viewed in the right context. Feedback such as "you stink" could be interpreted to mean that you did something poorly. Although it could be taken as an insult, also be aware that you were asking for their opinions from their viewpoint. It could mean that one of the resulting actions can be to improve a working relationship with another department.

Whatever the feedback, the final analysis should be compiled into a report to document the findings. That report must be shared appropriately within your organization. Executive management will likely be interested to make sure that the problem never happens again. Middle management and other departments might be interested in understanding more of the operational details and interactions within an organization for process improvement. Those involved might be interested so that they both see that their feedback was heard, but also to understand how they might have performed as well and what could be improved upon.

The ultimate purpose of the post-mortem report is to find common themes and areas for improvement. What needs to be done to minimize the impact of a similar incident and to prevent the same incident from reoccurring? The areas in which to improve can be technical in nature, but often you will find that they are more process-oriented. After you determine the actions that can be taken to prevent the problem in the future, make sure that someone owns those actions and implements them.

Although the post-mortem process might sound simple, there is more to it than just talking to people involved in the incident. To be effective and meet the needs of your own organization, take the time to determine what you hope to learn from an incident. That would influence what questions will be asked.

To be effective, the most important thing in post-mortem analysis is that it must not be used to assign blame. If the analysis is done to find who is to blame, people will not be honest in their answers because they will be afraid of losing their job. Such a post mortem is useless because nothing can be learned from it.

When starting the preparation for the post-mortem process, you must decide what will be analyzed. For our purposes, we can identify two main components that can be analyzed. The one is the incident itself, and the other is the IRT. Post-mortem analysis of the IRT should be focused on the team's performance and capabilities, whereas the analysis of the incident addresses all other aspects related to the organization. If your IRT is not a part of the organization that was attacked, your post mortem can cover only the team.

Incident Analysis

Post mortem of an incident is focused on things that enabled the incident and how the organization was capable of handling the situation. The purpose of this set of questions is to assess how the incident has happened; how can we prevent this class of incidents from happening again, and what was the business impact? We can divide questions into the following groups:

- **Technical aspects of the incident:** Why did the incident happen?

- **Identification of the incident:** Has the situation been recognized as malignant?

- **Notification process and interaction:** Have the right people been notified and was that done on time?

- **Network capabilities:** What was the impact on the network and computer systems?

- **Business impact:** What services were impacted, how fast were they restored, and what did that mean for the organization?

Following are some of the questions that can be asked within each group. They are given as an illustration and are not meant to be an exhaustive list.

Technical aspects of the incident:

- What enabled the incident to happen?

- Was it a vulnerability in an operating system or an application?

- Was there a patch for the vulnerability? Was it applied?

- Was the patch effective?

- If the patch was not applied, why not?

- What equipment was involved?

- What services were impacted (for example, the web server, database, DNS, and so on)?

- Was there any collateral damage?

Identification of the incident:

- How long did it take to recognize that an incident happened?

- Were there any other signs that could be used for faster incident recognition?

- Were the signs sufficiently unambiguous to identify the incident?

- What hindered a fast and accurate identification?

Notification process and interaction:

- After the incident was recognized, who was notified about it?

- Were the right people notified?

- Have people who could have been instrumental in handling the incident been contacted?

- Why were not all relevant people contacted?

- Were all people contacted at the right time (not too early, not too late)?

- Did the reporter have the necessary information to reach the right people (for example, phone numbers, email addresses, and so on)?

- Was there sufficient communication between those involved, especially for specific actions?

- Was the response from the IRT timely and adequate?

- Was the interaction with the IRT satisfactory (for example, courteous, accurate instructions, and timely)?

Network capabilities:

- Were the network and computers affected during the incident?

- What was the incident's impact on the system?

- Was it possible to segment the network to contain the incident?

Business impact:

- What was the business impact of the incident?

- What services were affected (for example, billing, ordering, and delivery)?

- Would a different network topology with more redundant server and services lessen the impact?

- How quickly was the service restored?

- What was the impact on the brand and customer satisfaction?

- Did the organization honor all its obligations (for example, payment and delivery on time, service level agreement, and so on)?

- Were there any legal implications of the incident?

IRT Analysis

This part of the analysis looks at the performance of the IRT only. You can divide this analysis into several aspects that should be investigated as follows:

- **Reporting procedure to the team:** How and when was the IRT engaged?

- **IRT's escalation and communication procedure:** How did the IRT escalate the case and involve other groups?

- **Incident handling:** How was the incident handled?

Within each of these groups, following are some of the questions to ask.

Reporting procedure to the team:

- How was the IRT contacted (email, phone, or pager)?

- Was the used means of the initial contact the most effective?

- Did the team receive all relevant and required information during the initial contact?

- Was the timing of the initial contact right (not too late, not too soon)?

IRT's escalation and communication procedure:

- Did the IRT reach the appropriate people (managers, technical specialists, lawyers, and so on)?

- Have these people been engaged appropriately and at the right time?

- How effective was the support from these people to the IRT?

- Would it be beneficial to involve more people? Why and whom?

- Did the IRT reach out to all required external organizations and teams?

- Did the IRT always have the correct information at hand when communicating to the other people and organizations?

- Was there sufficient and timely communication between those involved?

Incident handling:

- Was the incident diagnosed correctly?

- Was the reaction formulated appropriately?

- Was it possible to react more quickly?

- Did the IRT have the accurate topology and similar information in advance? How accurate was that information?

- Did the IRT have the required knowledge to handle such incidents?

- Were the proper resources engaged solve the problem efficiently?

Summary

Dealing with attacks is more than just applying an ACL on a router or patching an application. It is a process that needs to be constantly refined to remain effective. The purpose of this chapter is to provide a framework within which incident response can occur.

References

Burgoon, J.K. (1994). Nonverbal signals. M.L. Knapp and G.R. Miller (Eds.), *Handbook of Interpersonal Communication*, Second Edition (pp. 229–285). Thousand Oaks, CA: Sage.

Computer Misuse Act 1990 (c. 18), http://www.opsi.gov.uk/acts/acts1990/Ukpga_19900018_en_2.htm.

H.R. 3791, SAFE Act of 2007 (Referred to Senate Committee after received from the House), http://thomas.loc.gov/cgi-bin/query/D?c110:3:./temp/~c1102GrVYk::.

House of Lords Session 2005–06, Police and Justice Bill, http://www.publications.parliament.uk/pa/ld200506/ldbills/104/06104.31-37.html#j383A.

Server and Domain Isolation, Microsoft TechNet, http://technet.microsoft.com/en-us/network/bb545651.aspx.

Chapter 5

Incident Coordination

Chapter 4, "Dealing with an Attack," discusses facets to consider when responding to a computer or network security incident. Much of that chapter is devoted to working directly with individuals within your own organization to respond and deal with the incident.

Not all incidents are so simple. In some cases you will find yourself having to contact others external to your organization for assistance in dealing with the issue. If you were being attacked from sources in 15 countries across 5 different continents, where would you start? What if you found that a compromised machine from your site had been used to attack other targets in a number of countries across a number of continents? It often happens that an organization might not know that one of its own devices has been compromised, and you learn of it when another response team contacts you.

If your team is in a situation in which it needs to contact someone remotely, you might not always be able to reach the right party on the other end, or you might not reach a party at the remote end who cares or wants to help. Even though that can be the case at times, attempting to contact the remote end is certainly worth a try. This chapter covers such incident coordination.

Multiple Sites Compromised from Your Site

Several years ago, I worked an incident in which a number of Linux machines were compromised via an IMAP exploit. The attackers used the compromised machines to spread to other machines that existed at a number of universities, companies, and military sites. In working the incident, I needed to notify administrators at the other sites so that they could address the compromised machines at their sites and subsequently notify other organizations that their compromised machines might have infected. At that time that kind of activity was not so much widespread but today, this kind of example is a common occurrence.

One form of exploitation that has caught press attention has been various botnet-related activities. At its simplest, a botnet consists of a number of machines remotely controlled via a centralized control mechanism. The machines that join botnets are typically compromised through unpatched system vulnerabilities or insecure configurations, or by tricking an unsuspecting user to execute untrusted software. This creates the possibility for malicious software to be loaded on a machine, to register with a centralized controller, and continue attempting to spread to other machines on the network. The compromised machines are often used for spam and distributed denial-of-service (DoS) attacks, to name just a few ways how the compromised hosts can be misused.

If you find yourself or your organization in a situation in which you have a compromised machine, you might need to contact victims in another location somewhere else on the planet to alert them that they might have been compromised. Or the classical situation can occur in which you are the victim of a DoS attack, and you need to contact a remote organization for assistance in getting the attack stopped.

How to Contact Somebody Far Away

How would you go about getting hold of the responsible party? No comprehensive Internet directory exists with all of the right contacts listed. Locating the right person who can help can take determination and perseverance.

Chapter 6, "Getting to Know Your Peers: Teams and Organizations Around the World," focuses on getting to know your peers and introduces organizations such as FIRST, InfraGard, and NSP-Security. If the party that you need to contact is already a member of one of those organizations, your chances of getting in touch with someone who can help can be quite good.

But what if you are not so lucky? Several other methods that can also lead to someone who can help are given in the rest of this section. You must keep in mind that, generally speaking, there is no guarantee that people on the other end will be able to help you. Most of the time things are done on a best-effort basis and while people are willing to help they might not have time to actually do it immediately upon request.

Contact a CERT Local at the Remote End

Another approach can be tried in cases in which you can determine the geographical region from which an attack is sourced. Many national-level governments have established CERTs with responsibility for the entire country. In those cases, you might be able to contact a National Computer Emergency Response Team (CERT) and engage its help in seeking relief from the attack.

One place to start for locating a country-level CERT is from the FIRST website. FIRST currently offers an interactive map located at http://www.first.org/members/map/ that can be used to drill down and locate response teams from a particular country. The map on the FIRST site is currently limited to listing those teams that are members of the FIRST organization.

Another source you can use to locate CERTs within Europe is on the TERENA website: http://www.trusted-introducer.nl. There you can find a list of teams by country known to exist in Europe.

If those methods fail to help locate a team, another option is to simply try searching the Internet through your favorite search engine. Searching for the terms "computer emergency response" and including the country name in your search might return a match.

Standard Security Email Addresses

Organizations that adhere to RFC 2142 should have common email addresses for their domain similar to security@example.com or abuse@example.com that can be an additional avenue to seek help, especially if you want help from a service provider.

Standard Security Web Page

One proposal, which was a result of the efforts of the National Infrastructure Advisory Committee (NIAC), was for the creation of a "slash security page" for an organization. The slash security was not about slashing security; instead, it was a reference to the common URI notation for a website. The idea proposed was for an organization to have a contact page on its website that would list contact information for those within an organization who would handle security issues. Common examples of those groups might be information security teams, product security teams, physical and site security teams, or copyright and abuse handling teams. For a domain of example.com, the Slash Security page would be located at http://www.example.com/security/.

whois and Domain Name

whois is a utility that can be used to query the domain registration databases. When domains are registered, the registrar needs to maintain information about who to contact for that domain. A whois query on a domain will often return email, telephone, and physical address contact information for the technical and administrative contacts for a site. Those contacts can include an incident response team (IRT) for an organization because that team might not have responsibility for day-to-day management of the domain. For organizations that might not have an IRT, this administrative contact for the domain might be a start at reaching someone who can help. The usefulness of the contact information within whois depends on whether the incoming requests will get routed to the right individual in an efficient and expedient manner because the database's primary focus is for domain name registration. Example 5-1 shows output from a recent whois query on the cisco.com domain name.

Example 5-1   *Result of whois Query for the cisco.com Domain*

```
Registrant:
Cisco Technology, Inc.
   170 W. Tasman Drive
```

```
San    Jose, CA 95134
US
Domain Name: CISCO.COM
Administrative Contact:
    InfoSec             infosec@CISCO.COM
    170 West Tasman Drive
    San    Jose, CA 95134
    US
    408-527-3842 fax: 408-526-4575
Technical Contact:
    Network Services         dns-info@CISCO.COM
    170 W. Tasman Drive
    San    Jose, CA 95134
    US
    408-527-9223 fax: 408-526-7373
Record expires on 15-May-2009.
Record created on 14-May-1987.
Database last updated on 28-Nov-2006 22:53:55 EST.
Domain servers in listed order:
NS1.CISCO.COM              128.107.241.185
NS2.CISCO.COM              64.102.255.44
```

The preceding output lists two contacts that might help with an incident. One is infosec@cisco.com and another is dns-info@cisco.com. If nobody behind these two email addresses can help, they might be able to redirect you to someone who can.

If you were lucky, the whois database would contain the irt object. The "irt" stands for Incident Response Team, and that is the team you need to contact when dealing with an incident related to that organization. Assuming that an incident involves an IP address 131.130.1.101 and you use whois to find the contact, Example 5-2 demonstrates what you might see.

Example 5-2   *irt Object in RIPE NCC Database*

```
inetnum:        131.130.0.0 - 131.130.255.255
netname:        UNIVIE
descr:          LAN University of Vienna
descr:          Vienna University   Computer Center
descr:          Universitaetsstrasse 7
descr:          A-1010 Vienna
country:        AT
org:            ORG-VUCC1-RIPE
admin-c:        UK6107-RIPE
tech-c:         VUN1-RIPE
mnt-by:         ACONET-LIR-MNT
```

```
mnt-by:          AS760-MNT
mnt-routes:      AS760-MNT
mnt-domains:     AS760-MNT
mnt-irt:         IRT-ACOnet-CERT
status:          ASSIGNED PI
source:          RIPE # Filtered
```

Here you can see an entry mnt-irt: IRT-ACOnet-CERT. This means that ACOnet-CERT is the authority that handles all computer incidents coming to or from IP address range 131.130.0.0/16. Scrolling a bit down the page reveals detailed contact information for ACOnet CERT, as shown in Example 5-3.

Example 5-3   *Full Information About ACOnet-CERT*

```
irt:             IRT-ACONET-CERT
address:         Vienna University  Computer Center
address:         Universitaetsstrasse 7
address:         A-1010 Wien
address:         Austria
phone:           +43 1 427714045
fax-no:          +43 1 42779140
abuse-mailbox:   cert@aco.net
signature:       PGPKEY-800559FB
encryption:      PGPKEY-800559FB
admin-c:         TI123-RIPE
tech-c:          TI123-RIPE
auth:            PGPKEY-800559FB
remarks:         This is a TI accredited CSIRT/CERT
remarks:         emergency phone number +43 1 427714045
remarks:         timezone GMT01 (GMT02 with DST)
remarks:         https://www.trusted-introducer.org/teams/aconet-cert.html
irt-nfy:         cert@aco.net
mnt-by:          TRUSTED-INTRODUCER-MNT
source:          RIPE # Filtered
```

This particular example is used because ACOnet CERT was instrumental in the process of creating this object and driving its implementation. The irt object is optional, and not all organizations populate it. It is up to each individual IRT to request it from the registry and fill in the data. In addition to that, not all registries support the irt object. At the time this book was written, only RIPE NCC, AfriNIC, and APNIC support the irt object. It is unknown if and when other registrars will start supporting the irt object.

Who Is Your ISP?

Not all incidents will occur during business hours on working days. Even if it is business hours on a normal workday for you, that does not necessarily hold true for the remote end. It might also be the case that contact information for a site is out of date, or the person on the other end is not in the office for some reason. In cases like this, you might find it useful to do a traceroute to the remote site. The traceroute utility will attempt to return information about the path that network traffic takes between your site and a remote site. The path that is returned will contain the IP addresses of the devices that the traffic traverses on its way to the remote end. If those devices have had their IP addresses registered and they resolve to a real hostnames, you may use the whois utility to obtain contact information for your upstream service provider or the provider on the remote end.

There are cases in which the traceroute method might not work. Some providers may filter the ICMP traffic that some traceroute clients depend on, causing the traceroute to fail. If that turns out to be the case, you might need to contact your upstream provider for assistance in mitigating the attack. It can look at the path the traffic is taking through its network. Such information could be used to block the traffic at its ingress points or to contact neighboring providers to ask them to help mitigate the attack. Sometimes you might find that the service provider has contact information for its directly connected customers. If that turns out to be the case, it might be possible to get a misbehaving device some attention to address the problem.

Be aware, though, that many times an ISP might not have direct control over an end device. Its capability to assist might be to only filter traffic, and often this is only for a limited time. This should be taken into account if you are depending on upstream ISPs for mitigation assistance.

Law Enforcement

If you work with law enforcement on the incident, they might be able to assist as well. Some agencies, such as the U.S. Federal Bureau of Investigation, have legal attaches in embassies and consulates around the world. Many law enforcement agencies already have arrangements in place to work with their counterparts in other countries to combat international crime, of which electronic Internet attacks can be one example. Europol and Interpol can also be effective in finding the right people on the remote end to work with, but both of these agencies will support only other law enforcement agencies and will not work directly with affected individuals or organizations.

Working with Different Teams

As you work with other teams, many of which might be very remote from you, there are a few things to keep in mind. Although it might seem obvious, you need to be aware of time zone differences. Taking the continental United States as an example, there are four time zones: Eastern, Central, Mountain, and Pacific. If it is 12:00 pm in New York City (Eastern time zone), the corresponding time in San Francisco, California (Pacific time zone) is 9:00 am. Going international, things become even more interesting. The time difference between New York City and Tokyo, Japan, is 10 hours, so noon in New York City means that it is 2:00 am (the next day!) in Japan. If you include offsets for Daylight Saving Time into the calculations, it can be even more confusing.

The goal here is not to provide a tutorial on time zone calculations but simply to point out that geographical distance implies time differences that you need to take into account and be sympathetic to the individual on the other end because it might be an inconvenient hour for them. Also be aware that if the destination you are trying to reach crosses the International Date Line, it could be tomorrow or yesterday in their location. Sites such as http://www.timeanddate.com or http://www.worldtimezone.com are often useful for determining the time (and day of the week) in other time zones.

Another challenge you can come across are cultural issues. The world is composed of many cultures that celebrate different national and religious holidays. You might work during the Chinese New Year celebration or Brazil Carnival celebration, whereas teams in those countries have the day off.

Other cultures can have a different work week, too. Although it is customary in the United States to work Monday through Friday, other cultures might work Sunday through Thursday.

Also keep in mind that there are many aspects to languages that can be local to a region or specific to a profession. Just because two parties both communicate in English does not mean that they necessarily understand each other. Take care to be specific and clear in your message, avoiding the use of jargon or colloquialisms to prevent unnecessary confusion.

Keeping Track of Incident Information

For many IRTs, working only one issue at a time is a dream that will likely never come true. It is also the case that keeping mental notes or stacks of paper to track incident-related information will not only be inadequate, but also inefficient. A case tracking system is needed. A case tracking system can assign unique identifiers for an incident, provide a capability to search previous cases for similar qualities to a current attack, facilitate a workflow, and organize, collect, and store incident-related information in one location.

An additional benefit to such a system is the possibility of generating reports. These reports could be used to help senior management in an organization understand the scale of the problems faced. This might not only aid in making a business justification for additional resources, but can also help identify additional policies that might be required to mitigate the threats and risks to an organization.

If your organization does not already have a case tracking system of some type, you will likely need one. Several case tracking systems exist, both commercially and through open source. If your team cannot afford a commercial case tracking system, you should investigate some of the available freeware and shareware options. Request Tracker (RT) is one example of a case tracking system in use by a number of IRTs. RT is freely available at http://bestpractical.com/rt/.

If your organization has a case tracking system, you must determine whether you can use it or whether a separate system is required for the IRT. The answer to that question depends on criteria such as the physical security of the system, the need for compartmentalization of the information contained in the system, and the sensitivity of the information stored. Many teams, such as the Cisco PSIRT, have its own incident tracking system that is completely separate from other systems. This system resides on a separate server with limited access, strong authentication, and encrypted file systems.

Product Vulnerabilities

Thus far in this chapter, the focus has been on IRTs handling a scenario such as a DoS attack. What if, as a result of your own testing or from an attack, you discover a new unannounced vulnerability in a product?

Today these vulnerabilities get reported in a number of ways, ranging from a direct report to the vendor, to a coordination center for help, or through a public posting in an online forum. In theory, your goal should be to obtain a fix in the most efficient way possible. How would you go about getting that fix?

Many commercial and open-source product vendors have established product security teams that respond to product security issues and regularly release fixed software, patches, and security advisories for their customers. The second part of the book, starting with Chapter 7, "Product Security Vulnerabilities," is devoted to the topic of product vulnerability handling.

Commercial Vendors

The Cisco Product Security Incident Response Team (PSIRT) was established in 1995. The Cisco PSIRT handles security vulnerabilities in Cisco products and incidents in which people are trying to crack security in Cisco customer's networks. The PSIRT is responsible for generating Cisco security advisories, driving the resolution of security-related bugs in Cisco products, interfacing with external response teams (such as CERT/CC and other FIRST teams), and assisting customers in incident response.

Should a vulnerability be found in a Cisco product, the Cisco PSIRT can be reached at psirt@cisco.com. Other methods for contacting the Cisco PSIRT are documented at the following URL:

   http://www.cisco.com/en/US/products/products_security_vulnerability_policy.html

Cisco is not the only vendor to have a product security team. Other vendors offer similar teams. Hewlett-Packard (HP), Oracle, Microsoft, Silicon Graphics (SGI), Xerox, and Nokia all have their own product security teams, to name just a few.

Within FIRST, these product security teams have their own special interest group (SIG) where they meet and share experiences and best practices. The goal of this sharing is to improve the security of products and the delivery of fixes in a more predictable and industry-standard fashion. You can find more information on the Vendor Special Interest Group at http://www.first.org/vendor-sig/.

Another organization that occupies the same space as Vendor SIG is ICASI. The following description of ICASI is taken from its website:

> The Industry Consortium for the Advancement of Security on the Internet (ICASI) was formed as a non-profit corporation by a group of leading global IT vendors to create a trusted forum to address international, multi-product security challenges. This trusted forum extends the ability of IT vendors to address complex security issues and better protect enterprises, governments, citizens, and the critical IT infrastructures that support them.

At the time of writing, ICASI has six members: Cisco, IBM, Intel, Juniper, Microsoft, and Nokia. Further information about ICASI is available at http://www.icasi.org/.

Open Source Teams

Open source vendors often have their own security teams as well. Various Linux operating system distributions release advisories on a regular basis for software and services that might be installed on them. If you want to report a security issue to all Linux vendors, most, if not all of them, can be reached via the email address vendor-sec@lst.de.

Another place where you can report incidents and vulnerabilities related to the open source software is oCERT (Open Source CERT). More information about oCERT is available at http://www.ocert.org/. Details about an incident or an exploit should be sent to incidents@ocert.org, or you can use web reporting forms provided on the oCERT's website.

Coordination Centers

What if you do not know where to start? You think that you have found a vulnerability, but you do not know how to notify the vendor. Or maybe it is a problem that can affect multiple vendors.

Those cases are perfect examples in which a coordination center can be of assistance. Some of the country-level CERT organizations, such as the CERT Coordination Center (CERT/CC) based out of Carnegie Mellon University, the Centre for the Protection of National Infrastructure (CPNI) in the UK, the CERT-FI in Finland, the United States Computer Emergency Readiness Team (US-CERT), the Japan Computer Emergency Response Team/Coordination Center(JPCERT/CC), the Korea Emergency Response Team Coordination Center (KrCERT/CC), and the Australian Computer Emergency Response Team (AusCERT) can all assist with incidents in their respective countries and assist vulnerability reporters in getting in touch with the correct vendors and their product security teams.

Exchanging Incident Information

As you work with other teams, you often need to share common informational elements. The answers to the general questions of who, what, where, when, and how as they apply to the incident will likely need to be shared with another team attempting to assist you. If this information is sent over email, it should be encrypted.

Some of the information you likely need to share or be provided with if you are contacted by another incident response team follows:

- IP addresses of the devices involved, both sources and destinations.

- Autonomous System Numbers (ASN) of the sources and destinations.

- Information to identify the attack, such as an attack type, virus name, traffic parameters, or a sniffer capture.

- Time of the attack (start, end, and duration).

- Frequency of the attack.

- Impact of the incident.

- Information about why the attack might be occurring. This is important if the site reporting the problem is not the only target.

- Incident identifiers, such as internal case numbers, internal identifiers, or police report numbers.

- Contact information for the parties involved. Make sure to have multiple contact methods; email might not work if your network connection is down.

The need for standardized methods and formats for incident-related information sharing between teams has led to the development of several standards that an incident response team should be familiar with.

The first standard is a Common Vulnerabilities and Exposures (CVE) number, which is an identifier that refers to a specific vulnerability or exposure. A vendor might request a CVE number for a vulnerability to label it with a common identifier. Where the CVE number becomes most useful is in the case of a multivendor vulnerability. This situation occurs typically when there is a vulnerability in a commonly used service or protocol.

Similarly, another identifier exists to try to give a standard name to malicious software (malware) such as viruses, worms, and trojan horse programs. This identifier, the Common Malware Enumeration (CME), provides a common name for similar malware. In the industry today, vendors of antivirus products have dissimilar naming schemes. The names by which the various products identify the same piece of malware can be

completely different. To reduce confusion, CME numbers enable a common identifier for teams to communicate which malware specimen they are dealing with.

To further facilitate information sharing between IRTs, another format known as the Incident Object Description and Exchange Format (IODEF) exists. The purpose of IODEF is defined in RFC 3067 as "....to define a common data format for the description, archiving, and exchange of information about incidents between CSIRTs (Computer Security Incident Response Teams) (including alert, incident in investigation, archiving, statistics, reporting, etc.)." Even if your case tracking system does not support the IODEF format, it should at a minimum be used as a template for understanding the types of information that should be collected and possibly shared with other incident response teams that might be assisting you.

In situations in which you need to share vulnerability information, you can use the Common Announcement Interchange Format (CAIF). Some teams have analysis responsibilities for their constituencies. Others perform language translation on advisories passing them on to other teams. CAIF offers a common format that teams can standardize for feeding into automated case handling systems. By providing a standard set of data elements with each advisory using this format, those can be autopopulated into other systems that support the CAIF format.

Finally, international organizations for setting standards have also joined in. ITU-T has embarked upon creating a set of recommendations (that is "standard" in ITU parlance) to facilitate information exchange. This work is done within X.Cybex framework.

Summary

There is no shortage of ways to look for a response team at the remote location but, unfortunately, none of them guarantees the correct result. No universally accepted best practice exists for how to advertise an existence of an IRT, and even more worrysome, the need for IRT's existence is not universally recognized.

Information at the FIRST and Trusted Introducer websites is regularly maintained and is generally accepted as accurate.

References

Australia Computer Emergency Response Team, http://www.auscert.org.au/.

CAIF—Common Announcement Interchange Format, http://www.caif.info/.

Carnegie Mellon Software Engineering Institute, CERT Coordination Center, http://www.cert.org/.

Centre for the Protection of National Infrastructure, http://www.cpni.gov.uk/.

CERT-FI, http://www.cert.fi/en/index.html.

"Common Malware Enumeration," http://cme.mitre.org/.

"Common Vulnerabilities and Exposures," http://cve.mitre.org/.

Federal Bureau of Investigation, Legal Attaché Offices, http://www.fbi.gov/contact/legat/legat.htm.

FIRST.Org, http://www.first.org/.

ICASI, http://www.icasi.org/.

ITU, 2009. "ITU-T Newslog—Security standards group chalks two key achievements." Available at http://www.itu.int/ITU-T/newslog/Security+Standards+Group+Chalks+Two+Key+Achievements.aspx. [Accessed September 22, 2010].

Japan Computer Emergency Response Team Coordination Center, http://www.jpcert.or.jp/.

"Mailbox Names for Common Services, Roles, and Functions," http://www.ietf.org/rfc/rfc2142.txt.

oCERT—Open Source CERT, http://www.ocert.org/.

RIPE NCC, IRT Object FAQ. Available at http://www.ripe.net/db/support/security/irt/faq.html. [Accessed September 21, 2010].

"Security Vulnerability Policy," Cisco Product Security Incident Response, http://www.cisco.com/en/US/products/products_security_vulnerability_policy.html.

TERENA, http://www.terena.nl/.

"TERENA's Incident Object Description and Exchange Format Requirements," http://www.ietf.org/rfc/rfc3067.txt.

time and date.com, http://www.timeanddate.com/.

United States Computer Emergency Readiness Team, http://www.uscert.gov/.

"Vulnerability Disclosure Framework," http://www.dhs.gov/xlibrary/assets/vdwgreport.pdf.

WorldTimeZone.com, http://www.worldtimezone.com/.

Getting to Know Your Peers: Teams and Organizations Around the World

The previous chapter covers the various internal organizations a response team will likely need to interface with, such as public relations, attorneys, and executive management. The purpose behind involving those internal teams is to engage resources and specialized skill sets to deal with an incident internally. Collaboration between your IRT and key groups or individuals within your organization should be well established.

A sign of a mature IRT is one who not only has these relationships with other internal entities established, but also continues to cultivate them. These working relationships should be more than just mandated by senior management. It should be made clear to all involved why they are needed and the important role in the process that they will play.

Not all incidents can be handled using only internal resources. Often external resources might be required. Internet-based attacks are not limited by geographical boundaries. Attackers can be located in other countries, or it could be your next-door neighbor using compromised machines based in other countries.

You might find that in dealing with an attack, you need to contact your own Internet service provider (ISP), the ISP from which the attack is originating, the upstream ISP from the attacker, and DNS providers. You might also need to work with law enforcement organizations at both the local and national levels.

The IRT should seek out peers locally, nationally, and internationally that can assist when needed. There are additional benefits when working with other response teams outside of reacting to an incident. It might be possible for teams to share experiences, data, policies, tools, and expertise with each other. Reaching out to other teams and participating in external forums can help establish working relationships between response teams. You might find that other teams have been a victim of a similar attack. Other response teams might have information regarding the source behind certain attacks. A criminal investigator once told me, "I do not have to be an expert in everything; I just have to know who to call." The same is true for IRTs that are more effective when they do not operate in isolation.

This chapter introduces several external organizations that are useful to the IRT. The organizations introduced are in no way a complete listing but are useful starting points. You should find that participation in these organizations not only facilitates meeting new people and teams, but can also be a way to find and join other organizations that might be of value. Participation in forums such as the ones listed here requires a commitment of time and money. An additional travel budget might be required for the team to attend interesting events. In the end, any costs of participation are usually smaller than the costs of not having the necessary relationships established prior to an incident in which they are needed.

FIRST

Website: http://www.first.org

How to join: A candidate team must find two sponsors among the current FIRST members. Membership can be either full or liaison. Full members have voting rights, whereas liaison members do not.

Fee: An annual fee must be paid to maintain membership.

The Forum of Incident Response and Security Teams (FIRST) is an international nonprofit organization composed of response and security teams from around the world. Each year, FIRST holds an annual conference that attracts IRT members and security professionals from around the globe to meet and share research, project updates, experiences, best practices, and expertise with others.

FIRST holds smaller events such as Technical Colloquia (TC) in various regions internationally. Each TC provides a more intimate and interactive environment for teams to share and collaborate on similar subject matter as the annual conference but provides the flexibility for discussions and presentations on recent events and case studies.

Each TC offers hands-on training classes where members of a FIRST team share their expertise and knowledge directly with other FIRST team members. The TC program often contains updates on work in progress that might not be in a polished state as would typically be required for a larger conference presentation.

Other efforts within FIRST include offering training to prospective incident response teams and their members and best practice guides that can be used as a reference in your own organization. FIRST also has a number of special interest groups (SIGs), each focused on a specific area of interest. Through FIRST, members have an opportunity to shape new standards developed in ISO and ITU-T organizations.

FIRST stresses within its members that trust between teams and individuals is of paramount importance, and that incidents are best handled within a collaborative and cooperative manner. To facilitate this, FIRST provides several methods that members can use to communicate with other teams. The professional working relationships cultivated between FIRST member teams is often noted as the most valuable benefit for membership in the Forum.

APCERT

Website: http://www.apcert.org

How to join: There are two tiers of membership: general and full member. Any team can become a general member if it finds a sponsor (currently a member) and send a request to APCERT. The team can later upgrade its membership to full, which gives it voting rights. A sponsor is needed to either become a general member or to upgrade to a full member.

Fee: None.

The Asia Pacific Computer Emergency Response Team (APCERT) is composed of CERTs (Computer Emergency Response Team) and CSIRTs (Computer Security Incident Response Team) in the Asia Pacific region who have an interest in incident response and IT security. The operationally focused member teams within APCERT take a collaborative approach in dealing with electronic threats facing Asia Pacific economies and attacks on information infrastructures within the region. Its mission consists of several goals focused on increasing the international cooperation within the region with regard to information security. This includes the sharing of information and technology, insight that might be used for policy development, and developing measures to deal with large-scale or international network security incidents.

APCERT holds an annual conference within the Asia Pacific region, usually during February or March, to raise awareness of computer security issues and facilitate sharing of information and trends between incident response teams. Additionally, APCERT organizes local and regional workshops or seminars on information security and incident response.

TF-CSIRT

Website: http://www.terena.nl/activities/tf-csirt/

How to join: TF-CSIRT offers two tiers of membership: listed and accredited. Any team can become listed by sending the request to TF-CSIRT. To become accredited, the team must provide information about it and follow the procedure described at http://www.trusted-introducer.nl/ti_process/accredit.html. Only accredited teams have voting rights.

Fee: Listed members do not pay a fee. Accredited teams must pay a cost of the accreditation and, if successful, a yearly fee.

In the European region, the Trans-European Research and Education Networking Association (TERENA) is composed of organizations with a common interest in the uses of network infrastructure and services for research and education. TERENA sponsors a number of task forces, including the TF-CSIRT, which, according to its website:

> "...provides a forum where members of the community can exchange experiences and knowledge in a trusted environment. Participants in TF-CSIRT are actively involved in establishing and operating CSIRT services in Europe and neighboring countries.

The task force promotes the use of common standards and procedures for responding to computer security incidents. Common standards have great potential for reducing the time needed to recognize and analyze incidents, and then taking appropriate countermeasures."

The TF-CSIRT currently holds three meetings a year in various locations throughout Europe. Its activities are focused on Europe and neighboring countries. Meeting content typically consists of technical presentations, team updates, legal and policy consideration, and project status updates.

BARF

Website: None.

How to join: Open to teams that are members of FIRST and located in, or in the vicinity of, the Bay Area in California.

Fee: None.

The Bay Area Regional FIRST (BARF) teams are an important example of teams that realize the importance of maintaining professional relationships with other response teams. The group, composed of FIRST teams from the San Francisco Bay Area, meets once a month for dinner. This not only provides opportunities for teams to meet and network with other IRTs, but also allows them to do so in a more relaxed and informal setting. This smaller gathering of team members is kept fun and interesting by meeting in a different-themed restaurant each month.

InfraGard

Website: http://www.infragard.net/

How to join: To be accepted as a member, an applicant must be, among other things, a U.S. citizen, pass an FBI check, and be sponsored by an existing InfraGuard member, chapter, or partner. The complete process is described at http://www.infragard.net/member.php?mn=2.

Fee: None.

InfraGard is a program of the United States Federal Bureau of Investigation (FBI). This program, resulting from PDD-63 (see Chapter 1, "Why Care About Incident Response?"), seeks to create a partnership between the FBI, local and regional law enforcement, academic institutions, and private industry through which information is shared and levels of awareness are raised for the purpose of securing pieces of the national critical infrastructure within the United States. InfraGard meetings provide exposure and education that the attendees would have trouble getting elsewhere on cyber intrusions, exploited vulnerabilities, and infrastructure threats. The collaborative partnership becomes important when regionally significant events or local network break-ins are handled by the local authorities but could be part of a much larger attack on a critical infrastructure.

InfraGard chapters exist regionally, with meeting dates and the frequency that they meet set by the individual chapter. Nationally, the parent InfraGard organization holds an annual conference each year, attracting both chapter delegates and InfraGard members.

ISAC

Website: Information Sharing and Analysis Centre (ISAC) doesn't have a single website. The closest to that is ISAC Council's website at http://www.isaccouncil.org.

How to join: Different requirements might be applicable for each ISAC. Please consult requirements for the ISAC you would like to join.

Fee: Generally it is required but it can vary among ISACs.

Chapter 1 introduced Information Sharing and Analysis Centers (ISACs). In the United States, critical national infrastructures were defined by President Bill Clinton via Presidential Decision Directive 63 (PDD-63) on May 22, 1998. Those infrastructures included, but were not limited to, telecommunications, energy, banking and finance, transportation, water systems, and emergency services, both governmental and private. Around identified critical national infrastructures, 15 different ISACs[1] exist in the United States (as of September 2010). These ISACs provide a forum within a critical infrastructure for organizations to share information.

If necessary, the information to be shared might be sanitized to protect the reputation of those sharing it or to protect intellectual property that might be reflected in the information.

NSP-Security Forum

Website: http://puck.nether.net/mailman/listinfo/nsp-security

How to join: Team must be vouched for by at least two existing members.

Fee: None.

Network service providers (NSPs) worldwide have established the NSP-Security forum. NSP-SEC, as it is often referred, is composed of individuals responsible for responding to network security incidents in service provider networks along with product security team representatives from those vendors with equipment heavily deployed in those environments. NSP-SEC is operational in nature, responding to network-based attacks and compromised hosts in near real-time, collaborating internationally to mitigate and squelch attacks as close to the source as possible.

---

[1] Communications ISAC, Electricity Sector ISAC, Emergency Management and Response ISAC, Financial Services ISAC, The National Health ISAC, Highway ISAC, Information Technology ISAC, Maritime ISAC, Multi-State ISAC, Public Transit ISAC, Real Estate ISAC, Research and Education ISAC, Supply Chain ISAC, Surface Transportation, and Water ISAC.

The entire forum is structured around a mailing list (nsp-security@puck.nether.net) that is the main vehicle for information sharing. To improve and speed up communication, some of the providers use dedicated IP telephones.

Other Forums and Organizations of Importance

IRTs might need to use more organizations and forums. A short list of some of them is provided here. The reason why they are not covered in as much detail as the previous organizations and forums is that these are not strictly oriented to deal with computer incidents. Organizations and individuals mentioned in this section can be helpful in handling an incident, but their primary goal is something else.

The following forums and organizations are good to know because they, and people participating in them, can be helpful when dealing with an incident:

- Team Cymru is a group dedicated to making the Internet more secure. Simple and to the point. More information is at http://www.team-cymru.org/.

- Network Operators Groups (xNOGs) are forums for people who operate networks. The goal of these groups is to educate people and disseminate best practices and techniques in operating backbone networks. Multiple NOGs exist. Here are some of them:

  - NANOG: North America NOG, http://www.nanog.org

  - JANOG: Japanese NOG, http://www.janog.gr.jp/en/

  - NZNOG: New Zealand NOG, http://www.nznog.org

  - EOF: European Operators Forum, http://www.ripe.net/ripe/wg/eof/index.html

  - AfNOG: Africa NOG, http://www.afnog.org

  A more comprehensive list can be found at http://nanog.org/resources/otherorgs/.

- Internet Infrastructure Vendors Special Interest Group (Vendor SIG) and Industry Consortium for Advancement of Security on the Internet (ICASI) are two forums for computer and network equipment vendors—more precisely, for teams that deal with product security vulnerabilities. Their respective websites are http://www.first.org/vendor-sig/ and http://www.icasi.org. We will talk about them more in the second part of the book.

Summary

The IRT can call upon many organizations when handling a computer incident. This chapter presented only some more prominent organizations. Every IRT should make one of its priorities to join all relevant forums and introduce itself and get to know others. Sooner or later, you will need help from these other groups.

References

APCERT Operational Framework, http://www.apcert.org/documents/pdf/opfw.pdf.

FIRST, http://www.first.org.

Industry Consortium for Advancement of Security on the Internet (ICASI), http://www.icasi.org.

InfraGard, http://www.infragard.net/.

Internet Infrastructure Vendors Special Interest Group (Vendor SIG), http://www.first.org/vendor-sig.

ISAC Council, http://www.isaccouncil.org.

Presidential Decision Directives/NCS 63, Critical Infrastructure Protection, May 22, 1998, http://www.fas.org/irp/offdocs/pdd/pdd-63.htm.

TF-CSIRT, http://www.terena.nl/activities/tf-csirt/.

Chapter 7

Product Security Vulnerabilities

This chapter provides an overview of several topics related to handling product security vulnerabilities. Following are some main topics covered in this chapter:

- The definition of what constitutes security vulnerability
- Vendor's speed of producing remedies for the vulnerabilities
- Issues with applying the remedies in different environments

Throughout this and the following chapter, you will encounter terms such as *fix* and *patch*. For the purpose of this book these two expressions are equivalent, and their primary meaning is updated software and/or configuration to remove security vulnerability. However, these expressions also have, or can have, a second meaning: a change in the source code.

The expression "to make a fix" also refers to when a software engineer makes a change in the code to remove the root cause of the vulnerability. Sometimes the change can be as simple as changing a relation operator from **wile (counter=0)** to **while (counter>0)**, but it can also be as complex as re-architecting the entire product.

What the user receives to install on a system is usually packaged in a certain format to aid installation. That package can contain only a small portion of a code (a patch) that must be applied to an existing application (Microsoft's updates are probably the most known representative of this model) or an entirely new software release (Cisco uses this model). To prevent confusion when talking about a patch versus new (fixed) software release, we will use a generic term *remedy* to denote whatever users have to install on their system to remove the vulnerability. So, in the rest of this book, a remedy is what a vendor delivers to a user to remove a security vulnerability in a product. The expressions fix and patch will denote only a change in the code and configuration that engineering must make to remove the vulnerability from the software. The chapter does not discuss the relative advantages and disadvantages of the models for how remedies are delivered (that is, Cisco versus Microsoft model) and focuses instead on identifying and addressing product security vulnerabilities in an organized and effective manner.

The terms *product*, *software*, and *application* are interchangeable. Product is more generic because it encompasses not only software, but can also refer to a combination of software and hardware. It can also mean a service. Also, most of the processes described in the book are also applicable to hardware issues. What has not been covered are issues such as product recall, which are beyond the scope of the book.

Definition of Security Vulnerability

Security vulnerability can have several definitions. The National Infrastructure Advisory Council (NIAC) defines security vulnerability in its "Vulnerability Disclosure Framework" as

> ...a vulnerability is defined as a set of conditions that leads or may lead to an implicit or explicit failure of the confidentiality, integrity, or availability of an information system. Examples of the unauthorized or unexpected effects of a vulnerability may include any of the following:
>
> - Executing commands as another user
>
> - Accessing data in excess of specified or expected permission
>
> - Posing as another user or service within a system
>
> - Causing an abnormal denial of service
>
> - Inadvertently or intentionally destroying data without permission
>
> - Exploiting an encryption implementation weakness that significantly reduces the time or computation required to recover the plaintext from an encrypted message

U.S. National Institute of Standards and Technology (NIST) offer the following definition of vulnerability in its "Risk Management Guide for Information Technology Systems":

> Vulnerability: A flaw or weakness in system security procedures, design, implementation, or internal controls that could be exercised (accidentally triggered or intentionally exploited) and result in a security breach or a violation of the system's security policy.

Many more definitions exist for security vulnerability, but they tend to be variations of these two definitions. The one thing that can be noticed is that these definitions are more qualitative than quantitative in nature. That is not surprising because that is the only way the definition can be written. On the other hand, that can represent a problem when evaluating whether something is a vulnerability.

Following are three examples showing how practical these two definitions are. The vulnerabilities are default administrator password, weak cryptographic algorithm, and susceptibility to denial-of-service (DoS) attack.

- **Default administrator password:** Enables anyone who can access the device to exercise full control over it. This is security vulnerability by any of the two definitions because it enables an unauthorized user to access the device and modify it or, potentially, data residing in the device.

- **Weak cryptographic algorithm:** If you rely on a simple mono-alphabetic substitution as in a Caesar cipher to protect confidentiality of data, this would qualify as security vulnerability. Caesar cipher can be deciphered in a matter of minutes using nothing more sophisticated than a pencil and a bit of a paper. But what if, instead of a Caesar cipher, you use Data Encryption Standard (DES)? It is common knowledge that DES is broken, and information encrypted using that algorithm can be decrypted in a matter of hours or days given the sufficient computational power. A relatively inexpensive ($10,000 USD in 2007) machine, such as COPACOBANA, can break DES, on average, in 6.4 days (12.8 days worst case). For triple DES, it can take even longer than 12 days to decrypt the information by brute force. Now the question: If the confidential information must remain secret for only 30 to 60 minutes, is using DES to protect it security vulnerability? If breaking encryption takes two hours then DES might be sufficient for the purpose. What is obvious is that we can have a sliding scale that would mark when using DES becomes a product vulnerability. For some users, and for the purpose they are using the product, DES can be quite sufficient, whereas other users would consider DES a vulnerability for the purpose they are using it.

    A different algorithm might require a longer or shorter time period within which it can be broken. The question is, How can you to determine what timeframe (to break the encryption) constitutes security vulnerability? Is it a vulnerability if you can break the algorithm in 10 years? What if you need 100 years to break it? There is no universal answer to this, but it depends on how the encryption is used and on the data encrypted. And a vendor cannot know what data will be encrypted.

    Another issue that must be considered is how to use encryption. Using DES to encrypt passwords and then storing them in a file to which everyone has access (as used to be the case in Unix operating systems) should be considered a product vulnerability. That is because an attacker can mount an offline brute force attack that is devastating. Using DES as a part of Message Authentication Code (MAC), as used to be the case in Data Authentication Algorithm (DAA) in FIPS PUB 113 (now defunct) might not constitute a vulnerability even if protecting a file with DES is a vulnerability.

- **Denial-of-Service (DoS):** In this attack, a miscreant would consume a resource (for example, network bandwidth, central processing unit [CPU], memory, and disk space) so legitimate users could not perform their tasks. The NIAC's definition phrases this as "....a abnormal denial of service". The definition assumes an asymmetrical relationship in which an attacker uses relatively small effort to consume disproportionate larger amount of resources on the attacked device. Imagine a web server, with software running on the latest hardware with the fastest processor and a huge amount of memory. The device is connected with a Gigabit Ethernet interface to the network. All expectations are that this web server can serve a large number of connections per second. If an attacker can prevent the server from accepting any further connection by establishing ten connections per second, everyone would characterize that as a security vulnerability. But what if you now start to gradually increase the number of attacking sessions per second that is required to cripple the web server? At what number of sessions per second would unresponsiveness of the web server cease to be a vulnerability and become just a design or network limitation? Would that be at 100 connections per second? Maybe 1000, 10,000, or 100,000? Again, the answer depends on the information served by that web server, but that is something that a vendor cannot know in advance.

From these few examples, it should be visible that determining what constitutes a security vulnerability is not always easy and straightforward. Sometimes things must be put into a wider context to make a proper determination. Users can have different expectations and, if not fulfilled, may consider that as a vulnerability. Other times, how product or a feature is used can determine whether something is a vulnerability. This, however, does not mean that vendors should avoid improving products and removing such ambiguities even if they do not constitute a vulnerability in all cases. (For example, DES should be phased out no matter what.)

Severe and Minor Vulnerabilities

Why should you worry about security vulnerabilities in products? Because each of them represents a potential avenue for how your system can be compromised. Each vulnerability carries a certain amount of risk with it—the risk that an attacker will exploit the vulnerability and penetrate the system. The sad fact is that all complex products[1] contain vulnerabilities, and this is especially true when a nontrivial amount of software is involved. An organization typically deploys a mix of products from multiple vendors, so updating them requires coordination and resources. Each remedy must be tested to prevent introducing undesired side effects into the system. Testing requires people and time, and so does the final deployment of the remedy. For that reason, an organization must assign priorities to what products and what vulnerabilities will be fixed first, what second, and when.

At the same time, vendors are in a similar position. At any given point, vendors are dealing with multiple vulnerabilities. Ideally they should work on all of them at the same time, but that is not possible. Therefore, vendors also must make priorities about which vulnerability will be addressed first and which one will be next. Severe vulnerabilities will be given priority over less severe ones. So again, you are faced with the question: How can the severity of a vulnerability be determined?

Vendors can investigate technical characteristics of a vulnerability. How easy is it to trigger and what would be the consequences if exploited? In short, how bad is the vulnerability? Based on this assessment, a vendor will assign a severity to the vulnerability. That

---

[1] A few programs (as currently known) have only a few known severe vulnerabilities. Some of these notable exceptions are TeX, postfix, and djbdns.

can be done either descriptively (for example, Critical, Moderate, and so on) or using a numerical scale such as 0 to 3 or 0 to 10. This severity is later passed to the users so that they can use it in their evaluation.

What users are interested in more than severity of a vulnerability by itself is the impact to their system. The impact is directly related to the severity of the vulnerability but also depends on how a product is deployed. Vendors, in general, cannot assess the vulnerability impact on a given user's system because the vendor does not know how products are configured and deployed. The vulnerability evaluation is the process with multiple stages; the vendor starts it and the user must finish it.

To address this multi-staged approach, increasing numbers of vendors are adopting a system called Common Vulnerability Scoring System (CVSS), which has three components: base, temporal, and environmental. Each component is presented as a score on the scale from 0 to 10.

The base score, the technical side of vulnerability, states, "If all prerequisites for the vulnerability to be exploited exist, this is what attacker can achieve." Some of the things that an attacker can achieve are unauthorized access to data, modification of data, modification of the configuration, preventing legitimate users from using device or services, executing arbitrary code, and so on.

A temporal score gives information for how the vulnerability is changing with time. This aspect influences the urgency with which the vendor and user will address the vulnerability. For example, when a vendor published its advisory, the vulnerability was only theoretical, so it will be marked as such. A month later, a proof of concept code might be created, so the vendor needs to consider addressing the vulnerability sooner rather than later.

Taking base and temporal scores as the basis, users must add their specific deployment information to it to understand what impact the vulnerability has to the organization. This impact, in the CVSS jargon, is called the "environmental score." The environmental score modifies the base and temporal score. The result is a number that describes the severity of the vulnerability for the organization. This is easier to understand if we look at an example.

Assume that a device uses a Telnet protocol and that the implementation of the Telnet server contains a buffer overflow. This vulnerability enables an attacker to execute arbitrary code on the device and take complete control of the device. No authentication is required to exploit this vulnerability. From a technical perspective, this vulnerability is as bad as you can get. Its base score[2] would be 10 out of 10 (10 is the most severe and 0 is the least severe). It is also known that a working exploit exists "in the wild" (reflected by temporal score) so a user would like to address this vulnerability urgently. However, if all devices in the organization are configured so that Telnet protocol is completely disabled,

---

[2] The scoring components are Access vector–Network, Access complexity–Low, Authentication–None, Confidentiality impact–Complete, Integrity impact–Complete, and Availability impact–Complete.

the overall impact of the vulnerability to the organization is 0. No Telnet protocol means no impact on the organization, so you can schedule applying the remedy for this vulnerability at some later time.

This example demonstrates how combining the vulnerability's severity information from the vendor together with the deployment details, you can gauge the impact of the vulnerability to the organization. You can use this information to make decision about what vulnerability and which devices should be updated first, which second, and so on. More information about CVSS and further examples are available at http://www.first.org/cvss.

In CVSS, each vulnerability is considered on its own, independently from any other. The significance of this is explained in the following section.

Chaining Vulnerabilities

CVSS helps to assess the impact of a single vulnerability on the organization. That is great but not always sufficient. Consider the example with vulnerability in the Telnet server again. This time, in addition to it, assume that a second vulnerability exists. This second vulnerability is in the web server and enables the attacker to write an arbitrary file to the file system. The organization blocks all traffic to port 23 on the network edge so that nobody from outside the organization can establish a Telnet connection to a host within the organization.

If you use CVSS to evaluate the impact of these two vulnerabilities, you can come up with 0 for the Telnet vulnerability (because it is blocked on the edge) and a small number (that is, small impact) for the web server vulnerability because the data is pulled from the backend database on demand. Each of these two vulnerabilities, on its own, does not represent a high risk to the organization.

Now let's be creative and see what can be done if you combine these two vulnerabilities. You can use the vulnerability in the web server to create a file on the file system of the web server. The file will contain a Python (or Perl, PHP, or shell) script that the attackers will execute by accessing it remotely from their machine. The script will open a Telnet connection to the target host, create a new script on the target, and then execute it. This second script on the target host will make an outbound connection to the attackers' computer. The attackers now have access to the target computer. This scenario is depicted in Figure 7-1. From this example, it is visible that the combination of these two vulnerabilities poses a much higher threat to the organization than each of them individually. This is the way attackers operate. They use one vulnerability to gain a foothold, and then use other vulnerabilities to secure more control over the system.

Chaining vulnerabilities, using different vulnerabilities to infiltrate progressively further into the system and gaining more control over it, is something that we all must be aware of. Users must be aware of this because chaining can change the order in which vulnerability needs to be removed from the system. What might be several nonsevere vulnerabilities can become a severe issue if combined. The same is also applicable to vendors. Knowing which vulnerabilities can be used together can change the priority and the order in which they are being fixed. Figure 7-2 shows an extreme case of this.

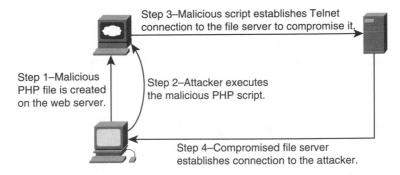

Figure 7-1 *Using Vulnerability Chaining to Compromise the Target*

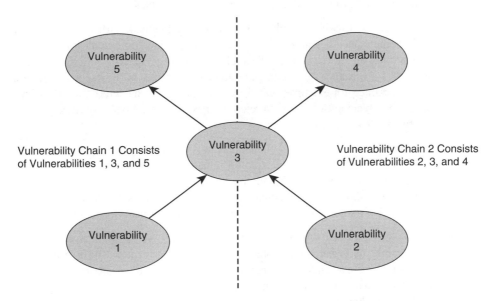

Figure 7-2 *Vulnerability Chaining Role in Fixing Prioritization*

Figure 7-2 shows two possible chains of vulnerabilities. Each chain consists of two vulnerabilities unique to the chain and one common for both chains. Each vulnerability by itself is not severe, so using the standard process, they can be fixed in, let's say, 6 months. If a vendor recognizes that vulnerabilities can be combined, as shown in Figure 7-2, and that by fixing a single vulnerability both chains will be broken, the vendor can increase the priority of the vulnerability at the intersection of two chains. By doing this evaluation and reprioritizing, the vendor can use its resources better and provide better protection for the users at the same time.

Unfortunately, performing such analysis is not a trivial task. Several commercial companies are claiming that they can do it if you buy their services, but the open literature on this topic is sparse. Good penetration companies will also use this technique when assessing the security posture of an organization, but so will attackers who are determined to compromise your organization.

Fixing Theoretical Vulnerabilities, or Do We Need an Exploit?

What is the difference between a vulnerability and an exploit? A vulnerability is just a condition that can enable an attacker to compromise the security of your system. An exploit, on the other hand, is a concrete manifestation, either a program or set of steps (a "recipe") that uses a particular vulnerability to compromise the system.

An exploit cannot exist without a vulnerability, but not all vulnerabilities have an associated exploit. Some vulnerabilities can be difficult or impractical to exploit for various reasons. Sometimes an attacker must collect a large sample of specific data (for example, the requirement for breaking certain cryptographic protection), or the injected code has a limited size and values (for example, only 5 bytes of printable characters can be injected), and so on. Such vulnerabilities are often referred to as theoretical because there is no exploit for them.

The biggest problem with theoretical vulnerabilities is that there are many smart people out there. If you do not know how to exploit a vulnerability, it does not mean that someone else would not find a way. For that matter, someone may already have found the way to exploit the vulnerability and is keeping that knowledge for herself. There are several examples in which a theoretical vulnerability can become practical overnight.

So how should a vendor deal with theoretical vulnerabilities? After all, there is no exploit for that vulnerability, so what is the problem? That, however, is the wrong attitude and is one way to differentiate a vendor with mature vulnerability handling processes from an inexperienced one. There is no such thing as an "entirely theoretical" vulnerability, as Microsoft learned a long time ago when, in 1992, handling a vulnerability reported by L0pth Heavy Industries. The initial response from Microsoft was that "...vulnerability is entirely theoretical" and, as such, is not high priority to be fixed. To prove Microsoft wrong, L0pth created an exploit using that vulnerability to compromise a computer. A vendor must treat every vulnerability equally, no matter whether an exploit exists.

Having a working exploit can be helpful. It helps to easily verify whether the same vulnerability is present in a different software release and also to verify whether the vulnerability is fixed. Even when an exploit is used for testing purposes, some limitations exist. The biggest limitation is that people become too dependent on it. The vulnerability becomes defined by the exploit, which is wrong. This can lead to a situation in which the vulnerability is fixed only partially or not at all. One vulnerability in a UDP-based protocol I worked on illustrates this very well.

I received an exploit for a UDP-based protocol that was able to crash a device running Cisco IOS. The protocol was using packet structure, as shown in Figure 7-3. The exploit would send a single packet where all fields were filled with zeros and the affected device would crash.

Version 1 Byte	Payload Length 2 Bytes	Payload

Figure 7-3   *Protocol Packet Structure*

The way to fix this vulnerability was to verify whether the protocol version was 1. If the protocol version contained any other value than 1, the packet was discarded. Testing with the exploit has confirmed that the vulnerability was indeed fixed, and everything was now ready to integrate the fix into all affected software releases. However, when the exploit was modified to send a packet where the protocol version was set to 1 and the rest of the packet was filled with 0s, the crash appeared again. It turns out that the modified exploit revealed the real root cause of the vulnerability: the length field was equal to 0.

This example shows the danger of relying solely on the exploit and when the exploit defines the vulnerability. Exploits can be useful to point you in a direction where to look for potential problems but they are not essential. Relying excessively on exploits to find and fix vulnerabilities is a road doomed to failure. All vulnerabilities must be addressed irrespectively of the presence or absence of an exploit because there is no such thing as theoretical vulnerability.

Internally Versus Externally Found Vulnerabilities

A vendor can learn about vulnerability in a product if it is found during internal testing or if someone from outside the organization reports it to the vendor. What, if any, difference does it make who discovers the vulnerability? Does the vendor need to treat them differently and why? Does this makes any difference to the users?

Look at this from a user's perspective first. In most cases, the user will learn about the vulnerability when vendors announce it together with a remedy for it. In the same advisory, the vendor might state how it came to know about the vulnerability (for example, "discovered during internal testing" or "reported by a researcher"). Assuming that the researcher is ethical, the user can hope that the researcher did not share the exploit with anyone else but the vendor. After all, an unethical researcher would not report the vulnerability to the vendor to start with. Therefore, the exploit might not be readily available in the wild. No readily available exploit equals a normal (not urgent) process of remedy deployment. The same line of reasoning applies if the vulnerability is discovered by the vendor, so it seems that, from a user's perspective, there is no difference in who discovered the vulnerability.

From the vendor perspective, things look slightly different. If the vulnerability is reported by a researcher, the vendor can hope that the researcher will not share this information with others, but the potential for that exists. Information disclosure can happen if the researcher makes one remark too many, and people who hear it then figure the rest. This happened to Dan Kaminsky in 2008 with his discovery of a vulnerability in DNS. Dan was not acting maliciously, but he gave away sufficient hints for Halvar Flake to join the dots. In short, Halvar was able to deduce the vulnerability Dan discovered in DNS without seeing Dan's research.

For internally discovered vulnerabilities, the way they are discovered can make a difference. If vulnerabilities are found using publicly available tools (for example, fuzzing tools such as the ones from Codenomicon or MuDynamics), someone else might have also purchased the same tool, tested the same product, and found the vulnerability. The tool is, or contains, the exploit, and because it is publicly available, the exploit exists in the wild. What if the vulnerability is found during source code analysis? If you are an open source vendor and use commercial products (for example, Coverity or Klocwork), as in the previous case, someone else can repeat the process and discover the same vulnerability. If the vendor does not make its source code available, it is harder for outsiders to find the same vulnerability using source code analysis—unless the source code is stolen, that is.

Let us now examine the entire situation again. No matter how the vulnerability is discovered, a vendor cannot be sure that nobody else knows about it. Being aware of that, users also cannot be sure that no exploit is publicly available. So it seems that who discovers the vulnerability should not make any difference in how vendors and users deal with it. The vulnerability must be treated equally no matter who discovered it and how.

Some vendors might be tempted to make the difference and try to treat them differently. Prioritizing externally found vulnerabilities over internally found vulnerabilities or providing remedies only for the upcoming and future release for internally found vulnerabilities are examples how vendors might behave. But that is not how things should be. There is always a reasonable doubt that someone else might know about the internally discovered vulnerability, so vendors should treat all vulnerabilites as externally discovered.

Are Vendors Slow to Produce Remedies?

The answer to this question depends on whom you ask. All respectable vendors would produce remedies (patches, fixes, and new software releases) without undue delay. As everywhere, some vendors would not behave this way. They will postpone fixing vulnerabilities or even deny their existence and try not to fix them. The behavior of these vendors is not a norm but an aberration. Luckily, the number of unresponsive vendors is getting smaller.

So let's repeat the question again. Are responsible vendors slow to produce remedies for security vulnerabilities? To answer this question, we must first look at the process of fixing the vulnerability.

Process of Vulnerability Fixing

Figure 7-4 shows the entire process of fixing any issue, including security vulnerabilities.

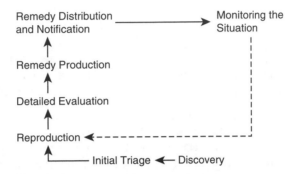

Figure 7-4 *Process of Vulnerability Fixing*

An abbreviated description of each step in the process follows, and you can find a more detailed discussion in Chapter 11, "Security Vulnerability Handling by Vendors." Discovery, or learning about the vulnerability, is the first phase. The vendor becomes aware of an issue. The exact avenue how it becomes aware is not important. At this stage, it is not known whether this is a real problem. In some cases, it might just be a mismatched expectation on the user's behalf. It is also unknown whether this issue is only some transient phenomenon or something that can be reproduced at will.

That is followed by the initial triage. Every product security team handles multiple vulnerabilities at any given time. To allocate resources accordingly, every new report must be prioritized, which is the purpose of this step: to provide quick assessment of the vulnerability so that the team knows whether this is something that must be worked on immediately.

Reproduction is the next phase. The term "reproduction" is taken in its most liberal form. In cases when the vendor posses an exploit or the report provides steps (or packets dump) on how to trigger the issue, the vendor will use that information to re-create what the report claims (for example, crash, arbitrary code execution, high CPU utilization, and so on). This is needed to make sure the issue is real and that it can be reproduced at will. In instances when the report is the result of source code inspection, the reproduction will amount to visually inspecting the source code and verifying that potentially dangerous code is present. Here the vendor does not need to create an exploit to trigger the vulnerability. It is not needed because the code inspection clearly shows that the potential for being vulnerable is present. Apart from just enabling us to re-create the issue, this step also helps us understand circumstances under which it is possible to trigger this issue. This information will be used when formulating workarounds.

A detailed evaluation is the following phase. Now when you understand how to reproduce the issue and what conditions must be met to trigger it, you can make an assessment about the report. Does it represent a security vulnerability or is it just a mismatched expectation? If the issue is real, vulnerability or not, it will be forwarded to software engineers to be fixed.

The remedy production comes next. This step consists of developing a fix and regression testing. A fix can be as small as changing one line of the code, or it can be as comprehensive as redesigning a part of the product. Occasionally, this step requires modifying the current standards, as was the case with the so called "TCP RST" vulnerability (see http://www.cisco.com/warp/public/707/cisco-sa-20040420-tcp-ios.shtml).

Regression testing comes after the fix is developed. At this phase, the fix is integrated into the product, and the product must be tested to make sure the fix has not introduced, or re-introduced, unforeseen problems. Although the fix has been tested during the previous phase, that testing was focused only to prove that the reported issue is addressed. Regression testing must now prove that the fix does not have any adverse influence on functions of all other parts of the product.

Remedy distribution is the next phase. After the vendor finishes with regression testing, the remedy is ready to be made available to users. Apart from the remedy, vendors also provide information about the issue that was fixed. If that were security vulnerability, vendors would normally make this a more visible event and publish a special publication (for example, Cisco Security Advisory, Microsoft Security Bulletin, and Oracle Security Alert).

After everything is finished, you must monitor for feedback from the field. It is possible that remedy will break some other functionality, and that was not discovered during the regression testing. It is also possible that the vulnerability is not complete and that the modified attack will still trigger the same issue. If any such adverse event is observed, the entire cycle must start again and the vulnerability must be reevaluated and retested.

What we have not considered is how long these steps can take.

Vulnerability Fixing Timeline

For a vendor, the clock starts ticking the moment its product security team becomes aware of the vulnerability. All vendors with mature processes and vulnerability handling teams will work without an undue delay, and almost all the steps require a relatively short time to complete.

One example that can illustrate a short timeline is a vulnerability with IOS HTTP authorization described in the Cisco Security Advisory at http://www.cisco.com/warp/public/707/cisco-sa-20010627-ios-http-level.shtml. After receiving the report about the issue, I reproduced it within 30 minutes. In the next 10 to 15 minutes, a few different IOS releases were tested to establish that the vulnerability was not confined to a single IOS release. The next step was to investigate the source code to gain an understanding of the scope of the vulnerability. After 2 to 3 hours of investigation, I not only fully understood the vulnerability but also discovered the root cause: The input values were trusted without sanitizing them and verifying that they were within the expected limits. The fix for this vulnerability was to verify that the input values were within the range of 0 to 15 inclusive. The fix was tested and, after verifying it, I was ready to open a bug and send all the information to the component owner. If we break this into the phases as per Figure 7-4, the timeline would look as in Table 7-1.

Table 7-1   *Timeline for Fixing IOS HTTP Authorization Vulnerability*

Phase	Duration of Each Phase
Discovery	Time starts now
Initial triage	10 minutes
Reproduction	45 minutes
Detailed evaluation	15 minutes
Developing the remedy	3 hours
Fix integration and regression testing	2–3 months

As shown in Table 7-1, the unofficial fix was ready within 4 hours of receiving the report about the vulnerability. Later that day, the HTTP component owner confirmed my findings and the fix. Everything was now ready to integrate the fix into an IOS image to ship to the customers. Three things were still missing: to identify which IOS releases must be fixed, were there any other products affected by this vulnerability, and regression testing. As it happens, this vulnerability affected all IOS releases supported at that time, so it was easy to determine which releases needed to be fixed—all of them. Approximately 1 week was needed to determine whether there were other products affected by this vulnerability. Now all that was left was to integrate the fix in all IOS releases and perform the regression testing. When taken across all supported IOS versions and hardware platforms, this step took the better part of the next 2 to 3 months to complete.

The preceding example is "on the light side," where determining the root cause and fixing it was easy. On the other side of the spectrum are cases that needed 1 or 2 weeks just to reproduce them.

What takes the most time is testing. Each update of the application must be properly tested before it is released to the general public. The worst that can happen is that the remedy for the security vulnerability will break some other application. Luckily, that does not often happen, but it is possible, as Apple and Microsoft, among others, have demonstrated on occasion when remedies they distributed caused computers to stop operating normally. To minimize this potential for bad remedies, vendors must test products and updates before they are released. This testing is known as regression testing and can take anywhere from 1 day to 1 week. That is how long it can take to test a single version of software on a specific hardware platform. If multiple software versions and hardware platforms must be tested, the total time required for the testing will grow. Obviously, multiple combinations of software and hardware are tested in parallel, but there are limits on how many things can be done simultaneously. Vendors supporting many products or multiple software releases can, literally, spend months in testing all different hardware and software combinations.

After the testing is done, the vendor is ready to publicly announce the vulnerability. The announcement can be either public (that is, posted to the public page on the vendor's website or posted to a public mailing list) or targeted only to the affected customers. Chapter 12, "Security Vulnerability Notification," is devoted to all things related to this topic, but for now, it is sufficient to say that the announcement itself is a short event. It is over in a few minutes, which is how long it takes to send it by email and post on the website, but the actual support work has just begun. Users will evaluate impact of the vulnerability to their environment and start applying the remedy. Invariably, this always generates questions that must be answered. Some of the more common questions are, "I am running version XY. Am I vulnerable?" or "How can I download the remedy?" or more serious questions such as "I have installed the remedy and now feature Z is broken. What should I do now?". If the product security team did its job correctly, the support part of the organization can handle all these questions with ease.

To summarize, different phases of developing a remedy take different amounts of time. Invariably, testing is always the slowest part of the process, but given its importance, it cannot be skipped.

Reasons For and Against Applying a Remedy

How fast can users apply remedies for vulnerabilities? Why are people still hit with malware that exploits old vulnerabilities for which the patch has existed for the past 5 years? These are interesting questions, and the answers to them are not always obvious. For this discussion, we will assume that users are aware that a remedy for the security vulnerability is available and that their devices are vulnerable. We will start by examining the risk of deploying a remedy and the potential consequences of a "bad" remedy—the one that unintentionally breaks unrelated applications.

Individual users at home can afford to apply remedies often and seldom verify them. That model, however, is not viable for a business. If my personal computer is rendered inoperative because a remedy for a security vulnerability has broken some of the existing applications, I am the only person who will be affected. I could not play my favorite video game for a day or two, but that is about the extent of the damage. If the same would happen to a business (that is, computers rendered inoperative after an update), the consequences will be much more expensive. To prevent this from happening, all organizations should first test every update (security-related or not) before applying it across the entire organization.

In small organizations, this can take a form of installing the update first on a single device and leaving it that way for a few days. If no adverse effects were observed, the update is then installed across all the organization. Larger organizations can have their own battery of tests that are executed against one or more test device in a nonproduction network. Only after all tests have passed will the update be installed throughout the organization.

The time for this testing to finish can take different amounts of time. It can be from 1 to 2 days to several months (3 to 6 months is not uncommon) and, in extreme cases, up to 1 year. This extreme case can be encountered in environments that deal with classified material (for example, an intelligence community or organization handling state secrets). In such environments, deployed devices must pass certification before they are deployed; only certain software and hardware releases configured in a particular way can be deployed. Changing software releases from 12.1 to 12.2 can cause a loss of certification and, subsequently, devices running a 12.2 software release cannot be deployed in the production network until this new configuration is certified. This certification process can take a long time.

On the other hand, if the remedy for the security vulnerability is not applied, the risk of someone misusing the vulnerability increases in direct proportion with the time the vulnerability remains in the system. The probability that someone will actually misuse the vulnerability also increases because with time, an automated exploit for that vulnerability might be produced. That would enable nontechnical users to easily exploit the vulnerability and cause damage.

Following are the more common reasons users do not apply remedies for security vulnerabilities:

- Users are not aware that a vulnerability exists and that they need to apply a remedy for it.

- Downloading the remedy is complicated or complex, so users just give up and do not retrieve it.

- Users do not know how to apply the remedy. They simply do not have the required technical knowledge and are not confident enough to try applying the remedy.

- Testing and certification take lots of effort for users, and resources are scarce at the moment. The remedy will be applied at some later time.

- Users thought about applying the remedy, but then something else came up and they never got back to it.

- The users' hardware platform cannot support new software (or software with the remedy applied). Reasons for the incompatibility can be insufficient memory, an old hardware revision, or the new software does not support the existing hardware.

Some of the reasons remedies are not applied can be addressed, and some already have been addressed. However, not all of them are under the vendor's control. Following is the same list but revisited from a solution standpoint:

■ **Uninformed users:** Vendors post information on their public web pages and public mailing lists. Many vendors also have separate mailing lists to which users can subscribe to receive notification on new security vulnerabilities. If applicable, products can notify users that new remedies, and other general updates, are available. (For example, both Apple's "Software Update" or Microsoft's "Windows Update" would open a new window and notify users of new updates.)

■ **Complicated installation process:** All consumer devices have a simple process to install updates. Again Apple and Microsoft are examples; both automated update installation to the point at which remedies can either be installed automatically or with a single click. It can hardly be more simple than that. For business-grade products this procedure might be more involved, but that would depend on an individual product. A tacit premise is that businesses will have dedicated personnel who would deal with this process.

■ **Users do not have knowledge or confidence:** In many cases, this is more the fear that users would not know what to do if something goes wrong after the remedy has been installed. The device was working fine, so it would probably continue like that even without the remedy. After all, none of the previous remedies were installed, and everything seems to be fine. The only thing a vendor can do is produce high-quality remedies and get it right the first time, every time. If the remedy quality is consistently high, users will have more confidence in applying them.

■ **Testing (user-side) requires resources:** The real issue here is that users do not trust that changing the system will not break anything. Although vendors produce more robust software and are improving their testing methodology, it will take a long time for users' perception to change. After the users' perception is changed and they have more confidence that the system will remain operative after applying the remedies, users might shorten or simplify their testing.

■ **Higher-priority task:** This can be a variation to the previously mentioned reason—lack of resources—but can also point to a different and more severe problem, such as a lack of internal organization. The support group must have an appropriate tracking system to avoid missing tasks such as applying remedies. Processes for risk assessment must also be in place so that security vulnerabilities can be appropriately assessed and ranked relative to other tasks. If the risk of a system compromise and the potential damage are high, that should ensure that applying remedies are given sufficient priority.

■ **Obsolete or insufficient hardware:** This plagues small and big organizations equally. There is anecdotal evidence that large organizations are worse offenders than smaller organizations. Here we have two opposing forces at work. Users would like to preserve their investment in the existing hardware, whereas vendors would like to support fewer software releases and move more customers to more recent platforms. Although this can represent a problem for security, it is something usually resolved through the sales and support channels. Vendors must work with customers to devise a plan to eliminate situations in which the existing hardware prevents installation of security remedies. This is also tied to the risk assessment process on the users' side. Relying on unsupported devices or applications is not a good business decision. Lack of spare parts or being unable to add a new feature can impair an organization's capability to deliver.

Question of Appliances

Nowadays most people understand that computer applications and operating systems must be updated to eliminate security vulnerabilities. That is accepted as a fact of life. All other noncomputerized devices do not need such special attention. They either work or get replaced when they break. But the problem is that computers, or computerized components, are installed into more and more devices. Computers are installed in modern elevators, trains, and cars. Closer to home, you can find computers in broadband modems and routers, and wireless access points, but also in your TV set top box (for example, TiVo and Apple TV), the television, game consoles (for example, Sony PlayStation), and mobile phones. And with each day, this list grows longer and longer. The problem emerging here is twofold. The first part is that people do not necessarily "see" these devices as computers, so they have different expectations toward them. The second part of the problem is that because these devices are becoming more pervasive, they are being used by less technically sophisticated users, and yet the devices are growing more complex.

Translating these two facets (device complexity and the need for updating) from the user's space into the vendor's space would give us education, notification, and ease of use. Vendors should educate users that devices must be updated and notify them when, and the process of updating the devices must be easy and error proof. In some instances, such as cable modems or TV set top boxes, the situation is relatively easy because these devices are maintained by a service provider. The service providers can always access the devices and make sure the latest remedies are installed. The problem arises when devices are wholly owned by users, as can be the case with mobile phones or is the case with video disk players (for example, Sony BDP-S550). In cases like these, everything is up to the users. Vendors can post notices on new vulnerabilities and remedies on various mailing lists and on their websites but, if users do not read them, devices will not be updated. The situation is probably even worse with devices such as video disk players. The majority of users would never consider that video players need to be updated. After all, the previous model was working fine for 5 years, and there was no need for updating.

Finally, for devices such as cars, updating software on computers embedded in them is not a trivial undertaking. Special equipment is required to interface with embedded computers and update the software. At this moment, the situation with computers in vehicles might not be that bad because these computers tend to run specialized versions of operating systems and applications. But that situation can change in a few years as more general-purpose operating systems will be used in embedded computers.

It would be great if we could have one model of how to notify users about security vulnerabilities and how users can apply remedies, but that might be just wishful thinking. We might end up with multiple models for dealing with security vulnerabilities in which each model is suited for a class of devices. Following are possible models:

■ **General-purpose computers:** This is the currently prevalent model in which users receive information on new updates automatically (for example, Apple's "Software Update" or Microsoft's "Windows Update"). Requirements for this model are that users can directly interact with the device, and the software is designed for remote and automatic update. Direct interaction requires a monitor and an input device (for example, keyboard, mouse, or touch screen). The device should have sufficient resources (memory and disk) to enable rollback after a failed update.

■ **Inexpensive devices:** Mobile phones are representative of this category. Instead of updating software on inexpensive devices, it might be easier just to visit the local store and exchange the device for a new model. Or instead of visiting a store, users can mail the device and receive a new one in the mail. General characteristics of these devices are that they do not need sophisticated ways to verify software, nor do they need rollback capabilities. All that is necessary is for users to receive a notification to upgrade the device.

■ **Third-party administered devices:** Representatives of this category can be TV set-top boxes, cable modems, and game consoles. Here, even if the user owns a device, it is still administered by the provider or vendor. Some games cannot be played on game consoles unless the operating system is updated. The service provider can push an update to the cable modems without the user's intervention; the same situation occurs with video content providers. Devices from this category must have all the characteristics of general-purpose computers with an even bigger emphasis on rollback capabilities.

Services such as Google search, Skype, or Cisco Webex also fall into this category. It is up to the service provider to keep the service free of vulnerabilities while users' participation in the process is minimal. More precisely, users do not need to do anything. The next time they use the service, all known vulnerabilities will be eliminated.

■ **Special-purpose devices:** Computers embedded in vehicles can fall into this category. Again, the rollback capability is important. What should be of high importance for this class is controlling the environment in which updates are performed and the integrity and validity of the remedies. The reason is fairly simple. How many people would like it that anyone who can come close to their car in a parking lot can upload an arbitrary application to it? Having trained staff in a garage to perform the update is certainly a better alternative. On the other hand, the process should not be too complex because current garages could not scale. They are designed to deal with normal wear and tear of the vehicle and a yearly checkup. Anything that would cause a much higher vehicle turnaround (for example, updating software on all cars twice a year) would break the model. Informing users about a vulnerability would represent a challenge because some of the devices will not be connected to the Internet. Vendors would have to use various methods, as we had a chance to see during the safety recall on some Toyota vehicles where the Internet, vehicle registrars, and newspapers were combined to deliver the message to the users.

These models are just a few examples of how the issue of notifying users of security vulnerabilities and applying remedies to the products can be addressed. This area is still open in a sense that there is no best practice how to do it. What is certain is that models presented here will be developed and tested in practice.

Summary

In this chapter, we have seen that security vulnerability, in general, may not be easily and universally defined. But for the identified vulnerabilities, vendors must produce remedies. All identified vulnerabilities must be addressed. The existence of an exploit for the vulnerability is irrelevant. If it does not exist now, it might be created in a few months or years or tomorrow.

After a vendor publishes a remedy, users can assess their exposure. This assessment can be done using CVSS, which can also help to determine priorities for the remedies to be applied first and in what parts of the organization.

Finally, as more devices contain embedded computers, we see a need to develop new models for how to update different classes of devices. The current model is successful for general-purpose computers and, with minor adjustments, for third-party administered devices. Extending this model to all appliances might be impossible, so the industry will end up using several different models for updating affected devices.

References

Cisco, IntelliShield Alert Manager. Available at http://intellishield.cisco.com/security/alertmanager/cvss. [Accessed February 11, 2009].

Cisco, 2004. "Cisco Security Advisory: TCP Vulnerabilities in Multiple IOS-Based Cisco Products." Available at http://www.cisco.com/warp/public/707/cisco-sa-20040420-tcp-ios.shtml. [Accessed September 20, 2010].

COPACOBANA, "COPACOBANA—Special-Purpose Hardware for Code-Breaking." Available at http://www.copacobana.org/. [Accessed February 9, 2009].

Darmaillacq, V., "Security policy testing using vulnerability exploit chaining." Available at http://www2.computer.org/portal/web/csdl/doi/10.1109/ICSTW.2008.37. [Accessed February 13, 2009].

FIRST—CVSS Special Interest Group, "Common Vulnerability Scoring System." Available at http://first.org/cvss/. [Accessed February 10, 2009].

FIRST—"Vendor Special Interest Group, 2008. Vendor-SIG response to ENISA." Available at http://www.enisa.europa.eu/doc/pdf/studies/NISbarriers/_2008-05-30_FIRST-Vendor-SIG_Comments.pdf.

"Is Kaminsky's DNS flaw public?" | Security—CNET News. Available at http://news.cnet.com/8301-1009_3-9996316-83.html. [Accessed September 19, 2010].

Jade, K. and McLean, P., 2005. AppleInsider | Latest Mac OS X Security Update breaks 64-bit application support (Updated). Available at http://www.appleinsider.com/articles/05/08/17/latest_mac_os_x_security_update_breaks_64_bit_application_support_updated.html. [Accessed March 24, 2009].

Kohlenberg, T., "A taxonomy & tool for automated vulnerability chaining and path discovery." Available at http://seattle.toorcon.org/2007/talks.php?id=11. [Accessed February 13, 2009].

Menzes, A.J., van Oorschot, P.C., and Vanstone, S.A., 2001. "Handbook of Applied Cryptography." Available at http://www.cacr.math.uwaterloo.ca/hac/. [Accessed February 9, 2009].

Microsoft, 2006. "You may experience problems in Windows Explorer or in the Windows shell after you install security update MS06-015." Available at http://support.microsoft.com/kb/918165. [Accessed March 24, 2009].

Ramaiah, A., Steward, R., and Dalal, M., 2008. draft-ietf-tcpm-tcpsecure-11—"Improving TCP's Robustness to Blind In-Window Attacks." Available at http://tools.ietf.org/html/draft-ietf-tcpm-tcpsecure-11. [Accessed February 17, 2009].

Toyota, 2010. Toyota Vehicles: Toyota Recall January 2010: Gas Pedal Recall / Toyota. Available at http://pressroom.toyota.com/pr/tms/toyota/toyota-consumer-safety-advisory-102572.aspx. [Accessed September 20, 2010].

US Department of Homeland Security, 2004. "NIAC vulnerability disclosure framework." Available at www.dhs.gov/xlibrary/assets/vdwgreport.pdf. [Accessed February 9, 2009].

US National Institute for Standards and Technology, 2002. Risk Management Guide for Information Technology Systems—NIST sp800-30. Available at http://csrc.nist.gov/publications/nistpubs/800-30/sp800-30.pdf. [Accessed February 9, 2009].

US National Institute for Standards and Technology, Special Publication 800-12: The NIST Handbook to Computer Security. Available at http://csrc.nist.gov/publications/nistpubs/800-12/800-12-html/. [Accessed March 30, 2009].

Wysopal, C., 2009. Time to Take the Theoretical Seriously. Available at http://www.securityfocus.com/columnists/490. [Accessed February 12, 2009].

Chapter 8

Creating a Product Security Team

This chapter deals with issues related to creating a Product Security Team (PST). Because the details about securing an executive's support, funding, and similar items are covered in Chapter 2, "Forming an IRT," this chapter does not go into those details again. The focus of this chapter is on items specific to a PST.

Why Must a Vendor Have a Product Security Team?

The answer to this question is quite simple—because we have not learned how to mass produce large and complex applications without errors. There are few notable exceptions to this rule, and only a handful of moderately complex (but not trivial!) applications are in constant use and apparently do not have security vulnerabilities. This is not for the lack of trying! There is an ever-growing body of research on how to design and write applications securely, and many major vendors are actively using this knowledge to remove a good deal of security vulnerabilities prior to shipping products to the market. The progress is being made, but vulnerabilities in products continue to persist. They persist either because the current tools and processes do not handle them properly or because of new research on the attacking side. In the same way developers increase their knowledge on how to remove vulnerabilities, there is parallel research into exploiting previously unknown vulnerabilities. Vulnerabilities also can be uncovered when the state of the art is advanced—that is, a novel way in which protocol is deployed might uncover a vulnerability, or new technology can bring to existence previously unknown concerns (for example, cryptography in a virtual environment in which you can move time back and reply the process). Therefore, it is unfortunate that you must expect that each application has a certain number of vulnerabilities in it.

After a vulnerability is discovered, it must be dealt with. Not having processes in place to handle product vulnerabilities, nor having people who know what needs to be done, is a recipe for disaster. Under these conditions the vulnerability will most certainly be mishandled or missed completely. That would be noticed by the users, who would change their buying preference accordingly. Handling security vulnerabilities is playing a more prominent role in purchasing process. Users are becoming more aware how important it is for them that vendors can manage security vulnerabilities effectively. Some governments are being proactive and helping users (in general and not only the public sector) to ask vendors the right questions. You can see one example of that in a recent document published by the Centre for the Protection of National Infrastructure (CPNI) from the UK. CPNI published a paper titled, "Security Questions to Ask Your Vendor," with 16 questions related to product security in general. Of these 16 questions, 6 are directly related to managing security vulnerabilities, including number 5, which reads

> Do you have a dedicated team to assess and respond to security vulnerabilities reported in your products?

It is almost certain that more governments will follow this initiative. Vendors can expect increased inquisitiveness from their existing and prospective customers on how they manage product security vulnerabilities.

Placement of a PST

The Product Security Team (PST) can be placed in multiple places within the organization. Some places, however, are better suited than others. Still, there is no universally best place. When looking across major vendors, their respective teams are situated in one of the following three places: engineering and development, a test group, and technical support. All these places are equally viable and suitable for establishing the PST. Although there are other possible places to establish the product security team, you need to focus on these three because they are the most common.

The subsequent text discusses reasons why certain places within the organization might be suitable for placement of the PST. You need to decide which scenario is the most applicable to your situation. In all cases, you can assume that the team is fully dedicated to handling only product vulnerabilities.

PST in the Engineering and Development Department

The engineering and development department is where all applications and products are designed and made. This department is also responsible for maintaining and improving applications and products. Following are the reasons why engineering is a good place to establish a PST:

- This is the place where vulnerabilities are fixed. No other place in the organization is better suited to fix vulnerabilities.

- Engineering knows the code; it is easier for them to identify where the vulnerability is.

- Engineering is responsible for introducing new processes into the development cycle.

On the other hand, the following are reasons for not establishing the PST within the engineering department:

- Having a product security team in engineering is a form of self-policing. The potential that the management might exercise increased pressure on the PST to ignore vulnerabilities, or classify them as nonissues, is great.

- Although the engineering department knows the code, it might not be well informed on how applications and product are deployed. Many vulnerabilities come to light only because products are deployed in a certain way.

PST in the Test and Quality Assurance Group

The test group is usually a part of the larger engineering department but tends not to be closely aligned with development. For that reason, the test group can have a degree of autonomy from the rest of the engineering organization. As the name suggests, the test group is responsible for testing. This testing is done after the product has been developed but before it is shipped to the market.

Following are reasons why the test group is a good place for the product security team:

- It possesses a degree of autonomy from the product development department that makes it more resistant to pressure from the development group to ignore security vulnerabilities.

- Many vulnerabilities are found during the testing, so this group has a good overview of all discovered vulnerabilities.

- The test group is testing all products (in contrast, a development team is responsible only for a single product or a single family of products), so it can analyze information across multiple products.

Following are reasons why the test group might not be best suited for placement of the product security team:

- The test group cannot fix vulnerabilities; it depends on development teams for that.

- Influencing development to change some of the practices, or to introduce new ones, can be difficult because the test group is an outsider. The test group is not part of the development proper, which can increase resistance to new ideas because it is pushed from the outside rather than proposed from inside development.

- The test group does not know the code. Testing is usually done as black-box testing, so people are not as familiar with the code as developers are. This unfamiliarity can prevent certain types of testing (for example, source code analysis) to be conducted. Additionally, analysis of root causes of vulnerabilities might not be as thorough as it should.

- The test group is not exposed to users and lacks information on how applications and products are deployed and used.

PST in the Technical Support Department

Technical support departments help users with any issues related to all products. In most organizations, this department is separate from the engineering and development department.

Following are reasons why the technical support department is a good place for the product security team:

■ Technical support intimately knows how products are being deployed and used by the customers. This can help in uncovering certain vulnerabilities occurring because of the specific deployment scenario.

■ This group is independent from engineering and development. That makes it resistant to pressure from development to ignore or downgrade vulnerabilities.

■ Support handles all products, so it has a good overview on which products are affected by which classes of vulnerabilities. This can help in formulating strategies to systematically approach the problem across all product ranges, rather than one product at a time.

Following are the reasons why technical support might not be best suited to host the product security team:

■ Influencing development to change some of its practices or introduce new ones can be difficult because the technical support department can be viewed as an outsider. Because the technical support department is not part of the development proper, this can increase resistance to new ideas because it is pushed from the outside rather than proposed from inside development.

■ Support is usually not well equipped to perform long-term and large-scale testing. This may prevent the team from identifying all products affected by a vulnerability. In that respect, the PST situated in the support organization will depend heavily on other groups to perform testing for them.

Product Security Team Roles and the Team Size

The size of the product security team depends, roughly, on how many vulnerabilities are to be dealt with and how many products are supported. The team's size also depends on what roles team members play within the organization. Additionally, the product security team must interact with several different groups within the organization. The level of the involvement the team chooses to have with each of the groups would also influence the team size.

The rest of this section looks at what other internal groups the product security team needs to interact with. This will be followed by possible team roles.

PST Interaction with Internal Groups

Members of a PST interact with almost all parts of the organization. Some of the more prominent groups within the organization are engineering and development, test group, technical support, sales, executives, legal, and public relations. Apart from being involved internally, the team must also be involved externally. The most significant external groups that the team must interact with are customers, other vendors, and coordinators. Apart from them, the team members can be involved with standardization bodies, policy setting and regulatory bodies, and law enforcement. Interaction with other vendors and coordinators are covered in Chapter 10, "Actors in Vulnerability Handling," in more detail.

The list of internal and external groups that members of the product security team should interact with is by no means exhaustive. There are many other groups, but the ones mentioned should be sufficient to show how product security permeates the organization. Also, given the number of groups, it is obvious that not all members of the product security team will be interacting constantly with all of them. Additionally, the involvement might not always be direct. Often the PST works with internal teams that would then interact with a wider audience. That is the only way that PST can scale.

When looking at different levels and depths of interaction between the PST and other groups, you need to understand that the PST does not need to own all actions. In other words, a PST must be involved and provide feedback and guidelines to various initiatives but does not necessarily need to be the group that either implements them or oversees their implementation and adherence.

PST Interaction with Engineering and Development

The obvious interaction with development is when working on fixing vulnerabilities. This is the most basic involvement with the engineering and development department. The following higher level of interaction is related to product design, coding practices, education of engineers, and development process improvements.

Given that the product security team sees all reported vulnerabilities, it is ideally placed to analyze them. This analysis can help with understanding the root causes of the vulnerabilities that, in turn, feed into product design, education, and process improvement.

PST Interaction with Test Group

Traditionally, the test group performs "positive" testing. One example of such a test can be to verify whether an application can receive a connection request. If you are talking about HTTP, this can be tested in a manner that the test application sends a request to fetch the top-level web page. If the tested application returns the top-level page, the test is considered successful. The reason why this kind of testing is sometimes referred to as "positive" is that it tests for known good events.

The PST can contribute knowledge toward "negative" testing. Negative testing is when you test for things that are outside the normal usage pattern. An example of a negative test can be how a particular vulnerability is triggered. That information can be translated either into a standalone test case (that is, test just for that particular instance) or as an input to develop a series of tests to cover the entire class of possible errors. This second instance, developing or improving test suites, fits quite well into a "fuzzy" testing category.

Fuzzy testing consists of sending malformed packets to the tested application. The expectation is that the tested application can handle all such packets without problems (for example, no crashes, normal CPU utilization, no performance degradation, and so on). These malformed packets can be either algorithmically generated, as is the case with IP Stack Integrity Checker (ISIC) test tools, or are separately coded, an approach taken by Codenomicon and Mu Dynamics.

Whatever the means might be, the resulting test cases should be made part of the regression test suite to make sure that all future product versions are immune to known vulnerabilities.

PST Interaction with Technical Support

The most valuable asset that a PST can bring to the technical support teams is knowledge of how to recognize a vulnerability and how to mitigate consequences of security vulnerabilities. When technical support receives a customer's case, it must be able to recognize whether the customer is suffering from a product vulnerability and, if so, provide mitigation. Also, if the support group thinks that it discovered a new vulnerability, it must be able to escalate that to the product security team for further evaluation.

Apart from helping technical support personnel in handling security incidents, the PST must constantly work to transfer the knowledge to the technical support group. That would enable the product security group to scale so that technical support can handle more, and more complex, cases independently and call upon PST only in very complex cases.

PST Interaction with Sales

The value that the PST can bring to the sales organization is multiple. Two most prominent values are the existence of the PST and help in competitive situations.

Occasionally, sales can encounter a situation in which a competitor is trying to win a sale by pointing out to a prospective customer that a particular product contains ostensible security vulnerabilities. Another variant of this maneuver is to point the prospective customer to a vendor's website, where information about various product vulnerabilities are listed. This is then accompanied by a comment that these products cannot be that good when so many vulnerabilities exist but its (competitor's) products are much better because their website does not list any product vulnerabilities.

To counter these situations, the PST can help the sales organization by authoritatively addressing whether something is a security vulnerability. An example of this are false positives that a vulnerability scanner (for example, Nessus, Retina) may report. Someone must verify such reports to establish whether this is a real vulnerability or false positive, and the PST is the right group to do so. This becomes even more relevant because the

U.S. government is making product scanning a mandatory part of the procurement process. Having a single point in the organization where all information about false positives is stored can ease and speed up the sales process.

The second way the PST can help the sales team is by its existence. Having an active PST is a sign that the organization has a certain level of maturity in dealing with product security vulnerabilities. Even the fact that the organization publicly admits having product vulnerabilities should be seen as beneficial rather than a disadvantage. If customers can learn about vulnerabilities, they can reassess their exposure and deploy mitigations. Hiding information about vulnerabilities does not imply their absence. It only means that customers are living with a false sense of security and cannot determine their security exposure. Additionally, if an organization does not have an active PST, it may be ill-equipped to deal with a situation when vulnerability is discovered. The organization might try to ignore the situation and, most likely, mishandle it later on. Both actions will leave customers exposed for much longer, thereby increasing a chance that they are compromised.

PST Interaction with Executives

A contribution that the PST can make to the executives is providing information about security trends in general, the situation and trends in the organization's products, and, finally, the situation in the industry related to the product vulnerability handling. All that can be translated into recommendations for concrete actions that the organization can take to improve its processes and security of its products.

Roles the PST Can Play and PST Involvement

Following are the roles that the PST can play within the organization:

- Handling existing security vulnerabilities

- Interacting with external product security teams, CERTs, law enforcement, and others

- Testing validity of security-related product fixes

- Security evaluation of existing products

- Security evaluation of new products during their design

- Developing fixes for existing security vulnerabilities

- Preparing and delivering education for engineers

- Handling customers' security incidents

- Involvement in standardization bodies

- Involvement in initiatives related to the protection of critical national infrastructures

- Developing and maintaining part of a regression test suite related to identified security vulnerabilities

The list is not exhaustive, but even this much shows that the PST can be involved in many different activities. Usually the team is not directly involved in all these activities because that would require a rather large team. What is often the case is that the PST selects several roles to actively pursue and be a contributor in all other cases.

It is common that the PST would focus only on the first three roles because they are the core competence of the team. Other roles might be filled if the PST has sufficient resources to do so.

PST Team Size

Despite the possible roles that the PST can take and other groups that it is involved with, the PST tends not to be large. In most cases, its major role is to coordinate people and resources within the organization and interface with external organizations and individuals. Many large vendors have teams with a size in the low teens, even though each of these vendors has tens of thousands of employees and is producing and maintaining hundreds of different products. The notable exception is Microsoft, which has a large security team. Having said that, the Microsoft product security team is not focused only on handling product vulnerabilities but is also active in various internal projects aimed at developing more secure products.

Virtual Team or Not?

The quick-and-easy answer is that the PST should not be a virtual team. Although the team can start as virtual (which was the case with many vendors), demands on the team members increase relatively quickly, so they spend more time dealing with product security matters than their original role. Another reason for establishing a separate team is that handling product security vulnerabilities is a specific job and has its own demands and requirements. The metrics used to measure a team's effectiveness differ from other groups within the organization.

The Cisco Product Security and Incident Response Team (PSIRT) is one of the teams that started as a virtual team within the Technical Assistance Center (TAC). All PSIRT members were working hard, and yet all of them had the worst performance measure in the entire TAC. The reason for this is that the same metrics to measure TAC performance were applied to PSIRT. One of the more prominent metrics for TAC is how fast a case is closed and how many cases are closed. The biggest difference between how TAC and PSIRT handle cases is depth. TAC would accept the case, diagnose the problem, and provide a solution in the reported software release only. If the remedy has to be integrated into other software releases of the same product, this would be left to the normal integration process where the fix would eventually, over a longer period of time, propagate into newer releases of the product. PSIRT, on the other hand, would also test whether any other product is affected by the same issue and then make sure that the fix is integrated into all supported software releases of all affected products. Given this much enlarged scope, people in PSIRT were able to handle fewer cases than any TAC engineer, and fewer cases (according to the TAC metric) translate into a worse performance.

A similar situation can be encountered if the PST is placed in any other group within the company. Given its unique requirements, the PST would need to be measured separately from any other group, so it is natural to make it a separate group rather than a virtual team.

Another issue that crops up in a virtual team is a unique skill set required for the PST. Again, from Cisco PSIRT experience, no support engineer is required to talk to the press or act as an expert witness. Closer to the technical side, TAC engineers support a few platforms and technologies, whereas PSIRT must take care of all platforms and technologies. Given these requirements, it might not always be easy to justify a team's training plan. If PST members are, hierarchically, part of the group that supports voice technology, why would they want to attend training on storage technology or clouds?

Overall, if your PST starts as a virtual team, you must treat it as if it is not a virtual team. Allow exceptions when measuring the team's success, training needs, travel, and special skill set. That way, you can grow it into a full, nonvirtual team.

Summary

This chapter deals with issues related to the creation of a product security team—more precisely, only to issues that are specific and unique for such the team.

The team's position within the organization must ensure a good measure of independence. This is required because the PST's priority can (seemingly) clash with business priorities; therefore, it is imperative that the PST is not directly controlled by the same managers responsible for development and shipping of a product.

The PST must interact with many groups within the organization and can play various roles. You need to select only a subset of roles that will be directly pursued by the team and be only peripherally involved in the rest. This has a direct consequence on the team size. Most existing PSTs are small. Many of them are not larger than 15 to 20 people, and some have even fewer than 10 people. The way these teams operate is to delegate much of the work to the appropriate places within the organization and retain the main coordinating role.

References

Codenomicon, "DEFENSICS. DEFEND. THEN DEPLOY." Available at http://www.codenomicon.com/. [Accessed May 18, 2009].

CPNI, 2010. "Security Questions to Ask Your Vendor." Available at http://www.cpni.gov.uk/Docs/Vendor_security_questions.pdf. [Accessed September 10, 2010].

Mu Dynamics, "Complete VoIP, IMS, IPTV Testing." Available at http://www.mudynamics.com/. [Accessed May 18, 2009].

Walia, G.S., Carver, J.C., and Nagappan, N., 2008. "The effect of the number of inspectors on the defect estimates produced by capture-recapture models." In Proceedings of the 30th International Conference on Software Engineering. Leipzig, Germany: ACM, pp. 331–340.

Xiao, S., "ISIC—IP Stack Integrity Checker." Available at http://isic.sourceforge.net/. [Accessed January 11, 2010].

Chapter 9

Operating a Product Security Team

This chapter deals with issues related to the daily operation of a product security team. In particular, it covers what requirements are specific to the product security team and how to address them.

Working Hours

Product security vulnerabilities can be discovered at any time of day but that by itself is not the worst thing. The worst is that a vulnerability can be exploited at any time. If that would happen, the product security team must be ready to respond on very short notice. This indicates that the product security team must work around the clock.

Although the team must have coverage around the clock, it generally is not required to have someone constantly in the office. In most cases, it is sufficient that a few team members can be reached at any time of the day, but it is not required for them to be in front of their computers at all times. Mobile telephones, especially the ones that can receive and send emails, are the perfect solution.

An additional reason why team members must be reachable and able to react comes to light when handling externally coordinated issues. Occasionally things might suddenly start to happen, and someone must be able to respond to the new development. We had a few cases where one of the affected vendors unilaterally decided to publicly disclose information about the vulnerability before the agreed-upon time. That vendor would usually inform the coordinator about that fact, and the coordinator would then try to notify all other involved vendors that information about the vulnerability will become public in a matter of hours. That kind of situation absolutely requires someone who can receive it and be able to make a decision on what should be done next.

Supporting Technical Facilities

The product security team has some specific technical needs. Some of them are related only to the team, whereas the others influence the entire organization. Three main areas are unique for the product security team: vulnerability tracking system, laboratory resources, and component tracking.

Vulnerability Tracking System

A vulnerability tracking system usually consists of a database where information about all vulnerabilities is stored. This tracking system can be either a commercial product or an open-source solution such as Request Tracker from Best Practical or any other equivalent product. Alternatively, an existing tracking system can be used, which is what many vendors do at the beginning. However, relatively soon they all migrate to some other solution, mainly because of heightened requirements for information confidentiality. In its simplest form, the vulnerability tracking system is only a database with a web interface that enables team members to store all information in a single place. Following are additional functionalities you can add:

- Managing incoming and outgoing emails, including handling encryption

- Drafting documents and enabling group review

- Lifecycle of a case; tracking the state the case is in, producing a timeline of previous and future actions

- Production of various reports

- Interfacing with companywide tracking report system

All these functionalities are self-evident and will not be described in great detail:

- **Managing emails:** The tracking system must be capable of accepting incoming emails and filing them to relevant cases. Users must also be able to compose and send emails via the tracking system. This can ensure that all information pertaining to a case can be easily found. As encryption is heavily used, the system must be able to decrypt, encrypt, and verify signatures of emails.

- **Document drafting:** Some of the cases will result in public documents (for example, Cisco Security Advisory) and the tracking system must provide facilities for drafting the document. Because each of these documents must pass an extensive review before being published, it is highly desirable if the tracking system can facilitate some form of collaborative environment in which multiple people can review and post comments about the document.

- **Case lifecycle:** Every case must pass through several stages from its creation until its closure. Some of these stages might be required to happen within a specified time frame. Keeping track of the current state of the case and what action must happen until the transition to the following state can greatly help to ensure smooth case handling.

- **Reporting:** This is self-explanatory. Some of the more commonly used reports can be a list of cases per state in the lifecycle, the time needed for transitioning between two adjacent states, and the rate of incoming cases.

■ **Interfacing with other databases:** This particular feature requires special attention, so the following section expands on it.

Interfacing with Internal Databases

So far I have not mentioned the relationship between the case tracking system used by the product security team and other tracking systems used by the organization. The two most important organization-wide tracking systems are one that tracks all customers' reports and the one used by software engineering to track software defects and new features. In most organizations, these two databases are separate. Notes about customers' cases are not mixed together with information on software defects and vice versa. What is possible instead is to cross link them. That way, a software engineer can see that a particular software defect is filled as a response to a customer case, and the engineer can read notes from the customer case. The opposite is also possible: a software defect linked to a customer case. It is important to note here that practically all the customer support staff and all software engineers can freely access both of these systems, and at least read all the notes.

The tracking system used by the product security team must also interface with both of the databases (software defects and customers' cases) but must be separate from each of them. The product security team receives information from different sources about possible vulnerabilities in supported products. Not only does the team receive information, it also receives fully functional exploits and time-sensitive documents that must be kept confidential until a certain date. For all these reasons, controlling who has access to information about security vulnerabilities is crucial.

This access must be limited only to people who need to know about this information. Obviously, all members of the product security team belong to this group, but not all software engineers need to know about all vulnerabilities. A software engineer must know about vulnerabilities filed against a product or component she maintains. Similarly, the customer support engineer should know only about vulnerabilities that a customer currently experiences in its system and nothing else.

Oracle has implemented this level of control really well. It has a special flag that can be assigned to either a software defect or a customer report. If assigned, this flag signifies that the report is a potential product security vulnerability. From that point on, only members of Oracle's Global Security Team can access the information. If confirmed that the report is indeed a vulnerability, it can enable specific people within the organization to access relevant parts of the information. This way, only people who have a need to know are privy to the information, which minimizes the possibility of accidental information leaks.

At this point, a tangent on information dissemination needs to be inserted. The previous text mentioned that engineers must know only the information pertaining to their particular product and nothing else. One school of thought holds that information empowers; so if more people know more, they can make better informed decisions. That is certainly true, but having access to too much information can lead to saturation and will not improve the situation (the proverbial drinking from the fire hydrant). The solution is to extract the pertinent information from different vulnerabilities, and then share that with the engineering teams instead of providing them with access to the raw information. To expand the earlier point, an engineer must have access to all technical information required to address the vulnerability in the product or component she is maintaining. Additionally, the engineer needs to know whether the same vulnerability is also present in other products or components and how it was addressed there. This additional information might help in devising a better remedy. The product security team might want to collect data on how much this additional information is used. If engineering teams do not use this extra information (for example, it never looked at it), some other mechanism, such as an internal developers' conference, should be established to foster communication between different teams because it is important to learn different approaches and their relative merits.

Laboratory Resources

Whenever the organization supports more than a handful of products, the product security team will face issues related to lab resources. More precisely, the issues can occur during re-creating reports on potential vulnerabilities. This is not a problem experienced only by vendors that make software that can be run on any hardware supplied by customers, but it is shared by vendors that produce software and hardware. All of them eventually end up supporting multiple hardware revisions running many software versions, and the vulnerability can occur in any combination of software and hardware.

Ideally, the product security team would have one of each software or device in its lab. That way, it can always test a report on the exact hardware and software combination as reported. Unless the organization has a very small set of supported products, this one-of-each approach can quickly become unmanageable. It becomes too expensive to maintain because some of the hardware will be used only occasionally. On the other hand, some other hardware models will be in high demand, so multiple units would be required to fulfill the need.

You can deal with this situation in two ways. The first is to share equipment with other groups within the organization, and the second is to use virtual equipment. No matter what approach is taken, the product security team always must have a small lab equipped with the currently most used (and most versatile) hardware models. If the organization produces software-only products, the team would still require several hardware configurations that resemble the most common configuration used by customers. Needless to say, that lab should be isolated from the rest of the organization's network to prevent a runaway experiment from taking down the organization's network.

Before looking at the main issues with the two approaches previously mentioned, let's investigate another important issue: the geographic location of the lab.

Geographic Location of the Laboratory

If all members of the product security team are located in a single location, this is not an issue. If, what is more likely, the team is scattered across the globe, or even a country, this issue becomes relevant.

Although today's technology enables remote device control, not everything can be done remotely. For things such as device remote powering on and off, numerous off-the-shelf solutions are available (for example, APC Power Distribution Units). Even for issues such as remote network rewiring (for example, connecting two devices that were previously not connected), you can find solutions. But what cannot be done[1] remotely is to physically change the configuration of a device, like inserting hardware modules, which requires someone to be physically present on a site.

Like every other remote lab, it also requires a mechanism to keep track of what equipment is currently used and the lab topology. More important, people using this lab must resist all temptations to make undocumented changes to the lab because that would defeat the entire system.

Shared Laboratory Resources

Shared lab resources are the answer to the high cost of maintaining a single lab with one of each software and hardware. The biggest issue with this approach is who has priority when the equipment is needed on a short notice. Also, unless the organization is small, it is to be expected that shared laboratories will be geographically dispersed, which might introduce an additional set of problems.

From the equipment usage standpoint, you can identify three phases during the lifetime of the vulnerability. The first phase is the initial testing that is relatively short in duration. During the second phase, the equipment is used only occasionally to test some corner cases or new ideas. This period is relatively long compared with the overall lifetime of the vulnerability. The last phase is just before and after the vulnerability is made public and customers encounter unforeseen issues. If everything is right, customers might not have any questions, but some last-minute testing before the vulnerability is made public is always needed. This third phase is also short lived.

What makes shared labs challenging is that the product security team might require the equipment for a prolonged time—anywhere from a few months to a year. And it is not the usage pattern that is the problem but the urgency with which the product security team needs the equipment, which is usually "right now."

---

[1] It can be done by introducing a remotely controlled robotic arm and video feedback, but the chance that the organization will opt for that kind of solution is slim unless it is in the business of producing robotic arms.

Virtual Hardware

Virtual hardware is possible through software emulators and simulators that can mimic behavior of a real hardware device and, optionally, enable the execution of any software on top of the virtual device. This is a great help because it eliminates the need for maintaining many different hardware models. You can also run multiple virtual devices on a single computer so that a single physical device can satisfy the needs of multiple users. You can usually run multiple instances of virtual devices in parallel and interconnect them. All this can bring great ease in working and reduce expenses.

The issue with using virtual devices is to be sure that the virtual device responds identically as the real device. Furthermore, any software running on a virtual device must behave identically as on a real device. Things can be further complicated if the issue is in a physical component of a device (for example, signal coding in an optical interface) or depends on event timing. Simulators can be especially inaccurate when handling multiple real-time, or near real-time, events.

The way to address these issues is to always make the initial testing on a real device and then repeat the same testing on a virtual device. If both results are identical, virtual devices can be used to test that, but only that, in the future. If a test needs to be modified, or a different feature tested, the process must be repeated again.

I learned this the hard way while testing routing aspects of a particular vulnerability. Despite all the assurances from software developers that the software module was not hardware-dependant, results from testing on the real and virtual device were completely opposite. Test on a virtual device would break routing protocol, whereas it would continue to work properly on the real device.

Third-Party Components

Reusing components and modules and using third-party libraries and software modules when software-only products are concerned is the norm in today's production cycle. The subsequent text uses the word "component" to describe both physical parts and software modules used to build a product. This imposes two requirements on the product security team. The first one is to know what component are used and reused and where, and the second is to regulate the relationship with component suppliers.

Product Component Tracking

"New vulnerability in OpenSSL is discovered. What, if any, is its relevance to us?" A question like this is often on an agenda of the product security team. It does not need to be OpenSSL; it can be Java, gzip, Apache HTTP server, Simple Network Management Protocol (SNMP) library, cryptographic library, or any of hundreds of other components woven into a product. The alternative form of the same question is, "This module is homegrown and is vulnerable. What other products use the same code?"

To get a feeling of the scale of third-party code usage, visit web pages either of organizations that are making these libraries (for example, a partial list of customers that use libraries from SNMP Research) or security advisories from CERT/CC or (after 2004) US-CERT. A good example is CERT/CC Advisory CA-2003-26 describing vulnerability in OpenSSL library. Reading the list of affected products can give you an idea of how third-party code is prevalent in today's products.

A system for tracking third-party components is not for the sole use of the product security team. That tracking system must be created and maintained by the engineering group within the organization. Additional benefits of such a system are the capability to find an existing module or a library that can be used or reused for a new product and to track usage of licensed third-party software. Both commercial and free-licensed components must be tracked in the system.

That information can also be used to keep track of obligations that an organization has toward the third parties. The obligations can be monetary (for example, paying royalties) or as specified in the license agreement (for example, publishing source code or correctly documenting component's usage).

For a product security team to do its job, the following information needs to be present in the component tracking system:

■ Component name and version.

■ Contact details of the component maintainer.

■ Contact details of the product maintainer where the component is used.

■ Product model and version where the component is first used.

■ Product model and version where the component is last used (that is, removed from the product).

■ Is the component used as-is, or has it been modified prior incorporating into the product? A high-level description of changes should be added.

■ Is the component third-party or developed in house?

The component tracking system should contain more pieces of the information, but they might be of secondary, if any, importance to the product security team.

Figure 9-1 illustrates some of the complexity that can be encountered when handling vulnerability in one component of a product.

In this example a fictitious product provides Transport Level Security (TLS) functionality. Initially, that functionality is provided by the RSA BSAFE 1.0 library. During the product development two new branches were created, and each of them uses a different library to provide the same functionality. The 1.1.1 branch uses OpenSSL while the 1.2.1 branch uses the RSA BSAFE 2.0 library. What is important to note is that, at some point, we have three software branches (releases) of the same product using three different libraries to provide the same functionality. The challenge of the product security team is to determine which library is used in which branch so that affected software releases can be identified.

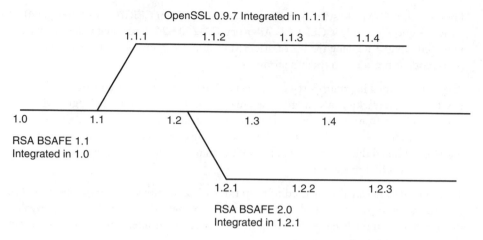

Figure 9-1 *Integration Points of Third-Party Cryptographic Libraries*

Another issue that can be encountered is forming a chain of suppliers. One case that the author handled is shown in Figure 9-2.

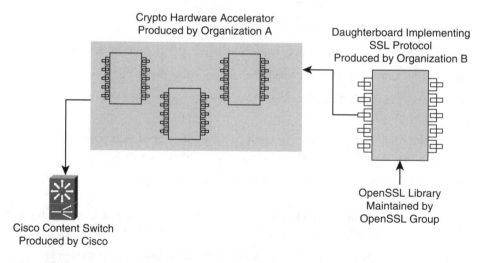

Figure 9-2 *Supplier Chaining*

It all started when vulnerability was discovered in OpenSSL,[2] and Cisco Content Services Switch (CSS) 1100 was identified as affected. CSS1100 uses OpenSSL as an integral part of a hardware cryptographic accelerator. That accelerator is produced by Organization A and is what Cisco integrates in the final product. On the accelerator, the OpenSSL library

---

[2] This is not a reflection on the quality of OpenSSL but is a mark of how widely it is used in many products.

was implemented in a special daughterboard produced by Organization B. Therefore, to fix the vulnerability in the Cisco product, it was necessary to first contact Organization B and ask it to incorporate the newest OpenSSL library in the daughterboard. Then Organization A was asked to update the accelerator with the new daughterboard, and finally, the Cisco product was updated.

It is clear that the product security team must be in frequent contact with various suppliers. The following section looks further into relationships with the suppliers.

Tracking Internally Developed Code

This is closely related to third-party component tracking but is about tracking usage of internally developed code. The class of the problem is the same, so the solution is similar. Again, you have a situation in which code developed for one product is reused in another product and, if vulnerability in the code is discovered, you need a mechanism to easily discover all potentially vulnerable products.

Relationship with Suppliers

When handling product security vulnerability, it is often sufficient just to ask the supplier to produce a fixed version of the component, and the fix will be incorporated. This is possible because it also benefits the supplier. Almost without an exception, the supplier also provides the same component to many vendors. If the supplier is promptly addressing security vulnerabilities in its component, it is viewed as proactive, and vendors would be more willing to use the component in the products. This is often the situation—often, but not always.

You might encounter two main exceptions for this case. One is when severity assessment of impact of the vulnerability differs, and the second exception is when the supplier is not responsive. Let's briefly examine both of them:

- **Different severity of impact:** We can use another example to illustrate this case. The vulnerability in question is TCP Reset vulnerability, described at http://www.cisco.com/warp/public/707/cisco-sa-20040420-tcp-nonios.shtml, and the product in question is CallManager. According to our assessment, the impact of this vulnerability to CallManager is moderate. The most exposed components are H.225 and H.245 signaling protocols. CallManager is based either on Microsoft Windows or the Red Hat operating system. The impact of the same vulnerability on a general purpose operating system as it is used in a standard home or small office working environment is minimal. Given this minimal impact neither Microsoft nor Red Hat could justify increasing priority of the vulnerability and committing additional resources to resolve it on an accelerated schedule.

- **Unresponsive supplier:** The number of suppliers belonging to this category is gradually becoming smaller but still persists at the moment. You can split this category into suppliers that do not acknowledge existence of the vulnerability, even if it can be demonstrated, and suppliers that are less responsive than expected. One example of the latter was encountered when dealing with a voice-related vulnerability. In that case, the supplier acknowledged the vulnerability but would fix it only in the new, up-coming version of its software scheduled to be published in approximately 8 to10 months. There was no solution offered for the software that was currently used by the customers because the supplier stopped maintaining that software version. And to top it all off, the new software could not be simply installed on the existing devices because of the memory requirements; new software needed more memory than the currently deployed devices had.

These two examples show that it is not always easy to address security vulnerabilities when dependency of third-party components exists. The only way to address this situation is contractually. You need to put specific clauses in the contract that govern how security vulnerabilities will be handled. One of the important things you need to pay attention to is product maintenance lifetime, as we experienced in the previous example with an unresponsive supplier.

This contractual way of addressing this issue is not applicable to free and open software because you have no one to sign the contract with. When using free and open software, the organization must understand that it might end up maintaining that particular component. This can happen naturally, as the organization genuinely wants to improve the component, or forcibly if the original component owner stops maintaining it. Another solution that does not include maintenance of free and open software is to switch to a different component. Even that is not without certain expenditures of the resources. You need to investigate which other component satisfies functionalities and then see how it can be incorporated into the existing and new products.

Summary

A product security team has specific requirements not shared with other teams within the organization. If the organization maintains many products and different product versions, lab resources can be an issue. Having a separate vulnerability tracking system is also required, as is the system for tracking where third-party components are used. Finally, it is not only how the organization functions internally but also how it interfaces with third parties.

References

APC Product Information for Power Distribution. Available at http://www.apc.com/products/category.cfm?id=6 [Accessed May 26, 2009].

Best Practical, Best Practical: RT: Request Tracker. Available at http://bestpractical.com/rt/ [Accessed May 26, 2009].

CERT/CC, CERT Advisory CA-2003-26 Multiple Vulnerabilities in SSL/TLS Implementations. Available at http://www.cert.org/advisories/CA-2003-26.html [Accessed June 1, 2009].

Cisco PSIRT, Cisco Security Advisory: TCP Vulnerabilities in Multiple Non-IOS Cisco Products—Cisco Systems. Available at http://www.cisco.com/en/US/products/ products_security_advisory09186a008021ba2f.shtml [Accessed June 1, 2009].

Free Software Foundation, Licenses—Free Software Foundation. Available at http://www.fsf.org/licensing/licenses/ [Accessed June 1, 2009].

SNMP Research, SNMP Research—SNMP Research Customers. Available at http://www.snmp.com/customers/customers.shtml [Accessed June 1, 2009].

Chapter 10

Actors in Vulnerability Handling

Vulnerability handling and managing is not something done solely by vendors. It involves multiple other actors, and each of them has a specific role in the overall process. The roles of individual players and interactions among them is changing and evolving over time.

This chapter investigates who the players in the vulnerability handling process are, what their roles are, how they interact with each other, and the current trends in how these relationships are changing. The main actors are

- Researches
- Vendors
- Coordinators
- Users

Researchers

"Researchers" is a catch-all word that encompasses all classes of people who are scrutinizing products for security vulnerabilities. Researchers can range from individuals who do this as a hobby, to organizations that buy research from others and then present it as their own, to well-funded groups who are paid by commercial organizations to government-funded outfits. In short, they are a rather disparate group of people with a common interest: finding vulnerabilities in a product.

Although their interest is common, their ulterior motives differ. In most cases, researchers are not a malicious group. If they discover vulnerability they will report it to a vendor—directly or indirectly through third parties. Although that information might be used to compromise systems on the Internet, the primary motive of the majority of the researchers is not gain through criminal activity; instead, they are more governed by a publish-or-perish motive. This leaves a small minority who perform research with the sole purpose of using that knowledge to commit criminal acts.

Vendors

A vendor is someone who is responsible for producing and maintaining a product. Vendors can produce a product (for example, a Cisco router) or provide a service (for example, the Google search engine), and they can do that for free or on a commercial, paid-for basis. This is another disparate group because a vendor can range from a single person to a multibillion-person global organization and anything in between these two extremes.

Although the proposed description of who a vendor is looks simple and complete, the reality is different.

Who Is a Vendor?

Before we proceed, let us ask one question, "Why it is important to know who is and who is not a vendor?" After all, delivering a remedy is all that matters. Although that is true, it is also important that people with criminal intent on their mind learn about the vulnerability as late in the game as possible. The general rule is that the more people who know about something, the chance for information leaking is higher. Therefore, only people and organizations that need to know about the vulnerability should be notified. Vendors are the obvious group that must be notified, which leads you back to the question, "Who is a vendor?" You can see that, as it is usually the case, no simple general answer exists. Not only that, but the answer is different if we change the perspective. From a user's perspective, a vendor is whoever sold the product. End of story. However, from the perspective of vendors and manufacturers, the answer can be quite different, which is the focus here.

The initial description of a vendor as someone who is responsible for production and maintenance of a product is a good start but needs further qualification. Following is a vendor ecosystem:

- **Direct production:** Hardware and software for a Cisco router is designed and produced by Cisco, so Cisco is a vendor.

- **Integrated components:** Closer inspection of Cisco routers reveals that some of the hardware components and software libraries are not designed and made by Cisco but by various third parties. Vulnerability in any of these components would require the appropriate third party to produce a remedy and Cisco to integrate it into a final product. Given the close integration of constituent components into a final product, you can still claim that Cisco is a vendor even when considering third-party components.

Needless to say that reusing third-party components can go arbitrarily deep. A third-party component can contain a module made by a fourth party that can contain yet another component from someone else, and so on ad nauseam.

Probably all modern operating systems work on this model where only a small part of it is written by an organization that is "the vendor," and all, or a big majority of, other parts (libraries, utilities and so on) are written and maintained by third parties. This is not limited to open-source vendors such as Red Hat or OpenBSD but is also present in commercial operating systems such as Apple Mac OS X and even Microsoft Windows.

■   **OEM or resellers:** Original Equipment Manufacturer (OEM) is the name for a company that buys a product from a second company, places its logo on the product, and sells it under its name. Reseller is a less ambiguous name for such a company. Although the reseller may appear as a vendor from the outside (that is, it sells and supports a product), it is not involved in the production or integration of a remedy for security vulnerability in a product. In this case, it is hard to argue that a reseller is a vendor.

■   **Value Added Reseller (VAR):** VAR is a reseller but it adds value to a product before selling it under its brand. Value can be added in multiple ways. Some of the values that can be added are customization (like translation of messages to a different language), additional functionalities (for example, new software or hardware modules added to the existing product), to integration with other equipment (with or without modifying or expanding functionalities of any integrated device or product).

VAR can be called a vendor depending on the level and scope of the modifications added to the initial product. However, because there is no clear demarcation line for how much modification must be added before a VAR should be called a vendor, this determination must be done on a case-by-case basis.

■   **System integrator:** This is a person or an organization who creates customized solutions out of products, devices, or modules from (usually) different vendors. System integration can involve different levels of component customization that can range from configuring devices in a specific way to developing new modules (software or hardware) to enable overall system functions.

Similar to VARs, system integrators can be considered vendors especially if vulnerability is found in modules and components produced by the integrator. Again, the decision of whether a system integrator is a vendor must be made on a case-by-case basis.

As you can see from the preceding examples, vendors come in all different shapes and sizes. There is no universal definition on who a vendor is from a nonuser's point of view. It is up to the parties involved in a process to sort that out, and the answer can change from one case to another. In all instances, a vendor is someone who can produce the remedy.

Vendor Communities

Despite troubles in determining who is a vendor, several vendors' forums are in existence today. Each of them is filling a slightly different niche and has a different composition and goals. The following list is by no mean exhaustive but provides only a brief snapshot of major forums.

Vendor Special Interest Group (SIG)

You can find the website of the Internet Infrastructure Vendors SIG (Vendor SIG) at http://www.first.org/vendor-sig. This forum operates under the FIRST (http://www.first.org) umbrella.

Vendor SIG goal is stated as

> ...to provide [a] forum for Internet Infrastructure Vendors. In this context, Internet infrastructure is considered to be Operating Systems, computer hardware, networking equipment and critical applications. This list is by no means exhaustive nor comprehensive.

The forum includes 30 vendors. It is a relatively informal forum and is open to teams handling product security issues. There is no membership fee, and to become a member of the forum, you must be vouched by at least two existing members. You do not need to be a member of the FIRST organization to participate in Vendor SIG.

At the time of writing, Vendor SIG was focused on contributing to several international standards from both ISO and ITU-T. These standards are related directly to handling product security (for example, ISO29147 "Responsible Vulnerability Disclosure") or related to it.

ICASI

According to the Industry Consortium for Advancement of Security on the Internet (ICASI) website (http://www.icasi.org), this forum

> ...intends to be a trusted forum for addressing international, multi-product security challenges. This trusted forum extends the ability of information technology vendors to proactively address complex security issues and better protect enterprises, governments, and citizens, and the critical IT infrastructures that support them. ICASI shares the results of its work with the IT industry through papers and other media.

This forum consists of six vendors. It has several membership levels, and to become a member, you must satisfy several criteria including signing a multiparty nondisclosure agreement (NDA) and be approved by the ICASI board of directors. ICASI members must pay a yearly fee to remain in the forum.

Because of the multiparty NDA, this forum can handle issues on a deep technical level. ICASI is currently focused on incidents and vulnerabilities that affect two or more ICASI member companies and to improve the state of the art in multivendor vulnerability handling.

IT-ISAC

The Information Technology—Information Sharing and Analysis Center (IT-ISAC) is one of several ISACs that cover various parts of U.S.-critical national infrastructure. Although the impetus behind forming ISACs was the U.S. government,[1] ISACs are run by private companies.

According to the IT-ISAC website (http://www.it-isac.org), it is

...a trusted community of security specialists from companies across the Information Technology industry dedicated to protecting the Information Technology infrastructure that propels today's global economy by identifying threats and vulnerabilities to the infrastructure, and sharing best practices on how to quickly and properly address them.

The IT-ISAC also communicates with other sector-specific ISACs, enabling members to understand physical threats, in addition to cyber-based threats. Taken together, these services provide members a current and coherent picture of the security of the IT infrastructure.

IT-ISAC consists of 23 companies. To become a member, you must be a U.S. company and be approved by the IT-ISAC board of directors. Different membership levels are defined and the yearly fee varies by the membership level. Most of the IT-ISAC activities are centered around weekly teleconferences and its email list.

VSIE

According to its website (http://www.cpni.gov.uk/Products/information.aspx):

The Vendor Security Information Exchange (VSIE) was formed in January 2005 to share confidentially mutually beneficial information regarding electronic security threats among the major companies involved in the ICT industry. The VSIE comprises members of major international companies in the ICT sector.

This forum is initiated by UK's Centre for the Protection of National Infrastructure (CPNI) and is loosely modeled on the ISAC model. VSIE is run by companies participating in the forum, but all meeting logistics is done by CPNI (UK government).

Membership and participation in the forum is strictly controlled, and the current list of members is not public. Each member company can participate with only two named individuals without substitutions. In another words, if none of two designated persons cannot attend the meeting, nobody else from the company can attend in their place. The majority of activities are centered around quarterly face-to-face meetings usually held in London in the UK. Membership is free, but to become a member, you must be approved by the existing members and CPNI.

---

[1] The initial idea of ISACs is outlined in the Homeland Security Presidential Directive/HSPD-7 in 2003.

Vendor Point of Contact—Japan

This is a specific forum run by Japan CERT/Coordination Centre (JPCERT/CC). The primary use of that forum is for JPCERT/CC to disseminate information about product vulnerabilities. The forum is focused on Japanese vendors and vendors with a strong presence in Japan. A partial list of vendors that are members of the forum is available at http://jvn.jp/en/nav/index.html.

There is no membership fee to belong to this forum. All members must register with the JPCERT/CC technologies they support and the point of contact that will be used for vulnerability coordination. That information is used by JPCERT/CC to determine which vendors need to be contacted if a vulnerability is found in a specific technology.

SAFECode

Citing its website (http://www.safecode.org/about_us.php):

> Software Assurance Forum for Excellence in Code (SAFECode) is a non-profit organization exclusively dedicated to increasing trust in information and communications technology products and services through the advancement of effective software assurance methods. SAFECode is a global, industry-led effort to identify and promote best practices for developing and delivering more secure and reliable software, hardware and services.

The forum consists of six members. To become a member, you must be approved by the SAFECode Board of Directors and the membership. All members must pay a yearly fee.

vendor-sec

The Vendor Security forum has grown around the vendor-sec@lst.de mailing list. Each of the members of the vendor-sec forum maintains one or more operating systems. These operating systems are usually open source (for example, Red Hat, BSD, Debian, or SuSe) but that is not a strict requirement.

To become a member, you must be voted in by the existing members. There is no membership fee. The complete list of current members is available only to the existing members. The forum discusses and coordinates security vulnerabilities in operating system core elements (for example, a kernel or libraries).

Coordinators

As more and more products support various Internet protocols, the potential for vulnerability to affect more than vendors increases. Whenever this happens, it is necessary to involve as many as possible affected vendors and start working on a remedy and coordinated announcement. This process is commonly referred to as vulnerability coordination or, more simply, only as coordination.

Coordination looks deceivingly simple. The coordinator should maintain a list of contacts with as many vendors as possible, contacting them when a new vulnerability is found, persuading them to develop a remedy within some reasonable timeframe, and making vendors agree on a date when the information will be publicly announced. Several big issues can occur that make coordination quite a challenge; a few are mentioned here.

The coordinator does not have any actual influence over a vendor. Each vendor can agree to be coordinated, but the coordinator cannot force a vendor to take any specific action. The coordinator cannot force a vendor to produce a remedy even if the vendor's product is affected by the vulnerability. Coordinators must be ready to work with vendors from all over the world. This introduces issues of working hours, local languages, and customs.

Often one vendor might request delaying the public disclosure date at the last moment. It is then the role of a coordinator to work with all other vendors to see if this delay is possible and then broker a new date.

Given all the preceding reasons why coordination is harder that it looks, the question is why are there coordinators at all? What is the incentive to become one, and why do vendors participate?

Vendors' Incentive to Be Coordinated

The reason why vendors consent to be coordinated is, first and foremost, to remove vulnerability from a product. It is in the vendors' interest to honor the gentleman's agreement with coordinators to ensure continuation of information feed on future vulnerabilities. We said that coordinators cannot force vendors to take any action, but the same is applicable in reverse. Vendors cannot force coordinators to do something either. If vendors are uncooperative, coordinators might decide to send information on future vulnerabilities to those vendors later in the process. This might give vendors less time to address the vulnerability. Less time usually translates into more resources and a higher urgency needed to accomplish the same task. Higher urgency equals more disruption and is something that all vendors try to avoid.

Some vendors do not publish security advisories to inform their users on security vulnerabilities. Instead they rely on the coordinators to publicize information about vulnerabilities and remedies. In effect, some vendors outsource publication and notification tasks to coordinators.

Coordinators' Business Model

Vulnerability coordination is not profitable activity. The biggest incentive to become a coordinator is access to information on product vulnerabilities before they are publicly available. Coordinators can learn about vulnerabilities via multiple routes. Both vendors and researchers might approach coordinators, or coordinators might conduct research and discover vulnerabilities.

Access to this kind of information opens additional multiple avenues. Coordinators can use the information for research, be it academic or commercial. Information can also be valuable to government agencies to evaluate exposure to security threats. Finally, coordinators might want to sell this information to its customers.

As much as selling the information might sound tempting, experience has shown that it is not the best option in the long run. Vendors appreciate if that information remains private until an agreed publication date because that will give vendors time to appropriately address the vulnerability. If coordinators publicize vulnerability information prior to the agreed disclosure date, vendors lose incentive to report vulnerabilities to the coordinators. This is especially troublesome for vendors because the majority of them do not habitually predisclose vulnerability to their customers. There are some exceptions, as with the Microsoft Security Cooperation Program, but generally vendors do not practice vulnerability predisclosure. Similarly, if researchers know that coordinators are selling that information and they are not compensated, researchers might lose incentive to report new vulnerability to coordinators.

Commercial Coordinators

There are no commercial coordinators in the full sense of the word. At the time of writing, no organizations have a charter to coordinate only various vendors. Some organizations do the coordination but only as a by-product of their main activity. Two of the most known organizations are TippingPoint and iDefense. The business model of commercial coordinators is to learn about new vulnerabilities before anyone does, and then sell that information to its customer base. Selling may be either as a direct knowledge (that is, vulnerability is in this software and module, technical details, and suggested workarounds if such are possible), packed in its own product (for example, IDS, IPS, vulnerability scanner, penetration framework, and so on) or a combination thereof. Whatever the case might be, customers of commercial coordinators have an expectation to learn about the existence of new vulnerabilities as soon as possible and before vendors produce a remedy.

Although these companies might provide a service valued by their customers, their performance as coordinators can be improved. These commercial organizations do inform directly affected vendors but usually do not try to identify and inform all other vendors whose products also may be affected.

Government and Government Affiliated

Some governments are also in the game of vendor coordination. This group is provisionally divided into government-run and government-affiliated organizations. The latter group has only two members: CERT Coordination Center at Carnegie Mellon University in Pittsburgh (CERT/CC) and Japan Computer Emergency Response Team/Coordination Center (JPCERT/CC). CERT/CC is classified as government affiliated because a good part of its budget comes from the Department of Homeland Security (DHS), and it is getting more and more intertwined with US-CERT (which is part of DHS). JPCERT/CC is a non-government organization but is largely funded by the Japan Ministry of Economy, Trade, and Industry.

Setting these minutiae (such as the source of the budget) aside, the group of teams in this government category actively working on vendor coordination is rather small. The following teams belong in this category:

- CERT Coordination Center (CERT/CC) in the United States of America

- Centre for the Protection of National Infrastructure (CPNI) in the United Kingdom

- Finnish Communication Regulatory Authority (FICORA) in Finland

- Japan Computer Emergency Response Team/Coordination Center (JPCERT/CC) in Japan

Open-Source Coordinators

This group contains only one team: Open Source CERT (oCERT), which is a group of volunteers who are willing to help big and small open-source projects with vulnerability coordination. Not only that, but oCERT can also help with security research and assessment. To receive this service, a vendor must register with oCERT. The registration is free and serves to confirm the contact details.

Other Coordinators

The only other team doing global vendor coordination is the Australian Computer Emergency Response Team (AusCERT). It was active several years ago, but global vendor coordination is not something that it is currently involved with.

Users

Users are the ones who use a product, and at first look are relatively passive actors in the entire process. That, however, is not the case. Users do have a role. The obvious one is to vote with their feet (that is, to migrate when they perceive situations to be more beneficial elsewhere) and punish irresponsible vendors by not buying their products. That and applying remedies to devices is under their control.

We can divide users in two distinct groups: home users and business users. Each of these groups has a slightly different view on security vulnerabilities.

Home Users

Home users tend to value ease of use more than anything else. Plug-and-play is the best possible approach as far as they are concerned. Devices should automatically check for security and other updates and notify users when they are ready.

At this point, it is tempting to push the boundary a bit further and automatically install all new updates without the users' intervention. Tempting as it might be, that would not be the best course of action. Some users do have sufficient knowledge to make a selection for what updates need to be installed, and depriving them of that choice would be wrong. Another reason is that users should be given a chance to back up their information before applying an update. If an update is applied automatically and something goes wrong, users might be left with an inoperative device and potentially lose data.

Business Users

Business users can be provisionally divided into small and large. Small businesses generally have similar requirements and needs as home users. This is not surprising because they have fewer resources to devote to securing the business because all energy is spent on serving their customers.

Large business users, on the other hand, tend to prefer features (capabilities) over everything else. They have people dedicated to IT security who have expertise and knowledge needed to configure and operate a complex system.

Equipment Usage

What complicates this division of home and business users is that large businesses are also using home-grade components in their systems. The biggest driver for this is the equipment cost and a mobile workforce. Devices targeted to the home market tend to cost much less than business-grade devices. Using consumer devices in a high-demand environment does not have to represent a problem if planned correctly and as long as realistic expectations are placed on the consumer-grade equipment.

Traditionally in a home environment, people do not expect high availability especially because many users still switch off equipment after use. It is also assumed that the majority of users would not have sufficient knowledge to configure devices, so consumer-grade devices will either be missing some features or existing features will be nonconfigurable. From a support perspective, the majority of users will have basic questions, and support can be geared toward that. In practice, this means that it can take longer for a business user to escalate a support case (for example, move beyond questions like, "Have you turned on the device?"). Development priorities can also be different than for a vendor of business-grade equipment. It should not be surprising if, for a vendor of consumer devices, interfacing with Apple iTunes or developing new video codec takes priority over deep packet inspection. After all, more home users are interested in audio and video than traffic filtering.

From a security standpoint, prospective vulnerabilities are treated the same in all types of equipment. If identified, security vulnerabilities will be fixed. The difference is that, for home users, vendors rarely back port remedies in older software releases. The remedy is in a new software release only, and to protect yourself, you must upgrade. In contrast to this, for business-grade devices, remedies are backported into older software releases.

What is now changing the state of the play is the mobile workforce. More employers allow people to work from home, and these people are having different expectations from a stereotypical home user (as previously described). These new home users expect high uptime, high availability, and increasingly high bandwidth. They are also asking for more security features and more secure software. All this is gradually starting to blur the differences between consumer- and business-grade devices.

Interaction Among Actors

Interaction among actors in vulnerability handling is interesting—even more so because this is one of the rare environments in which most of the actions and dealings are done based on an honor system. Only a relatively small part of interactions and requirements are mandated in some way, while the rest is strictly based on a gentlemen's agreement. Formal regulation exists almost exclusively only between vendors and users. That regulation can take a form of laws (for example, equipment and applications used in medicine or public transport) or contracts drawn between a vendor and user. Interaction between any other groups (for example, vendors and coordinators or researchers and vendors) is completely unregulated.

The only way this honor system can function is if all involved parties trust each other. It takes a long time to build trust, but it can be destroyed in an instant. Communication and setting expectations is something that can help build trust. Knowing the expectations of each of the players and being aware of actions they intend to take can significantly contribute to building trust and reducing unpleasant surprises.

Despite this lack of regulation, things are happening relatively smoothly and without too many mishaps. One instance when things tend to get out of balance is when a new coordinator appears and tries to coordinate vendors on a global scale. Luckily, other coordinators and vendors are quick to help the new entrant, and things settle back to normal in a short period of time.

One relatively recent trend is that national governments are becoming more and more aware of the extent to which they are dependent on networks and IT in general. That awareness results in thinking about creating government CERTs and mobilizing resources to protect national critical infrastructure if an attack occurs. Unfortunately many governments are also making common mistakes in the process. Following are some of the more common ones:

- Assuming that nobody in the country is handling computer-related incidents and that everything must be done from the beginning. Quick search on the FIRST website (http://www.first.org) is all that is necessary to find out whether there is an existing team in a particular country.

- Government wants all information about all attacks and all incidents in a country, which is a nice goal but not easy to achieve for a new team. Existing teams already do have working relationships with others and simply do not see value in sharing information with governments. Even if they would like to share information with governments, there are many practical details that must be worked out before any information sharing can commence, and usually none of them are in place. Some of these details are what information to share, when, in what format, how to protect it (in transit and on the recipient's end), who will have access to it, and so on. Things can be especially interesting when some information becomes classified and yet people would like to share it quickly and securely.

■ Attacks stop on national borders. Thinking how we can simply put some kind of a wall around a country and protect everything within shows a lack of understanding of how intertwined things are. Some politicians show signs of improvement in this area. Several people in the European Commission are now fully aware that computer-related incidents can easily affect more than one EU member country, and that it cannot be easily confined to a single member country. However, there is still a notion that the whole of the EU can be isolated from the rest of the world.

■ Governments want to know everything about all security vulnerabilities in all products deployed in their critical national infrastructures (CNI). They also want to be able to talk individually with vendors on how to protect their CNI. Unfortunately, vendors cannot easily scale to this level of individual communication because there are many governments but only a handful of major vendors. If governments would find a way to trust each other, this could be a much easier task to accomplish. It would be sufficient to place all interested parties in a single room and discuss the topic only once, especially because practically all governments are asking the same questions and receiving the same answers.

■ Governments want to be involved in vulnerability coordination. There are several issues with this idea, not the least one being that having hundreds of such coordinators is untenable.

This trend of increased government involvement is a relatively new factor, and how things will develop is still unknown. Governments have a tendency to regulate things, but the reality is that regulation is not always the answer.

The last to mention are standardization efforts. The International Organization for Standardization (ISO) and International Telecommunication Union—Standardization (ITU-T) are working on multiple cybersecurity-related standards. Work in ISO is spread across multiple Working Groups, whereas ITU-T is more focused within Study Group 17, Question 4 (see http://www.itu.int/ITU-T/studygroups/com17/sg17-q4.html). ISO is working, among other things, on a standard on "Responsible Vulnerability Disclosure," which will be published as ISO 29147, whereas ITU-T is working on a Cybersecurity Information Exchange Framework (Cybex – X.1500). Within the Cybex framework, ITU-T is looking to propose usage of structured data formats by adopting a host of XML schemas developed mainly by MITRE and a few schemas from other sources, and to introduce mechanisms for transmitting the data and ensuring its authenticity and integrity.

Summary

Vulnerability handling is becoming a more and more involved process. What used to be a relatively clean playing field with only a few players now is becoming a crowded terrain. Vendors, coordinators, and researchers are still in the core of the process and are the main actors. Governments are trying to get in the game, and there are multiple standardization efforts related to the vulnerability handling and information exchange. All that guarantees an exciting time with lots of opportunities to shape how things will be done in the future.

References

Cisco, 2004. "Cisco Security Advisory: TCP Vulnerabilities in Multiple IOS-Based Cisco Products." Available at http://www.cisco.com/warp/public/707/cisco-sa-20040420-tcp-ios.shtml. [Accessed November 16, 2009].

Cisco, 2008. "Cisco Security Advisory: Multiple Cisco Products Vulnerable to DNS Cache Poisoning Attacks." Available at http://www.cisco.com/warp/public/707/cisco-sa-20080708-dns.shtml. [Accessed November 16, 2009].

Cisco, 2009. "Cisco Security Advisory: Transport Layer Security Renegotiation Vulnerability." Available at http://www.cisco.com/warp/public/707/cisco-sa-20091109-tls.shtml. [Accessed November 16, 2009].

FIRST—Vendor SIG, 2006. "Guidelines for Vendor—Coordinators Relationship." Available at http://first.org/vendor-sig/vendor-coordinators-guidelines-public-v1.0.pdf. [Accessed November 23, 2009].

FIRST, FIRST—"Improving security together." Available at http://www.first.org/. [Accessed November 16, 2009].

ICAI, ICASI. Available at http://icasi.org/. [Accessed November 16, 2009].

ITU-T, "ITU-T Study Group 17—Question 4/17 (Study Period 2009-2012)." Available at http://www.itu.int/ITU-T/studygroups/com17/sg17-q4.html. [Accessed December 31, 2009].

Microsoft, "Microsoft Security Cooperation Program (SCP)." Available at http://www.microsoft.com/industry/publicsector/government/programs/SCPabout.mspx. [Accessed September 1, 2010].

MITRE, 2010. "Making Security Measurable." Available at http://makingsecuritymeasurable.mitre.org/. [Accessed September 1, 2010].

MITRE, "MITRE—Applying Systems Engineering and Advanced Technology to Critical National Problems." Available at: http://mitre.org/. [Accessed December 31, 2009].

Naraine, R., 2003. "Security Flaw Finder Severs Ties with CERT." InternetNews.com. Available at http://www.internetnews.com/dev-news/article.php/1577001/ Security+Flaw+Finder+Severs+Ties+with+CERT+.htm. [Accessed December 14, 2009].

oCERT, "oCERT.org—Open Source CERT." Available at http://www.ocert.org/about.html. [Accessed September 1, 2010].

Chapter 11

Security Vulnerability Handling by Vendors

This chapter covers the process of handling security vulnerabilities. Although this description is strongly influenced by an existing process used by Cisco, this text is not the exact description of the process used by Cisco. This chapter deviates from Cisco practice in places and introduces new elements. The purpose of this chapter is to provide a description of a general vulnerability handling process that can be adopted by many vendors rather than a detailed description of the process of a single vendor.

Known Unknowns

It was Mr. Donald Rumsfeld who used the phrase "known unknowns," and we will have to borrow it here. A certain level of nonobjectivity exists in handling security vulnerabilities. One of these nonobjective issues is who else knows about this vulnerability. Vendors can act only on the things they know. When a new vulnerability is discovered during internal testing a vendor might assume that nobody else knows about it unless information to the contrary becomes available. Of course, it's possible that someone else also knows about that particular vulnerability. It is also possible that this vulnerability is actively used to compromise devices, but unless vendors possess concrete information to that effect, it is reasonable to assume that nobody else knows about that vulnerability and that it is not being used by miscreants.

It was important to say this before going any further because it helps frame a backdrop against which vendors make their decisions. Consider this when you read security notifications published by a vendor. A statement saying, "no known malicious use of vulnerability," might be interpreted as actually saying "no known malicious use as far as we know, but not discounting the possibility that it is being used."

Sounds like a good candidate for "known unknowns."

Steps in Handling Vulnerability

Vulnerability handling processes differ from vendor to vendor, but the basic outline is the same. Figure 11-1 shows the schematic for the process.

- Discovery of the vulnerability

- Initial triage

- Reproduction

- Detailed evaluation

- Remedy production

- Remedy distribution and notification

- Monitoring the situation

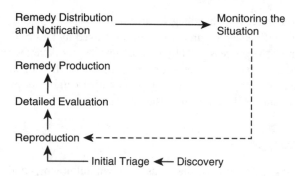

Figure 11-1 *Generalized Vulnerability Handling Process*

Subsequent sections cover each of these steps in more detail.

Discovery of the Vulnerability

Vendors can learn about a vulnerability in a multitude of ways. It can be discovered internally during development or testing, or it can be reported by a customer or a researcher. A vendor can read about it (for example, blog, email post, or newspaper), be informed by a coordinator, or told by another vendor. Although the avenue how a vendor learns about vulnerability seems unimportant, it does a play certain role in how the vendor might handle the vulnerability. More about that in the "Remedy Production" section.

What is common among vendors is that, after a vulnerability is known, it will be fixed. Timeline and availabilities of remedies for various software releases depend on many factors, but vulnerability will be addressed. If any vendor chooses simply to ignore the existence of a vulnerability, it is doing so on its own peril. Vulnerability will not cease to exist by itself if it is ignored. Vulnerability will be misused; customers will suffer and eventually take their business elsewhere.

Initial Triage

The next step in the process is the initial triage. Its purpose is to determine how severe the vulnerability is and whether it is a vulnerability at all. Initial triage is done without reproducing the vulnerability. This introduces a possibility for misclassifying the issue (for example, a severe vulnerability will be judged as a low severity issue or vice versa), but experienced people rarely make that mistake.

A growing number of vendors use Common Vulnerability Scoring System (CVSS) for the initial triage. A complete description of CVSS is available at http://www.first.org/cvss. For the current purpose, a CVSS score consists of three metrics (parts) and, for initial triage, we are concerned with the first two: basic and temporal metrics. Basic metrics describes innate technical characteristics, whereas temporal metrics provides information of exploitability and exploitation of the vulnerability.

Base metrics is divided into the following elements:

- **Access vector:** Can vulnerability be triggered remotely?

- **Access complexity:** How difficult is it to trigger vulnerability if the attacker has access to the vulnerable system?

- **Authentication:** Does the attacker need to be authenticated to trigger the vulnerability?

- **Confidentiality impact:** What would be the impact on the confidentiality of the system if the vulnerability is exploited?

- **Integrity impact:** What would be the impact on the integrity of the system if the vulnerability is exploited?

- **Availability impact:** What would be the impact on the availability of the system if the vulnerability is exploited?

Temporal metrics is divided into the following elements:

- **Exploitability:** Describes the existence of an exploit and its availability.

- **Remediation level:** Is a remedy for the vulnerability available?

- **Report confidence:** The level of confidence placed in the vulnerability report and the accuracy of technical information contained in it.

Each of the metrics (base and temporal) has a number between 0 and 10. A higher number designates a more severe issue. For the purpose of the initial triage base metrics is all that is needed. However, it is considered good practice to assign a score to temporal metrics at the same time.

There is no universal rule that would tell where the cut-off point is between vulnerability and nonvulnerability. In other words, when looking at the base score, you cannot state that, for all vendors, a score less than 4 does not represent vulnerability. This cut-off point should be established by each vendor separately. For the purpose of this text, assume that 5 is the cut-off point. If vulnerability has a base score less than 5, it is not considered vulnerability. If the base score is 5 or higher, it is considered a security vulnerability. An example of a low-scoring vulnerability is that an administrator can add an invalid parameter to a configuration command that then renders the device completely inoperative until it is rebooted. This can be done only on the console, and the user must authenticate twice: first as a user and then as the administrator. When this information is entered into CVSS calculator the vulnerability would be assigned a base score of 4.3. The attacker must possess an administrator's privileges and have console access. If someone has administrator's rights, it is possible (by definition) to have full control of the device, and it is not necessary to use this vulnerability to render it inoperative. Given all this, we can say that, although the vulnerability is present and must be corrected, it can probably be done via a normal process.

Reproduction

If the report scores sufficiently high after the initial triage, it must be reproduced. Reproduction is important for two reasons: to confirm the report and to collect more technical information about the issue.

Confirming the report is not about not believing other people's experience; in more than 15 years of Cisco PSIRT existence, no one intentionally made false reports. It is about reproducibility. To find out what is going on, you must be able to reproduce the report at will, or at least with a certain degree of success.

Even if a report cannot be reproduced every time, that does not reduce its validity. It is not uncommon to have a series of events, each preparing the stage for the next, until the last event triggers the vulnerability, but when tested in isolation, none of the events by itself will trigger the vulnerability. If the events must happen with certain timing, it might not always be possible to reproduce the issue every time, but that does not affect the severity of the issue.

While trying to reproduce the report, we are also collecting more information. What are the exact requirements to trigger the issue? How must the device be configured to be affected? What does the trigger packet look like? Are there any variations? Can some other packets/events trigger the issue? These, and many other questions, will be answered during the reproduction of the report. All that information can be used in the later stages of the process, some in the detailed evaluation and others when devising workarounds.

Reproduction can be done on real or virtual devices. Using virtual devices is convenient because it enables quick changes of the environment and because you can simulate a small network on a laptop while sitting on a beach. But a virtual environment is not always a good substitute for the real devices. If events must happen in a certain order or timing, you might not be able to reproduce the report in a virtual environment. This is especially true if the issue is triggered at the hardware level. If virtual devices are used for reproduction, you must be sure to know the limitations of that environment. Even then, you should perform a final check on real hardware, just to be on the safe side.

Detailed Evaluation

If a vulnerability scores higher than the cut-off point (5 in our case), it must be further evaluated. Initial triage is just a first filter to help differentiate nonvulnerabilities from vulnerabilities but, when that is done, you must delve deeper into the vulnerability. A deeper understanding of the vulnerability can help you determine the affected devices/systems/applications and devise workarounds and understand triggers and consequences.

In some cases, the outcome of a detailed evaluation might be to reclassify the vulnerability as a low severity or even a nonvulnerability. One such example is a Cisco Security Notice on Internet Key Exchange (http://www.cisco.com/warp/public/707/cisco-sn-20030422-ike.html). When Cisco PSIRT received the initial report it claimed that it is possible to brute force the preshared password used during Phase 1 of establishing an IPsec connection. Base score for this issue was either 5.4 (if high complexity is assumed) or 7.1 (for medium complexity) and, according to the score, this is a moderate to severe vulnerability. The reason why it was not treated a vulnerability is that detailed analysis uncovered that this particular attack scenario had been considered during development of the IKE protocol and the risk associated with it was deemed acceptable. As a result of this, the reporter was advised to bring the issue to the attention of IETF together with the reasons why the risk might have changed since the IPsec protocol was created.

In almost all cases, detailed evaluation includes the creation of an exploit. Exploits are not mandatory to prove the presence of the vulnerability but are useful because they can be incorporated into test suites to prevent reoccurrence of the same vulnerability. To some extent, the presence of an exploit can be counterproductive because it can constrain people when thinking about vulnerability—both during the investigation and correction. In both instances, there is a tendency that the exploit is the ultimate proof if the device is vulnerable (or not). People tend to focus on the exploit instead of on the underlying root cause; it is not uncommon to overlook that the slightly modified attack can still trigger the vulnerability.

Remedy Production

After vulnerability is confirmed and a detailed analysis performed, a remedy can be produced. Recall that a remedy is not only a fix (for example, a change in the source code or the configuration) but the process of producing the remedy also includes regression testing, packaging in a form suitable for distribution, and testing its installation. Depending on the number of different software releases supported, this step can take a variable amount of time to perform. It can be done quickly for a small number of software releases, or it can take considerable time if many software releases must be updated. Also, the code change itself can range from simple (changing < to <= or simple array checking) to complex changes in a protocol design, as was the case with TLS Renegotiation vulnerability.

Depending on a vendor, producing the fix can be performed by the people on the product security team or by the software developers. In the former case, the argument is that the product security team is the expert in security and that it can produce a remedy of higher quality. This limits the number of people who know the technical details of the vulnerability, thus limiting the risk of a leak. The argument for the latter case is that software developers know their code the best and can produce a remedy much faster than someone who does not work on it every day. Having someone with less knowledge about the overall code modify the source code increases the potential for product instability and adverse side effects. Apart from technical reasons for and against each of the approaches, you need to consider one more thing. Mandating that the product security team produce remedies will increase the size of the team, whereas surrendering the remedy production to developers will enable the product security team to stay small. There is no "right" or "wrong" approach for this but only different avenues to achieve the same goal.

Ideally, remedies for all vulnerabilities will be produced immediately. In practice, given limited resources, the vendor must decide which vulnerabilities will be dealt with first and which ones can wait. Two components influence this decision: the base CVSS score and whether the vulnerability is reported by an external researcher.

As previously said, the base CVSS score describes intrinsic technical characteristics of the vulnerability and, all things being the same, the vulnerability with the higher base score should be handled first. What can modify this decision is who knows about the vulnerability. If it is reported by an external researcher, or there is credible evidence that details are known outside the vendor, the urgency with which the vulnerability should be dealt with can increase. The priority of the vulnerability remains the same (that is, it did not became any worse from a technical perspective) but the vendor might decide to deal with it before some other vulnerabilities of the same, or even slightly higher, priority (severity). One of the reasons for an urgency increase is that external knowledge increases the chance of an information leak and exploitation. Another reason is that an external research would like to present the findings at some of the conferences that then introduce a hard deadline. If possible, a vendor should work with the researcher to meet the conference deadline. That effort can help establish the vendor's good reputation and make researchers willing to work with the vendor in the future.

What is important to emphasize is that external knowledge can influence the urgency with which the vulnerability is dealt with only if the vulnerability itself is of a certain severity and taking into account what other vulnerabilities are currently being handled. A low-severity vulnerability does not deserve to be handled before a high-severity one, no matter who knows about it.

You might wonder why a vendor would not take into account where and how the product is used when prioritizing work on a vulnerability. The short answer is that the vendor, generally speaking, does not know where products are used. Here are a few examples to illustrate this. A Linksys wireless access point can usually be found in a home environment but can also be used in a nuclear power plant. The same switch can be deployed in a medium-sized organization and a Boeing 787 airplane. A CRS-1 router can be found only in large installations, but that can be a stock exchange or a massive multiplayer online role-playing game data center. Unless a vendor is specialized in a niche product, it is not easy to determine where and for what purpose it is used. If a vendor would have only two products, such as a child's toy robot and hospital radiation machine, it would be natural to prioritize vulnerabilities in the radiation machine over the toy. However, in most cases, the distinction between products is much less pronounced.

Remedy Availability

All customers should be able to obtain a remedy against security vulnerability free of charge. A long time ago, Microsoft tried to charge for remedies, but it was quickly dissuaded from that practice. Giving away remedies for security vulnerabilities for free has its price, too. Users should be entitled only to free remedies but not necessarily other kind of fixes and updates (for example, new functionalities). Availability of nonsecurity-related fixes and updates differs from vendor to vendor. For example, Apple and Microsoft give them away, whereas Novell would like to charge for them (but still give security remedies for free).

What stance a vendor takes on nonsecurity updates usually depends on its business model. It tends to be that if the product itself is free, the vendor would try to recoup the cost by charging for support. This support might not include remedies for security vulnerabilities.

Another aspect of remedy availability is how to deal with situations in which a single product is affected by multiple vulnerabilities. The general rule is to plan for maximum flexibility but propose the safest options. In other words, a vendor should make all individual remedies available but suggest to users to apply cumulative remedies. To illustrate this, look at Table 11-1.

Table 11-1 *Fixing Multiple Vulnerabilities in a Single Product*

Vulnerability	Patch			Fixed Software Release		
	P1	P2	P3	1.2a	1.2b	1.2d
HTTP	X	—	—	—	—	X
SSL	—	X	—	—	X	X
TCP	—	—	X	X	X	X

Table 11-1 shows two different situations that can be encountered. The first one is when the remedy is distributed as a patch (columns P1 to P3), and the second situation is when the vendor provides a new software version (the last three columns). Looking at the patches, you can see that patch P1 fixes a vulnerability in HTTP, P2 in SSL, and P3 in TCP. Similarly, software release 1.2a has fixes for a TCP vulnerability, 1.2b for both TCP and SSL, and finally release 1.2d for all three vulnerabilities. Please note the difference that each patch (P1, P2, and P3) are separate and are not cumulative, as is the case with new software releases; that is, P3 fixes only TCP vulnerability but not SSL or HTTP.

When making remedies available, a vendor should always suggest to users to either apply a cumulative patch (P1, P2, and P3 all together) or upgrade to the software version 1.2d. Either of these options can provide maximum protection because all known vulnerabilities will be removed. At the same time, the vendor should make individual remedies available so that users can apply only what they think is appropriate for their environment.

The downside of applying cumulative remedies is that customers will install remedies for functionalities that might not be currently used. However, that is also the advantage because these functionalities can be used at some time in the future. And when that happens, it is not likely that users will recall that not all remedies were applied.

This idea of applying cumulative remedies can be extended to a situation in which multiple, but separate, applications are vulnerable to multiple, potentially distinct, issues. It can be argued that, even in this situation, it is better to patch all vulnerabilities even if some of the applications are not used. Again, users might start using some of these applications at a later time but not recall that the application has not received all remedies. Another possibility is that a new feature in one application might start using a vulnerable application.[1] In both cases, the net result is that a system that was relatively safe can now be easily exploited. The alternative to patching all applications would be that each application, upon start, verifies whether it contains all remedies and, if remedies are not applied, either refuses to execute or only warns the user of that fact. Similarly, the same should happen if one application wants to use another application. A check should be made and, if remedies are not installed, execution should be terminated.

A contra-argument to applying remedies to all applications is that the remedy itself can introduce vulnerability. Although that is true, and it happens on occasion (for example, Sony with its XCP Digital Right management software), such instances are rare. It is much more likely that users will start using a vulnerable application than the remedy introduces a new vulnerability.

Remedy Distribution and Notification

Customer notification, and especially public notification, is the most visible step in the entire process of vulnerability handling. In this context, notification means to make affected users aware of the security vulnerability and of the remedy. Different vendors will handle notification in various ways. The common thread among all vendors is that each of them claims that their particular notification method is best suited for their customers. The best part of that claim is that it might even be true!

The next chapter deals with various details related to the notification process and the document itself, so for now, remember that producing a good notification on security vulnerability is a serious undertaking. It requires lots of effort and good teamwork to consistently produce high-quality documents.

---

[1] An application can encrypt data and is currently using its own, built-in cryptographic libraries. There is also a system cryptographic library that users are currently not using that contains security vulnerability. If the next release of the application starts using a system cryptographic library instead of its own, the entire system suddenly becomes vulnerable.

Monitoring the Situation

Although monitoring is listed last, it is something that must be constantly done after vendors learn about the vulnerability. Vendors must look for signs of malicious exploitation, information leaks, and efforts to (re)discover and modify the vulnerability. Depending on which event occurs, vendors might modify priority and urgency of the vulnerability or be forced to premature public disclosure.

A good source of information are support cases opened by the customers. If vulnerability is being encountered by the customers, it is highly probable that someone will report that to the customer support. Various public mailing lists are also worth monitoring. Many of them tend to be rather verbose, so if possible, this monitoring should be either automated or outsourced. What is invaluable and irreplaceable are personal relationships with prominent researchers and other important figures in the computer security field. Any important information will always find its way to these people first and only afterward to public mailing lists. Being close to these people can enable vendors to receive notification sooner than relying on public sources and to receive more precise and more detailed information.

Monitoring is also required after the notification has been published. This is to ensure that notification contains sufficient information, without negative side effects of the remedy and existence of an exploit. If the notification does not contain sufficient information, there will be an increased number of support cases. In that case, the product security team should modify the notification to better inform the customers. Similarly, if the remedy will break some other features in the product, or prevent interoperability between products, the product security team will have to take this on board and work with engineering to correct the remedy. Finally, the notification may be updated if an exploit has been created and used in the wild. This information can be used by customers to reprioritize applying the remedy in their environments.

Summary

This chapter gave an overview of a process for how vendors can handle security vulnerabilities. The process is common among all major vendors, but the exact steps within each phase can (and usually do) differ. Public notification and the remedy are the visible results of that process. Of these two, notification on security vulnerability is more prominent because it explains the situation and is read by humans.

References

BBC, 2003. BBC NEWS | World | Americas | Rum remark wins Rumsfeld an award. Available at http://news.bbc.co.uk/1/hi/3254852.stm [Accessed October 12, 2009].

Cisco, 2009. "Transport Layer Security Renegotiation Vulnerability—Cisco Systems." Available at http://www.cisco.com/en/US/products/products_security_advisory09186a0080b01d1d.shtml [Accessed September 2, 2010].

Wood, M., 2005. DRM this, Sony! - CNET.com. Available at: http://www.cnet.com/4520-6033_1-6376177-1.html [Accessed October 17, 2010].

FIRST—CVSS SIG, 2007. CVSS v2 Complete Documentation. Available at http://www.first.org/cvss/cvss-guide.html [Accessed October 12, 2009].

Chapter 12

Security Vulnerability Notification

Public notification on security vulnerability is the most visible outcome of the work done by a product vulnerability handling team. It is also a prominent and disruptive event for customers. This chapter discusses various issues related to the production and publishing of security vulnerability notifications. To simplify matters, they are referred to only as a notification or a document. For the purposes of this chapter, publication means making information known outside the vendor; more precisely, that means product users and the general public.

Producing a good notification is no trivial matter, and a vendor needs to experiment until the right formula is found. Making changes to the notifications and processes surrounding it is good, but it must be done in a controlled manner. Users expect stability and are quick to rely on certain aspects and features of the notification and make their own processes and procedures based on these features. By changing notification features, vendors can inadvertently break these processes, which hinders the users' ability to quickly react to the notifications.

Types of Notification

After a vendor starts notifying users on security vulnerabilities, it quickly becomes apparent that one size does not fit all. One type of notification is not sufficient for all purposes. These purposes can be as follows:

- Severe security vulnerability has been discovered and one or more products are vulnerable.

- Minor security vulnerability has been discovered and one or more products are vulnerable.

- Severe security vulnerability has been discovered but none of the products are vulnerable.

These three notification types differ in how a vendor expects users to react. In the first case, a vendor would like customers to take notice and react. In the second and especially third case, customers might not need to take any action.

You can now ask a question, "If a vendor does not want a customer to take any action, why does it need to publish a notification?" The answer is to provide an authoritative answer, stop users from guessing what is the impact of the vulnerability, and prevent them from opening support cases to clarify the situation.

Publishing some kind of notification for a minor vulnerability is usually the result of a researcher publicly announcing the vulnerability. In this context, "minor" means that either the vulnerability is hard to exploit, even though the consequences would be severe if it could be exploited, or it is relatively easy to exploit but the impact is not big. An example of the former can be seen at http://www.cisco.com/warp/public/707/cisco-sr-20080516-rootkits.shtml, "Rootkits on Cisco IOS Devices," which discusses severe issues but relies on planting software that has been tampered with. An example of the latter can be seen at http://www.cisco.com/warp/public/707/cisco-sr-20090925-axg.shtml, "Unmatched Request Discloses Client Internal IP Address," which describes an issue of minor severity.

Finally, there is a question on publishing a notification in a case when none of the products are affected. Generally, a vendor should refrain from doing this because that can easily run out of control, but an option for doing this must not be ruled out. Assume that a severe vulnerability has been discovered in Network Time Protocol (NTP) as implemented by ntp.org, and given how widely that implementation is used by various vendors, a majority of vendors will be affected by it. However, products may use modified NTP code, and that modification, by chance, removes the vulnerability so the products are not affected. This is the situation in which a vendor might consider publishing a notification that none of its products are affected by that particular vulnerability.

When a vendor considers different types of notifications, they need to be distinctive. This distinction is usually done by using a different graphical layout of the document because the content is practically the same (for example, vulnerability description, affected products, remedies, and workarounds). Users must not be in any doubt what kind of notification they are reading and what is expected from them. Additionally, it should be possible for these different notification types to coexist on a same web page or close to each other. Forcing users to visit multiple different parts of a website to find particular notifications (or an absence of it) is a bad design. All security-related notifications must be at one place (for example, http://www.vendor.com/security or linked off that page) to make it easy for users to locate relevant information.

When to Disclose Vulnerability

The publication timing has two aspects. One aspect is related to periodicity of the publications, which is covered in the "Scheduled Versus Ad Hoc Notification Publication" section later in this chapter. The other aspect is what constitutes a trigger to disclose information about a specific vulnerability. Will the information be released this month or the one after or next year? This section focuses on this latter aspect.

A succinct answer to the question of when to publish security notification is when the remedy exists either for all (if the number is relatively small) or for a majority of most deployed software releases. When either of these conditions is met, the vendor is considered ready to "go public." In practice, it looks like this.

Most major vendors maintain many different software releases for, optionally, multiple hardware platforms. The number of these different releases can be anywhere from high teens to multiple hundreds or, as is the case with Cisco IOS, to a few thousand. Occasionally, a vendor can encounter a vulnerability that is present everywhere, or at least in a huge majority of software releases, which means that each software release must receive the remedy. If a vendor supports only a handful of software releases, the expectation that a remedy will be created for each of the software releases is not unrealistic. When that number of supported software releases becomes sufficiently large, a vendor must make a decision on which software releases should receive the remedy first, which second, and so on, and also whether the remedy will be produced for all software releases. The reason for this prioritization is the always-present possibility that the information about vulnerability will become public prematurely. If that happens, the vendor would like either the most important (however this might be defined) or the majority of customers to be protected.

The most used metrics for this prioritization is the number of deployed releases; that is, how many installations of software release 1.0 exist versus release 1.2. This can be further differentiated as the number of users or the number of software instances. Having a single user that has deployed 100 instances of a particular software and 100 users each using only a single instance of the software might or might not be equivalent. Another metric that can be used is which releases are used by organizations that provide critical functions. In the latter case, the vendor must be in a position to understand how customers deploy its products, which might not always be the case. An example of this second metric might be a situation in which the majority of customers (for example, more than 85%) use software releases 2.3 and 2.4, but it is known that all banks use release 1.5. Although banks constitute less than 15% of the overall number of customers, a vendor might decide that version 1.5 must receive the remedy first before moving to produce a remedy for other software releases.

The original answer contains the phrase "....majority of most deployed software releases," which means that vendor might decide not to have a remedy for all software releases at the time of publishing. In cases like this, the vendor would usually include wording like "To obtain a remedy for release X, please contact the support team or your representative" in the notification. This means that if a customer needs a remedy for version X, the vendor will create it on demand. If nobody asks for a remedy for version X, the vendor would not make it. This behavior has a dual purpose: It frees some resources on the vendor side and also gives a signal to users that if they use software version X, they should consider moving away from it.

Another trigger for publishing the notification is when the customer well-being is in jeopardy. This can happen when vulnerability is being widely exploited or if vulnerability becomes public, and the risk of it being exploited is high. Additionally, not only that the risk of exploitation is high but also the consequences of the exploitation are severe.

In such cases, the vendor should immediately publish a notification with whatever information is available. This should happen even if the vendor does not have a remedy available. The main reason for this action is to provide authoritative source of information. When people are told that something bad is going on, they will try to find all information available. Usually, and especially at the onset, all sorts of information will float around, and most of it will be incomplete, inaccurate, and distorted, be it by design (for example, intentionally spreading misinformation to gain something) or by chance. If a vendor remains silent on the matter, its users will rely on possibly misleading information that might expose them even further. To prevent users from relying on hearsay, it is imperative that the vendor publishes authoritative information for its products.

Such notification would usually contain information on how to recognize whether users are affected by the vulnerability, a technical description of the same, and workarounds if they exist. As always, it is important to publish only information verified to be correct. It is expected that such emergency notification will be updated relatively frequently but, between updates, customers will rely on what is published. If that information is wrong, customers might make their situation worse than it is. For that reason, the vendor might consider adding information on what is not yet confirmed. An example can be stating that "...vulnerability can cause a denial-of-service condition. Potential for executing arbitrary code is being investigated but is not confirmed at this time." However, the vendor must be careful with what it is saying in the notification, because inevitably some users would interpret this example as saying that remote code execution is possible but the vendor just does not want to say that.

Amount of Information in the Notice

A notification must contain sufficient information for users to understand the vulnerability and be able to assess how it affects their systems and, at the same time, not disclose too many details to make its exploitation trivial. The notification must also be written as simple as possible.

Disclosing a sufficient amount of information can be achieved in a majority of instances. It is usually sufficient to state that "a specific packet can crash application/device" and give an indication if authentication and authorization is required to trigger the vulnerability. This provides the assessment of requirements for triggering the vulnerability and consequences but without giving away details of how to actually trigger it. What can disclose more information are workarounds.

A workaround is a measure that can be taken to make triggering vulnerability harder or prevent it from being exploited completely. Depending on a product and the vulnerability, the workaround can disclose almost all details of how to trigger the vulnerability. A good example of this can be seen in the "Cisco IOS Interface Blocked by IPv4 Packets"

Security Advisory, available at http://www.cisco.com/warp/public/707/cisco-sa-20030717-blocked.shtml. Given the nature of the vulnerability, it was not sufficient just to say, "IPv4 packets can block an interface," because the workaround would be to block all IPv4 packets from reaching the device, which is clearly not acceptable. An acceptable workaround was to list specific protocol types that can cause an interface to be blocked, which then directly provided all information needed to exploit the vulnerability.

Vendors must also be aware that if the remedy is distributed as a patch, researchers can (and probably will) reverse engineer it and learn about the vulnerability that way. Snort (http://www.snort.org) is a great illustration of how quickly this can be done. In less than six hours from the moment Microsoft published patches, they were able to reverse engineer patches and produce a Snort signature. For "easier" cases, this can be done even faster. Even though some researchers have abilities and knowledge to deduce vulnerability details from patches, remember that only a relatively small number of people and organizations are capable of doing so. The majority of miscreants is not in that league, and you don't want them easily attacking others.

The best way to gauge whether a sufficient amount of information is present in the notification is to ask customers for their feedback and to monitor support cases opened against the disclosed vulnerability. If you notice that many customers ask the same question, it is a sure sign that the notice must be immediately updated. The ideal outcome is when no support cases were opened to clarify what the notification wanted to say and customers are applying remedies, and there are no signs of vulnerability actively exploited. When you reach close to this state, you are disclosing the right amount of information.

Disclosing Internally Found Vulnerabilities

Some vendors would publish notification only for externally reported vulnerabilities. Users would not be notified on vulnerabilities found internally. Not that internally found vulnerabilities would not be removed—they would, but the vendor would not notify users about them.

Reasoning for not disclosing internally found vulnerabilities revolves around the premise that users are better served if fewer people know about them. A vendor can monitor various public and pay-for services to establish whether knowledge about vulnerabilities is "out in the wild." Monitoring support cases opened by the users can also give an indication of whether any of the internally found vulnerabilities are triggered. In the absence of signs that the vulnerability is externally known, a vendor can simply integrate the remedy into an upcoming software release (but not necessarily into old, but still supported, releases), and after users upgrade, they will be protected.

Notifying users about internally found vulnerabilities will draw attention to them. Miscreants can then reverse engineer the remedy and create exploits that can then be used to attack customers. Obviously, if a vendor learns that an internally found vulnerability is being exploited, the vendor will publish a notification because at that point, it will be an externally known vulnerability.

The school that advocates notifying users about internally found vulnerabilities argues two things: 1) you cannot be sure that the vulnerability is not being misused but without visible traces and 2) that users do not upgrade regularly. The first issue is that you cannot be sure that a particular vulnerability is not being misused already. Miscreants might have developed an exploit that would compromise the system without leaving any visible traces (for example, noticeable performance degradation or unexplained crashes). In this case, a vendor would not notice support requests against internally found vulnerabilities because users would not know that they were compromised.

It is common knowledge that a majority of users will not upgrade their systems regularly. That is true even when an upgrade can be fully automated (for example, applying patches on Microsoft Windows operating system). Left on their own schedule, users would run old software as long as it provides required functionality despite the number of security vulnerabilities in the system. Public notification on vulnerabilities therefore serves as a trigger for reluctant users to upgrade. It is true that miscreants can also learn about vulnerabilities and (potentially) develop exploits. However, because users are also aware of the miscreant's abilities, this increased threat of exploit existence only strengthens the case for an immediate system upgrade.

Open-source vendors are a separate category because all changes to the code they make are completely visible to everyone who cares to look. If an open-source vendor addresses an internally found vulnerability, knowledgeable users can deduce what has been changed and why. From that standpoint, open-source vendors would better serve their customers if they always disclose internally found vulnerabilities.

Public Versus Selected Recipients

The first thing to clarify here is that any notification sent to customers is considered a public notification. It is public because the vendor cannot effectively control the information. In a more narrower sense, public notification means broadcasting information to the general public, users, and nonusers. The following text uses public notification in this narrower sense.

After a vendor produces the remedy, the goal is to inform affected users about it hoping that users will take appropriate remedial actions. There are multiple ways how to approach this notification, and for a change, these approaches are not conflicting. It all boils down to whether it is possible to identify all affected users.

If a vendor can identify all users affected by the security vulnerability and be sure that these contacts are technical people who can evaluate the notification, it is sufficient to send a notification only to them. This model of notification is called "selected recipients" because only affected users are targeted. This model is often used, among others, by startups or small vendors. They can do that because such vendors tend to have close ties with their customers and know most of them by their names. Another class of vendors that can use this notification model is when a product is a service. Examples of this category are Cisco WebEx, Google Mail, and all Software-as-a-Service (SaaS) and cloud computing offerings. Extending this notification model further, you can also argue that the vendor needs to notify only users who use the affected component or feature and not all users. A fictitious example of this scenario would be notifying only users that actually deploy Border Gateway Routing Protocol in their networks rather than all users of Cisco routers. Alternatively, a vendor can notify only customers that fit into a certain profile, such as a large ISP or a financial institution. This profile of who will be notified does not need to be permanent and can change depending on the vulnerability.

Detractors of a notification model in which only selected user are informed about security vulnerability would often say that the vendors who use that model are hiding their vulnerabilities. Furthermore, prospective customers cannot gauge by themselves how such vendors are handling vulnerabilities in their products. Often such arguments are voiced by researchers and academia. Taking into account researchers' motivations, it is easy to see that this notification model deprives them of information and impedes their work. On the other hand, this notification model also provides less information to miscreants.

Prospective customers of vendors who publish notifications only to their users can, presumably, ask these vendors to disclose details about the vulnerability handling process and list of recently handled vulnerabilities. Responsible vendors should not have problems disclosing that kind of information. Conversely, if the vendors will not disclose any details related to the vulnerability handling, that would almost certainly signify a vendor that does not handle vulnerabilities well or at all. The vulnerability handling policy should be public irrespective of the notification model used by the vendor. The prospective user should also consult policies by other vendors (for example, Cisco, Microsoft, or Oracle) to see how responsible vendors with mature processes handle security vulnerabilities. The number of vulnerabilities that actually affect a product is not relevant by itself. A product can indeed be affected by two to three vulnerabilities in the past 24 months. What is more important is to ask for evidence of how many reports on potential vulnerabilities have been handled and the reasons why these reports do not affect the product.

Returning to the notification models, the second model is public notification. In this model, the vendor provides notices on its public website visible to everyone. Additionally, such vendors would often mail the notice to various public mailing lists. The reason why vendors would like to use this model lies in the inability to identify all affected customers. This situation can arise if products are sold via third parties (for example, partners and retail), and it is not possible to identify the actual users.

Advocates of this notification model compliment its openness, whereas critics point out that a) miscreants are learning about vulnerabilities and are able to create exploits, b) not all customers receive the notification, and c) some customers receive too much irrelevant information. Now look at the critic's arguments more closely.

The argument that miscreants also learn about vulnerabilities is correct. For a discussion of why that might not be too big of a problem, see the previous section, "Disclosing Internally Found Vulnerabilities." In short, if users know that miscreants are in a position to misuse vulnerabilities, this might provide additional impetus to an upgrade or apply workarounds.

It is also true that even with public notification, not all users receive the information. However, all reputable vendors that employ this notification model provide sufficient information on how to access notifications on security vulnerabilities. This is clearly visible from the product's documentation and, where applicable, the product itself might have features to display security notifications to the user. So, although it is not possible for a vendor to identify all customers, the vendor must provide the means for customers to view and receive that information.

The last critic's argument is that users receive irrelevant information that distracts them from their daily work. If you look at the volume of notifications that users might receive, and assuming a heterogeneous environment, you can estimate that number to be approximately 200 messages per year. That would translate to, approximately, one notification per working day. Hardly a high volume. Second, if users would like selective notification, they would need to provide vendors with sufficient details on used products and their configuration. That information would enable vendors to notify users only on relevant events, but the onus is on users to provide and maintain that information. However, a majority of users cannot provide and maintain that information.

To conclude this section, both notification models—public and selected users only—are mandated by the vendor's ability to identify affected users. Methods are not mutually exclusive, and the vendor can use both of them if they are adequate for the purpose. And, to repeat, the purpose is to notify affected users. Any other fringe benefits that notification may bring (for example, advancing research) are certainly a bonus but are secondary to helping users.

Vulnerability Predisclosure

Vulnerability predisclosure means that some users will receive notification on security vulnerability sooner than others. It is possible to have multiple "tiers" of customers, and each tier can be notified at a different time. Theoretically you could define arbitrarily many tiers but, in practice, two (most common) or three tiers are used. This implies that some users are more "valuable" or "important" than others. The biggest issue is how to define criteria to divide customers. Before looking at the motivation of why a vendor would like to predisclose information to a subset of customers, let us say that this discussion assumes that there are no legal obligations on a vendor to predisclose information to a particular customer or set of customers. Some vendors might be contractually obliged to notify certain users about security vulnerabilities before the information becomes public. Reasons why a vendor would make such an arrangement are beyond the scope of this text.

The main reason for predisclosure is the severity of consequences if the vulnerability is exploited. Consequences are that either users might suffer directly (for example, an inoperative hospital system for dispensing prescriptions can prevent the hospital from functioning) or its users might suffer indirectly (for example, patients in the hospital might get worse if they cannot be given their medicine).

Now, let's examine how we can go about making criteria for selecting which users will be notified in advance of the others. What is important is to select a criteria as objectively as possible. After the criteria is selected, the vendor would ideally use an independent and external source of information for the actual ranking of customers. Looking at various institutions that are important in everyday life, you can make something like the following list:

- Hospitals, fire departments, and emergency services

- Police

- Armed forces

- Energy sector (electricity, oil, natural gas)

- Transport (road, rail, air, water)

- Utilities (water, waste)

- Financial sector

- Communication (radio, TV, Internet)

- Government

These important services correspond to parts on Critical National Infrastructures (CNI), and many governments already have them defined. In a majority of cases, all parts of CNI can be affected by a vulnerability that would necessitate notifying all the CNI. To compound this, because global vendors operate in many countries, they would need to prenotify all parts of CNI in all countries they have presence. For a large vendor, this can present a tangible and intractable problem.

To make this problem easier to deal with, a vendor might focus on only a portion of its users and decide that only a subset of it would receive prenotification. An example of this might be if Cisco decides that only Internet service providers (ISP) would be eligible to receive prenotification because without them, the Internet would become a set of unconnected networks—that is, cease to exist as the Internet we know. One measure of ISP "rank" is how many Autonomous System Numbers (ASN) originate or transit through it. The higher number of ASNs means more fragments will be left and that ISP stops operating. However, even this approach is fraught with dangers, as the presentation by C. Labovitz given at the NANOG 47 conference showed. According to the presentation, until 2007 only ISPs were in the top 10 list according to the number of originating or transit ASNs. But the current data in 2009 shows that Google is now at number 3 on the list, and Google is not an ISP. But if Google would stop operating now, the Internet would still remain interconnected and the majority of Internet users would be able to perform their tasks providing they do not use Google search. This is to show that even an objective criteria can change over time and that it must be reevaluated periodically.

Overall, constructing actual criteria on who will be prenotified is a complex task, as the previous example illustrates. Instead of attempting to define criteria, following are the characteristics the criteria itself must possess:

- Must be as objective as possible. Imagine that you would have to defend it at a court of law, so make it as universal as possible (for example, "top 10 ISPs but not Google" is a bad criterion).

- Use external and independent information sources to eliminate bias. (The "ATLAS 10" list from Labovitz's presentation is a good example.)

- Must be created with global application in mind. Major vendors operate on a global scale, so criteria must accommodate the situation (for example, "all countries but not XY" is a bad criterion).

- Must be periodically revised because an environment can change with time.

- Do not use metrics such as purchased equipment and services or revenue in your criteria. That will be tantamount to blackmailing and punishing small users, which will hardly be a justifiable criterion.

- Keep the number of recipients of prenotification and tiers of notification small. If you need more than two tiers of notification (for example, selected and everyone else) and if the number of users in the first tier is more than a handful, you should revise your criteria.

Another issue is that many of the organizations that would be considered for prenotification are global. If a vendor would notify one organization in any single country (assuming that the CNI model would be used), the information will be spread within the notified organization and across national borders. This is logical as devices in one country are connected to the devices in another country. To protect itself, the organization must apply the remedy to all affected devices no matter in which country devices are situated.

The next effect you need to consider is interorganizational versus intra-organizational links. If prenotification would force an organization to make changes, but only on systems within the organization that do not interface to any outside system (intra-organizational), the change might go unnoticed. If, however, changes must be made to the systems that interface systems outside the prenotified organization (interorganizational), it is likely that other organizations will notice that something is going on. When these other organization see public announcements some time later, they will make the connection between these two events.

This can easily result in a scenario in which at some future time, an organization (call it "Minor Corp.") that has not received prenotification would notice activities at the "Major Corp." that was known to have received prenotification in the past. Noticing activities, Minor Corp. can conclude (rightly or wrongly) that another vulnerability is being patched and then start reacting. It can start asking everyone what is happening, which can lead to false rumors. At this point, even if Major Corp. or the vendor tells privately to Minor Corp. that nothing is going on, the situation might not improve. Minor Corp. can assume that the vendor and Major Corp. are in cahoots, and they would obviously deny whatever is going on. When false rumors start, it is impossible to discern real information, especially if the only authoritative source—the vendor—is silent during that time. False rumors can prompt even more organizations to start taking actions they perceive as something that will protect them, but in reality, these actions might have no effect (in the best case) or actually decrease security and stability.

Prenotification has its place but must be planned carefully and used rarely. Only a few examples of why prenotification is a complex matter have been presented. If a vendor wants to experiment with prenotification, it should expect that the first one or two attempts will be messy and likely escalate out of control quickly. For that reason, the vendor must be prepared to stop prenotification and notify all users. It is much better for users to receive correct information rather than allow them to act on rumors.

Many vendors avoid prenotification because of all complications related to it and opt for a model in which everyone is notified at the same time.

Scheduled Versus Ad Hoc Notification Publication

This is another issue that depends on users and how quickly they can react after receiving information about vulnerability. The reaction process at the users' side after they receive notification can be described as follows:

- Information received; the clock starts ticking from now.

- The system must be evaluated in the light of this new information. Are any devices affected? What is the additional risk to the system by this exposure? This analysis can be done relatively quickly—probably within a few days or a few weeks.

- A decision must be made on the optimal course of action. Will the remedy be applied? Which devices will receive it? Will mitigation be applied and where? This decision can be made in a matter of days.

- Testing of the remedy and workarounds is done next. No serious organization will just blindly update its devices without previous testing. Testing can take anywhere from weeks to months.

- Applying the remedy and workaround comes next. This is again done over the course of days and weeks because not all devices are updated at the same time. This is done to preserve overall system stability; some unforeseen issue might cause devices to crash even after the remedy has passed all testing. In some environments, updates cannot be applied at any time, but they must be planned in advance or even agreed with other organizations to which devices are linked.

It was important to present this process to emphasis that vulnerability notifications are disruptive to the organization that receives them. To minimize disruption, organizations would like for things to happen in an organized way so that they can plan for them. In practice, this means that organizations would like vulnerability notification to happen according to a schedule. That is the reason why Cisco has "IOS bundles" twice yearly, why Oracle has quarterly patches, and why Microsoft has its "second Tuesday in a month." Some organizations do not agree with this policy and demand that vendors publish notifications as soon as a remedy is ready. Their argument is that a notification schedule introduces a delay during which their systems are vulnerable and susceptible to attack—an argument that certainly has its merits.

The answer to the question, "Should a vendor use ad hoc or scheduled notification?" depends on the speed users can react. If users can finish the entire process in a short period of time with minimal disruption, notifications can be published ad hoc. If users need a significant amount of time to go through the process, a scheduled release is preferred. As we see, the answer is tied toward what is best for customers. Are customers best served by notifying them immediately, or is this unrealistic and does a regular cadence actually mean that more customers are applying the remedies?

This is not to say that these two options are mutually exclusive. A vendor should use both methods. The default method should be scheduled notifications, even if users can handle the notification quickly. The main advantage of a schedule is that it enables key personnel to be available during the expected notification time so that information can be quickly analyzed and assessed. On the other hand, if a severe vulnerability is encountered and is being actively exploited, a vendor should notify its users as soon as the remedy is available (and in critical instances maybe even before the remedy is produced) no matter the notification schedule. This mix of models, where the scheduled notification is the primary and the ad hoc secondary model, is something that more vendors are embracing, and it is very likely to become the predominant model throughout the industry.

Vulnerability Grouping

The question of vulnerability grouping is of more significance to vendors that produce multiple products but can also be relevant to vendors with a single product. The question here is how to best present multiple vulnerabilities that affect multiple products. Alternatively, you can phrase this question as, "How can you present multiple vulnerabilities that affect a single product?"

Let's start with the main question and assume that we are dealing with a situation, as shown in Table 12-1, and we want to announce all vulnerabilites at the same time.

Table 12-1 shows five products (A–E) that are affected by vulnerabilities that can be divided into five categories. Not all devices are affected by all vulnerabilities, and the question is, "Should we publish notification per product or per protocol?" You can assume that vulnerabilities are independent from each other.

If you decide to create notifications per product, you can have a situation as shown in Table 12-2.

Alternatively, you can decide to divide notifications per protocol, and then you will have the situation shown in Table 12-3.

Table 12-1 *Multiple Vulnerabilities Affecting Multiple Products*

Protocol/Technology	Products				
	A	**B**	**C**	**D**	**E**
SSL	—	Vulnerable	—	Vulnerable	—
HTTP	Vulnerable	Vulnerable	—	—	Vulnerable
SIP	Vulnerable	—	Vulnerable	—	—
BGP	—	—	Vulnerable	—	Vulnerable
TCP	Vulnerable	Vulnerable	Vulnerable	Vulnerable	Vulnerable

Table 12-2 *Notification Per Product*

Product A Affected By	Product B Affected By	Product C Affected By	Product D Affected By	Product E Affected By
HTTP	SSL	SIP	SSL	HTTP
SIP	HTTP	BGP	TCP	BGP
TCP	TCP	TCP		TCP

Table 12-3 *Notification per Protocol*

SSL Affects Products	HTTP Affects Products	SIP Affects Products	BGP Affects Products	TCP Affects Products
B	A	A	C	A
D	B	C	E	B
	E			C
				D
				E

Inherently, there is nothing wrong with either of the approaches. The real issue is which one can help customers better. If customers think in product terms, division per product is a better fit. If, however, customers think in terms of protocols, that division should be used.

Thinking in terms of product versus protocols depends on deployment. The more specialized and narrower the use of a product is, the more it is considered in terms of its functionality rather than as a device. Consider a general-purpose computer used exclusively as a web server and another one as a workstation. Although both of them can be the same device model, the former is thought of more in terms of its functionality (for example, web server, PHP), whereas the latter is thought of as a device (for example, Sun Ultra 27 Workstation), even if it also might have a web server running on it.

The only other guideline in this area is that after you decide which division will be used, you should stick to it for the planned notifications. The next time you have a similar situation with multiple products and protocols, you can use a different division for the notifications. An example of this mixing would be to publish one notification that would advise on vulnerability in TCP in all products and then publish an additional notification for each product. (For example, Product A is affected by HTTP and SIP vulnerabilities.) All this is also related to the format for how notifications are presented, which the following section covers.

The alternative question is how to present multiple vulnerabilities in a single product if the vulnerabilities are unrelated. If Product A is affected by vulnerabilities in HTTP, SIP, and TCP, should you publish three separate notifications, each for a single vulnerability, or one notification covering all three vulnerabilities? You can also ask, "Do we need to list all vulnerabilities in the notification or only a subset?" as a related question. The way to approach these questions is always to consider what would be the best for the customers. Before that, let us answer why we are even considering these questions.

That answer is simple: complexity. Listing multiple vulnerabilities in a single document can lead to a long and complex document that is hard to understand. Splitting vulnerabilities across multiple notifications can create excessive cross-referencing between the documents, which makes them harder to read and understand.

Knowing this, it is easier to answer the original questions. If information about vulnerabilities can be presented in a sufficient condensed form, presenting them in a single notification would be the preferred option. If at least a single vulnerability demands a complex and prolonged description, then each vulnerability should be covered in a separate document. Again, mixing styles is discouraged. If you decide on one style (all in one or each vulnerability separately), then stick with it for the current notifications. You can change the style when faced with the similar situation in the future—depending on the vulnerabilities—but things must be kept consistent within a given notification instance.

The last question we have to address here is whether you need to list all vulnerabilities or just a subset. In the previous example, Product A is affected by vulnerabilities in HTTP, SIP, and TCP; do you need to list all of them? The reason why you might not want to list all vulnerabilities would be to reduce the complexity of the notification.

There is no clear answer to this question, and it would depend on the situation. Ideally, a vendor should always list all vulnerabilities. Customers might not be affected by some of them, and it might suffice just to apply workarounds instead of upgrading or patching a device. Workarounds tend to be less intrusive and easier to implement. If you would not list all vulnerabilities but only some of them, customers might either be forced to perform an unnecessary update or will not update and be left susceptible to compromises.

On the other hand, many customers are reluctant to upgrade their devices, so forcing them to do so can actually improve the security of their systems. However, this course of action is possible only if the vendor is absolutely certain that listed vulnerabilities will trigger the wanted course of action at customers. Looking at the example in which Product A contains vulnerabilities in HTTP, SIP, and TCP, you might say that listing only TCP-related vulnerability should suffice and that listing the other two vulnerabilities is superfluous. This decision could be valid but only if TCP vulnerability is severe (for example, pass-through traffic can lock up a device, or remote code execution is possible and an exploit is available) and there is no workaround. If a workaround exists, many users will apply it to buy time until an upgrade that would still leave them vulnerable to HTTP and SIP issues is applied. That would be clearly an unacceptable situation, so if there is a workaround for TCP vulnerability, you need to list all three of them in the notification.

The last option that can be encountered is having multiple vulnerabilities in the same component; for example, five vulnerabilities in HTTP. Assuming that all five vulnerabilities are addressed by the same remedy, the vendor might decide not to list all five of them in the notification but only one or two of the most severe vulnerabilities. The purpose of this is to reduce the complexity of the notification. If customers decide to upgrade, they will be protected against all five vulnerabilities. If customers decide not to upgrade based on the information about the most severe vulnerability, knowledge about the remaining four nonsevere issues would not change the situation. Again, the vendor must think what course of action would serve customers the best and then act accordingly.

Notification Format

When talking about the notification format, you need to consider several aspects, such as medium, type (for example, text, PDF), structure (for example, free text, XML), and graphical layout.

What is closely related to this question is the notification distribution. All vendors rely on email and the Web as avenues for delivering the information to users. Additionally, some vendors also offer Real Simple Syndication (RSS) feeds and product self-check features in which a device (or application) automatically checks the vendor website for updates.

Notification Medium

The medium will almost always be electronic. It is expected that users will receive notifications via email and be able to read them on the vendor website. Nonetheless, a vendor must have a contingency plan for how to distribute notifications and remedies on physical media. This contingency can be used in catastrophic events such as a complete Internet meltdown, in which large parts of the Internet are fragmented and inaccessible.

Currently, the most practical physical media are CDs or DVDs. Universal Serial Bus disks are also an option, but they can be more expensive than CDs. Dealing with physical media also requires that the distribution logistics are worked out, but that is beyond the scope of this book. The reminder of this section focuses only on electronic documents.

Electronic Document Type

An electronic document can be stored and distributed in multiple formats, such as the following:

- Text only
- Hypertext Markup Language (HTML)
- Adobe Portable Document Format (PDF)
- Proprietary formats (for example, Microsoft Word .doc)

The decision of which format, or formats, will be used depends on what is the most convenient for customers and what can present information in a legible and easy-to-understand way. Being convenient for customers, in this context, means that notifications can be read on a variety of email clients and without requiring installation of additional applications.

Both of these requirements are satisfied by using a text-only format. Unfortunately, a text-only format is also the least expressive. Possibilities of how to emphasis certain parts of the text are limited, and presenting schemas is difficult and impractical at the best. Luckily, a survey of email clients' usage from June 2009, shows that top 10 clients can display graphics and HTML documents. This means that vendors can abandon text-only notifications in favor of graphically advanced formats such as HTML.

The use of more complex formats, such as PDF or proprietary formats, should be discouraged because in most cases it would require installation of additional applications, and not all of them might be available free of charge. Mandating that customers pay for an additional license just to receive and read notifications on security vulnerabilities is a sure way to drive customers away.

Because of its ubiquity, HTML is the best candidate. It enables expressiveness that a text-only format lacks and can link other documents and elements (for example, pictures) into the documents. The only drawback is that the resulting document will be larger than its text-only equivalent. This can be significant for customers who do not have access to high-speed connections (for example, dial-in modems or General Packet Radio Service [GPRS]) or rely on nongraphical communication devices to receive timely notifications (for example, pagers or older models of mobile phones). For these reasons, vendors should use a combination of text-only and HTML documents for notifications of security vulnerabilities.

Electronic Document Structure

Here we consider an internal document structure rather than how document content is structured (for example, summary, description, and so on). The document internal structure can be either free text (that is, no internal structure) or structured by using Extensible Markup Language (XML).

Most vendors start by using nonstructured documents for their notifications because they are easy to create either in a text-only or HTML format. Unstructured text is easy for customers to read and understand, so it would appear that we have reached a perfect solution. Unfortunately, this is not the case when customers need to deal with a large number and, potentially, variety of devices.

After a customer's system reaches a certain size, a need for full- or semi-automatic notification parsing becomes evident. Multiple notifications from many vendors in different formats, products with different numbering schemes, and patch or update conventions—all this can be time-consuming for people to handle manually. To resolve this situation, vendors should consider moving away from unstructured text toward structured text.

Out of several XML schemas (CAIF, DAF, IESPP, OVAL, and VuXML) developed for this purpose, it seems that only Open Vulnerability and Assessment Language (OVAL) is currently maintained. OVAL is also proposed for adoption by ITU-T and is expected to become an official ITU-T recommendation as a part of the X.1500 Cybex framework.

The biggest advantage of structured text over unstructured text is that structured text can be parsed by applications. This can help customers automate certain steps in the evaluation of received vulnerability notifications.

Usage of Language in Notifications

Consider the following aspects of language use in notifications:

- Style of the language (for example, formal versus informal)
- Literariness of the language (for example, poetic versus academic)
- Translation into other languages

Because all these things are interrelated, we will treat them together. It is not possible to exactly prescribe the right style for the notifications, and over time, every vendor will find its own style that feels right. Generally, the resulting style tends to be bland and factual. Somewhere between a formal and informal style but definitely not poetic. Following are guidelines to help while searching for the right style.

The sentences should be short and the vocabulary constrained. Be consistent in expressions used throughout all documents. Do not use overly academic language unless you are absolutely certain that your audience will understand it. The vendor must be cognizant that some people that will be reading the notification have only basic technical knowledge of how the device or application works and what the Internet is about.

The user base of every large vendor is international, and large portions of your users do not speak whatever language the vendor has chosen to be the official language. That alone dictates that style must not be complex or poetic but factual and more akin to the style used by good newspapers (not tabloids!). Always remember that a certain portion of recipients will use online translators such as Babelfish or Google to translate the notification into their language. If you never used machine translators, please do try them to get an idea of what kind of text your customers might be reading.

Although the preceding advice might sound wrong for those who like to have variety in a language, it is the right thing to do for the customers. I used to pride myself on using different phrases to explain the same thing within the Advisory, even sneaking in a few Latin phrases in some of the Security Advisories. ("Cum grano salis" was one of them and an odd "sic" was added for good measure.) All of them were removed a few years ago when we were updating the documents, and rightly so. It can be hard for non-native speakers to understand a pithy style of the notifications without requiring them to tackle old Latin phrases.

If possible, the vendor should translate the notifications into different languages. Given the number of spoken languages, it is impossible to translate the document into all of them, so only those spoken by the majority of the customer base will suffice. Translation requires that the text of the notification be finalized well in advance of the planned publication date to allow for correct translation. Using constrained vocabulary, specific phrases, and template text can ease and improve the quality of the translation. Finally, each translated notification must contain text stating which version of the notification is authoritative (that is usually the version written in the vendor's chosen official language) and a pointer to it.

Push or Pull

Is it better that the vendor sends notifications to customers (push model) or that affected devices fetch that information itself (pull model)? The answer is "yes." Both models are valid, and vendors should use whichever is more effective in informing users about vulnerabilities. The vendor can also use both models but probably not for the same product.

The push model is good because it can be configured to suit users' needs. If the vendor uses email or RSS to send the notification, the users can automate the process so that after the notification is received, it is parsed and, depending on its content, different people are alerted about the notification. These alerts can be sent to their pagers; automated voice messages can be sent to their mobile phones; and emails can be sent to their addresses. All that can happen within seconds after receiving the vendor notification. Less-sophisticated users can read the notification the next time they check their email or browse a website, which might be several days or weeks after the vendor published the notification.

A pull model means that a device will periodically check whether a new notification is published and then notify the user about it. That way, users can learn about the notification as soon as they turn the device on. This method is less amenable to automation than the push model unless users reverse engineer the mechanism for how the device checks for new notifications. After this reverse engineering is done, it should not be hard to automate the process of receiving and preprocessing the notification, as was the case with the push model. But there is more. The following analysis is applicable to some extent to both models but is more applicable to the pull model.

To receive information about a notification, the device must be connected to a communication network. Ideally, the device should be constantly connected to the communication network; if that is not the case, it must be connected frequently enough so that the period between when the notification becomes available to when it is detected by the device is minimized. We will call this a "freshness" principle.

Although a device can inform users about events in various ways (for example, light, tone, vibration), the best way to convey information about security vulnerabilities is to display it on a screen. The reason for using a display is the complexity and importance of the information; however, just presenting the information is not sufficient. In a majority of cases, users would need to react to the notification. The expected reactions are to agree or decline remedial actions. Optionally, users can choose which remedial actions will be allowed or declined. This requirement assumes capabilities for users to interact with a device. We will call this "interactivity."

Not all devices satisfy these criteria—that is, have a display and a way the user can directly interact with the device. In some instances, that is done on purpose because devices might be prohibited from initiating or receiving connections from outside a closed network. Interactivity requirements can be violated by the product design (as in cable modems) where it is not envisaged that the user would directly interact with the device, so a direct interface is missing. Additionally, a device can be assembled from multiple parts, and each of these parts might require updates. Computers are prime example of this class of devices. A standard computer would have a processor, BIOS, network interface card (wired or wireless), and a video card, and each of these components should be able to be updated. Many users are not even aware of the existence of these subcomponents (which is an acceptable position) and none of the components can directly interact with a user. For devices, and components of devices, that do not have direct interface, users need to use a helper device to enable the process of receiving the notifications.

This helper device can be either a separate device or the aggregated device itself. For example, a home wireless access point can be managed by a home computer, and a central server can manage network infrastructure devices of a service provider. For a computer's components, that helper device can be the computer itself. This model with the helper device is already in use by several vendors, such as Cisco and Juniper for routers and other networking devices. The helper device in this case is the user's computer where the notification is received and which is used for the remedy download. That helper device must satisfy the principles of freshness and interactivity.

In summary, a vendor should use whichever model (push or pull) is more suitable. The suitability is determined by who the users are and device characteristics. Generally, home users prefer a pull model because it is more convenient. Enterprise users, on the other hand, lean more toward a push model. Device characteristics, as described under freshness and interactivity principles, provide additional constraints on which the notification model can be used.

Internal Notification Review

Before it is published, the notification must be reviewed to ensure that it contains all the necessary information and that it is accurate. At the beginning of the Cisco PSIRT operation, this review was done within the team. We would get together on a telephone and discuss the notification. After the team agreed on the content, the notification would be published. The current review process in Cisco PSIRT is more involved and takes more steps, but the end result is improved notification.

Following are groups of people, apart from the product security team, who should be involved in the notification review:

- The developers, a group that develops and maintain the product, always must be the first on the list. Unless the vendor has only a few products, it is hard for any single group to know all the products in great details. People who maintain the products are bound to know all about them and can provide technical details related to the vulnerability.

- People who provide customer support for the given products must be involved. For a larger vendor, the entire support organization will not be involved, but at least senior people must be included in the review cycle. Although developers know how the products are made, a support group can give an insight into how the products are used by customers. It is not uncommon for users to deploy the products in a different manner than developers have envisaged. Deployment method matters because it might make triggering vulnerability harder or easier. A deployment method can also influence workarounds, as I found out in one of the first Security Advisories that I wrote. It was about Cisco Discovery Protocol (CDP), and the workaround that I originally strongly suggested was to disable CDP on all devices. The immediate comment from the support people was that the workaround was not acceptable because a huge percentage of customers were running CDP for network management purposes and the IP voice solution, as designed at the time, would stop functioning if CDP was not running.

- Some vendors might have dedicated support people for certain strategic customers. If that is the case, a subset of that group should be involved in the notification review. If customers that have such support arrangements belong to different business lines (for example, service providers, financial institutions, and retail), the review group should cover all lines of business. Such composition helps bring diversity of deployment methods that improves the notification. In one particular vulnerability, Cisco PSIRT was recommending blocking certain traffic as a workaround. All the reviewers were fine with the workaround except the person who supported government installations. He noticed that if the workaround was applied, some devices used for secure voice communication would also be blocked, so parts of government structures would lose the ability to talk over secure telephone lines.

- Legal people must also be involved. Some of the words or phrases habitually used might have a specific meaning in the legal world. As a test, here are two examples. Is it better to say, "We found a defect in our product" or "We found vulnerability in our product"? If two competitors work on producing a remedy, would you say that they "cooperated" or "collaborated"? If you are not sure about the "answers," talk to your company lawyers. You might be surprised what they will tell you. If possible, have one or two people from the legal department who will be designated to review all draft notifications. After both sides go through the initial period of learning how the other side works and thinks, the review gets much easier and faster.

- A press relation (PR) group should be included, not as much to provide feedback but to prepare responses for the press and key people within the organization. Depending on who you are, a notification on security vulnerability might become news. Your PR group must be aware that a notification is pending and what it is about. It must have a chance to prepare its standing response in case journalists contact you for more information. In one extreme case, Cisco PSIRT had a situation in which it published a Security Advisory toward the end of January. Some of you might know that the end of January is when the World Economic Forum has its annual meeting in Davos, Switzerland. John Chambers, the CEO of Cisco, was on the stage at the time when the Security Advisory was published. Journalists in the room were quick to find that out and asked John to comment on the Security Advisory. Your PR group knows about such high-profile appearances and can help prepare these people in advance. One thing is certain—whatever you do, you do not want to make your CEO look unprepared in a room full of journalists.

Additional groups can also be involved in the entire process of creating the notification; the previous list is not exhaustive. For example, someone would have to proofread the notification and verify whether it conforms to your company guidelines for publishing. If it is translated into another language, translators will have to be involved.

Whoever you decide to involve in the review process, it must be clear to everyone that the product security team is the one who "owns" the notification. All these different groups can provide the input, but it is up to the product security team to decide what will be included in the final document (technical facts aside). The more people reviewing the notification, the more suggestions there will be. It is easy to make suggestions on how to modify the document, especially because the reviewers usually will not bear the consequences if something is not right with the notification.

Notification Maintenance

Occasionally, the published notification needs to be updated. That is usually because some new information came to light that is deemed significant enough to be presented to the customers. Practically all notifications from vendors that publish them have a "History" or "Revisions" section in their documents, but is that all there is to it?

It is not. A vendor must make two major decisions related to notification maintenance. The first one is when to change the document revision number, and the second is whether users need to be notified of the change. Notifications from all vendors have revision numbers (for example, 1.0, 1.1, and so on), with the idea that when the document is changed, the revision number will be incremented. The first question the vendor must answer is what changes warrant a revision number to be incremented. If the change is only cosmetic, such as when the original document included only "TCP" and is updated to read "Transmission Control Protocol (TCP)," is it necessary to increment the revision number? If the answer is that cosmetic updates will be silently made, it must also be decided what constitutes a noncosmetic update.

Ideally, a vendor will never make silent updates to the document. It is much easier not to think of whether an update is cosmetic, but simply increment the revision number and document the change every time the notification is updated. Some customers have automation in place that downloads every notification a vendor has on its website and compares it against the previous copy that customer has stored locally. That is how customers safeguard themselves from silent updates.

The next question is when will users be notified about changes in the notification? In other words, what changes warrant republishing the notification? It is usually a major change in the content, such as when a new product is confirmed to be vulnerable, or if a product that was previously considered to be vulnerable turns out not to be affected. Availability of a remedy might also constitute a major event and necessitate notification republishing.

Whatever the criteria are, the vendor should document them and make its users aware of what they are. Notifying users of a change in the notification is a disruptive event for the users and, as such, it should be minimized. If you force your users to mobilize their resources needlessly one time too many, they will stop paying attention to your future notification. That is the situation that must be avoided.

Access to the Notifications

Finally, we look at the issues related to the access to the notification, including the maintenance of the list of the recipients, static versus dynamic URLs, and whether access to it must be protected. The answers to these questions are partially dependant on the vendor disclosure policy, as previously discussed in the "Public Versus Selected Recipients" section.

Starting from the recipients, the users are the only people who can nominate who, on their side, will receive the notification. This is valid for both the push and pull models of distribution. In the pull model, the user might decide that only a selected device will be allowed to receive notifications directly and all other devices only after the remedy is made available internally within the organization. This requires users to configure their products and selectively enable or disable the auto-update feature. In the push model, where the vendor sends out the information, users must be able to subscribe or unsubscribe themselves to that service.

Many of today's websites generate content when it is requested and use dynamic URLs. This means that the same document might have a different URL every time it is retrieved. The vendor must make provisions that all notifications are also accessible using static URLs, which enable users to bookmark them, other vendor documents can reference them, and the notification can also be referenced from online newspaper articles.

Finally, we ask the question, "Do notifications need to be freely accessible to everyone, or should people who want to see them be registered with the vendor and have a special username and password to access them?" This is very much tied with the disclosure model. If the vendors make their notifications accessible to everyone, it makes sense not to require users to register on the vendors' website to read the notifications. If the vendor makes the notification available only to their customers, it is natural that a username and password will be required to see the notifications. If, however, vendor uses both models, it should follow the same logic for the website access. Notifications that were sent to everyone should be available without registration, whereas notifications sent only to the customer should require registration.

Summary

Creating a good notification system about security vulnerability is more complex than many vendors initially suspect. You need to consider multiple aspects and potential consequences of various ways how notifications can be produced and presented. Given a multitude of things and decisions that need to be made, a vendor should not expect to get it right the first time around. It is natural to make mistakes, but the vendor must learn from them. It is crucial to talk to users and ask for feedback at any opportunity because that is the only way to improve.

References

CampaignMonitor, 2009. "Email client popularity—Email Stats & Reports—Email Clients—Campaign Monitor." Available at http://www.campaignmonitor.com/stats/email-clients/. [Accessed November 2, 2009].

CERT-Verbund, Deutsches Advisory Format—DAF. Available at http://www.cert-verbund.de/daf/daf_description.html. [Accessed November 2, 2009].

Cisco, 2003a. "Cisco Security Advisory: Cisco IOS Interface Blocked by IPv4 Packets." Available at http://www.cisco.com/warp/public/707/cisco-sa-20030717-blocked.shtml. [Accessed November 9, 2009].

Cisco, 2003b. "Cisco Security Advisory: Cisco IOS Software Processing of SAA Packets." Available at http://www.cisco.com/warp/public/707/cisco-sa-20030515-saa.shtml. [Accessed October 19, 2009].

Cisco, 2003c. "Cisco Security Notice: Response to BugTraq—Internet Key Exchange Issue" [IPsec Negotiation/IKE Protocols]—Cisco. Available at http://www.cisco.com/en/US/tech/tk583/tk372/technologies_security_notice09186a008016b57f.html. [Accessed October 19, 2009].

Cisco, 2008. "Cisco Security Response: Rootkits on Cisco IOS Devices." Available at http://www.cisco.com/warp/public/707/cisco-sr-20080516-rootkits.shtml. [Accessed November 14, 2009].

Cisco, 2009. "Cisco Security Response: Unmatched Request Discloses Client Internal IP Address." Available at http://www.cisco.com/warp/public/707/cisco-sr-20090925-axg.shtml. [Accessed November 14, 2009].

Cisco, Products & Services Security Vulnerability Policy—Cisco Systems. Available at http://www.cisco.com/en/US/products/products_security_vulnerability_policy.html. [Accessed October 26, 2009].

Cisco WebEx, WebEx: Web Conferencing, Web Meeting, Video Conference, Online Meeting Services. Available at http://www.webex.com/. [Accessed October 26, 2009].

Dragoon, J., 2009. Upcoming support changes—NOVELL FORUMS. Available at http://forums.novell.com/novell-community-forums-stuff/community-chat/386700-upcoming-support-changes-post1858218.html. [Accessed November 8, 2009].

FIRST—CVSS SIG, 2007. CVSS v2 Complete Documentation. Available at http://www.first.org/cvss/cvss-guide.html. [Accessed October 12, 2009].

Google, Google Mail. Available at https://mail.google.com/. [Accessed October 26, 2009].

GSMA, GPRS ~ GSM World. Available at http://www.gsmworld.com/technology/gprs.htm. [Accessed November 2, 2009].

Labovitz, C., McPherson, D., and Iekel-Johnson, S., 2009. ATLAS Internet Observatory 2009 Annual Report. Available at http://www.nanog.org/meetings/nanog47/presentations/Monday/Labovitz_ObserveReport_N47_Mon.pdf.

Microsoft, Microsoft Security: Microsoft Security Response Center (MSRC) | Security Engineering. Available at http://www.microsoft.com/security/msrc/whatwedo.aspx. [Accessed October 26, 2009].

MITRE, Common Configuration Enumeration (CCE): Unique Identifiers for Common System Configuration Issues. Available at http://cce.mitre.org/. [Accessed November 2, 2009].

MITRE, CPE—Common Platform Enumeration. Available at http://cpe.mitre.org/. [Accessed November 2, 2009].

MITRE, CVE—Common Vulnerabilities and Exposures (CVE). Available at http://cve.mitre.org/. [Accessed November 2, 2009].

MITRE, OVAL—Open Vulnerability and Assessment Language. Available at http://oval.mitre.org/. [Accessed November 2, 2009].

NIST, National Vulnerability Database CVSS Scoring. Available at http://nvd.nist.gov/cvss.cfm?calculator&version=2. [Accessed October 19, 2009].

NIST, The Security Content Automation Protocol (SCAP)—NIST. Available at http://scap.nist.gov/. [Accessed November 2, 2009].

ntp.org, ntp.org: Home of the Network Time Protocol. Available at http://www.ntp.org/. [Accessed November 14, 2009].

Oracle, Security Vulnerability Fixing Policy and Process. Available at http://www.oracle.com/technology/deploy/security/securityfixlifecycle.html. [Accessed October 26, 2009].

RUS-CERT, U.O.S., CAIF. Available at http://www.caif.info/. [Accessed November 2, 2009].

Sourcefire, Inc., Snort: Home Page. Available at http://www.snort.org/. [Accessed November 9, 2009].

US-CERT, 2005. US-CERT Vulnerability Note VU#312073. Available at http://www.kb.cert.org/vuls/id/312073. [Accessed November 8, 2009].

Vidrine, J.A., 2005. VuXML. Available at http://www.vuxml.org/. [Accessed November 2, 2009].

Chapter 13

Vulnerability Coordination

Although it might not look like it, vendors are getting better at removing vulnerabilities from their products. Through a combination of better product design and more comprehensive testing, vendors are removing many vulnerabilities from their products before they are shipped. What is on the rise are vulnerabilities found in protocols, as demonstrated with vulnerabilities in TCP (in 2001, 2004, and 2009), DNS (2008), and TLS (2009). Because of their nature, vulnerabilities in protocols affect many vendors, so the industry needs to cooperate more closely when dealing with such vulnerabilities. A similar situation arises with vulnerabilities in widely used applications and libraries such as the ones from Adobe, Apache, NTP.org, OpenSSL, RSA, and others. Given widespread use of this software, an error in any of them is bound to affects hundreds of vendors.

This chapter covers the need for vendor cooperation, potential obstacles in this cooperation, and how that cooperation takes form. The case is presented only from the vendors' point of view.

Why Cooperate and How to Deal with Competitors

Vendors are in a business of making a profit and, for many vendors, this is a zero-sum game—someone will either buy a product from Vendor A or Vendor B. If my product has been bought then I gain, and other vendors selling the same product will lose. Given this, what is my incentive to cooperate with other vendors and to actually help them make their products more secure?

Vendors should compete on features and not on security vulnerabilities. Using arguments such as, "Our competitor is vulnerable to this but we are not," is not something on which a purchasing decision should be based. Every vendor has its own share of security problems; its products are vulnerable, too. If you ever encounter a vendor that claims to not have any security vulnerabilities, it is certain that multiple vulnerabilities are present in the product, and many of them are probably severe. Not only that, but that vendor does not have processes to deal with security vulnerabilities, and most likely is not doing any meaningful security testing.

However, vendors can differentiate how they handle vulnerabilities in their products. Depending on how mature and effective vendors' processes are, there is a difference in the way product vulnerabilities are handled. Vendors with better processes should have more internally discovered vulnerabilities. (Some vendors might not report statistics on internally discovered vulnerabilities.) Their relationships with external researchers tend to be better, and these vendors are more responsive than vendors with immature processes. Also, the quality of remedies tends to be better (that is, fewer bad fixes) in vendors with mature processes.

Where security vulnerabilities are concerned, there is no such thing as a competion. The only competition, in this case, are miscreants but not other vendors. To better understand that, we must look at things from the users' standpoint. Any system, from home to large enterprises, is composed of products from multiple vendors. Users always look at the system in its totality rather than separate sets of products from different vendors. Although it used to be easy to divide system into computers, computer network, and telephony, that division is becoming more tenuous as time passes. Computer network and telephony are nowadays practically the same, and computers are also becoming more abstract and more a part of the network. If any part of the system can be compromised, there is a good chance that some other parts of the system can be compromised, too. For users, this is a bad thing—and it is especially bad if one vendor intentionally allows that to happen. Switching perspective and looking from the vendor standpoint, we can ask several questions related to this topic.

What I am getting by working with other vendors? Better technical insight into the problem and solution. In addition to that, a higher assurance that the remedy from one vendor will not break functionalities in products from other vendors. There are concrete examples to back up these claims. To address TCP Reset vulnerability (see http://www.cisco.com/warp/public/707/cisco-sa-20040420-tcp-ios.shtml), a change in the TCP stack was introduced. At that time, there was a concern that the change might cause interoperability issues with products from other vendors or, more to the point, that Cisco and Juniper routers could not "talk" to teach others or that Microsoft Windows could not connect to computers running the Solaris operating system. To make sure that no interoperability issues were present, an interoperability event was organized where it was tested that all these products will continue to communicate with each other after changes in the TCP stack were made. More recently, we had "DNS Cache Poisoning" and "TLS Renegotiation" cases in which multiple vendors collaborated on the remedy. It is interesting to note that, in the DNS case, this collaboration helped correct an invalid assumption made by a major operating system vendor that prevented it from releasing an incomplete remedy. Had this vendor worked in isolation, its customers would have had to upgrade twice in a short period of time.

Why should I wait with an announcement if I am ready and other vendors are not? Different vendors need different amounts of time to produce the remedy, and some of them publish announcements according to a schedule (for example, once a month or once a quarter). So, if one vendor has produced a remedy now, why should it wait for the next few months and then announce it together with the rest of the affected vendors? The answer to this is that customers use products from multiple vendors in their systems.

After a single vendor publicly announces the presence of a vulnerability, it is relatively easy to establish whether it is vendor-specific or an industrywide issue. If vulnerability affects multiple vendors, miscreants will start working on exploits for products that are suspected to be vulnerable but without remedy. Such unilateral decisions to publicly announce vulnerability can make collective customers easier targets and force other vendors to scramble and rush their production of remedies that, in the worst case, might lead to incomplete remedies, so customers will have to apply them more than once. This is not a good way to establish solid relationships with other vendors, especially because the next time the situation can be opposite. The old dictum "Never impose on others what you would not consider yourself" (Confucius, Analects XV.24) is still valid.

What should I do if my customers are under active attack? This would be an exception from waiting for other vendors. If customers are actively targeted and that particular vulnerability is being exploited, a vendor should publicly announce the existence of the remedy, even if other vendors are not ready yet. In this case, vulnerability is already being misused, and vendors must try to contain damage as much as possible.

Who Should Be a Coordinator?

In theory, anyone can act as a coordinator. In practice, coordinating vendors on a global scale requires a fair amount of effort that not everyone can put in or is willing to do so. A vendor should not try to act as a coordinator because that can create a potential for lawsuits and an inability to recoup the cost.

Assume that vendor "Big Corp" discovers a vulnerability in its product, determines that it can affect other vendors, and decides to initiate an industrywide coordination. It is practically impossible to contact all vendors that might be affected by the vulnerability because there can be so many of them, and no worldwide global registry exists to determine which components are used in their products. Not informing the "Small Shop" about the vulnerability leaves an opportunity for it to sue Big Corp. Small Shop can try to prove that Big Corp deliberately decided not to inform it about the vulnerability. Furthermore, Big Corp is trying to use the vulnerability information as a competitive advantage and gain market share at the expense of Small Shop. It is far from certain that such a hypothetical case would succeed in a court of law, but why take that risk at all?

If a vendor decides to attempt the coordination, it would have to devote some resources into that. In short, it will have to assign two or more people for that task, and these people will expect to be paid for their work. Now the question is how a vendor can recoup the cost from performing the vulnerability coordination. If the vendor performing the coordination would try to directly monetize the information (for example, sell it as an "intelligence feed" or build it into its product's intrusion detection system), other vendors would not like it. The reason for the objection is that it would put the coordinating vendor into a privileged position because it will know other vendors' vulnerabilities and that can give it a competitive edge. Other vendors might also feel that it is not fair disclosing information about vulnerabilities in their products (the Golden Rule again). So if a coordinating vendor would like to monetize information, it needs to find a way that would not alienate it from other vendors. That usually means publishing and using the information only after the vulnerability is publicly released. But, by that time, the value of the information has dropped because now everyone knows about it, so the expected return to the coordinating vendor is lower. Overall, the coordinating vendor needs to invest in the coordination but without a hope to recover the cost. This, however, does not preclude a vendor from doing the coordination for purely altruistic reasons.

These two reasons, potential for lawsuit and cost, are usually sufficient to dissuade vendors from doing vulnerability coordination on a global scale. That is also the reason why currently most respected coordinators are government-sponsored.

Another option, not yet fully realized, is for a not-for-profit organization to fill the role of a coordinator. From the vendor perspective, if it is capable of coordinating correctly, nongovernmental and not-for-profit organizations would be the best option. That would remove government influence and an incentive to sell vulnerability information. Additionally, not being a vendor, such neutral coordinators would not have a conflict of interest nor vested interest in any particular vendor. Industry Consortium for Advancement of Security on the Internet (ICASI) is making the first steps toward that direction, but it is still too early to say whether ICASI will be willing and capable of filling the role of a neutral coordinator. Another organization that has potential to perform such a role is the Forum of Incident Response and Security Teams (FIRST), but it seems that it does not have the will to do it.

How to Coordinate Vendors on a Global Scale

This section lists some difficulties and successes encountered while being coordinated by various coordinators in numerous cases. Although this section presents how a situation looks from a vendor perspective, some of the lessons learned are a product of informal and semi-formal discussion with coordinators. Nonetheless, the information is far from complete, and there are more lessons that coordinators have learned but are not captured here.

Vendors Never Sleep

Let me rephrase this slightly—at least one vendor is working at any given time of the day or day in a week. A good coordinator must be ready to work on the same 24×7 schedule. It is absolutely unacceptable for a coordinator to simply stop working on Friday afternoon and be unreachable by any means until 9:00 a.m. on Monday morning. It is not necessary for coordinators to have someone in the office at all times, but they must be reachable at any time of a day. It goes without saying that the same requirement stands for all vendors, big and small alike. Even if a vendor is not working, someone from the vendor's product security team must be reachable at all times.

The worst thing that can happen is that information on vulnerability leaks, and a decision must be made immediately on what to do next. In cases like that, key players (the coordinator and major vendors for that product/technology) should be able and capable of having a quick discussion. After a decision has been reached, and especially if the decision is to prematurely announce the vulnerability, the coordinator must be able to reach all involved vendors and notify them of the new development. It does not feel good to start your work week with information that all other vendors already have published their notifications, and you have hundreds of customers asking what the situation with your product is.

Be Sensitive to Multicultural Environments

Local customs must be respected and processes adapted to accommodate for a multicultural environment. This is important for coordinators and vendors if they want to work together. Some of the things that a coordinator should pay attention to when working with vendors are as follows:

- When communicating with a vendor on a one-to-one basis, use the vendor's native tongue if possible.

- If possible, offer limited help with the translation of key documents to the vendor's native tongue.

- Avoid using absolutes and imperatives in communications (for example, "This device will always be compromised. You must develop a fix for that."). Not everyone will find it easy to push back and argue differently.

- Try to pick a time and date for telephone/video meetings so that it suits most vendors.

- If possible, provide local telephone numbers for teleconferencing so that vendors do not need to dial international numbers.

Although these might sound like small things, they will go a long way in establishing goodwill between the coordinator and vendors.

Use Good Communication Skills

Coordinators must have good communication and "soft" skills. They must deal with many different vendors, and each of these dealings will have its own challenges. It might be language, lack of technical understanding, unwillingness to respond, inadequate responses, or thousand of other challenges.

Recall that coordinators cannot force a vendor to do (or not to do) anything; yet the coordinator has taken upon itself to produce a consensus among vendors. Trying to agree on common timetables when the vulnerability will be announced is not a small feat. Things can get even worse when a few vendors ask for an extension of the agreed-upon deadline. Coordinators not only need to persuade all other vendors to postpone the announcement, but also a new date for the public announcement must be negotiated.

This also means that coordinators must be firm on occasions. It should not be possible for a minority of vendors to delay the public announcement indefinitely.

No Surprises

Coordinators should explain their policies and procedures to vendors. Ideally, that should be done in advance, but that might not be always possible for new coordinators. Vendors do not like being surprised by unexpected actions. Things like that can backfire because this intricate dance is based on trust. Vendors need to trust the coordinator to do the right things, and the coordinator needs to trust vendors in return. This is all based on an agreement that each side will do its best and not harm others in the process.

In practice, coordinators should state how to handle vulnerability information, what the default timeline is, what actions will be taken, who has access to the information, and what expectations are on vendors and researchers. This does not need to be an exhaustive document but sufficient enough for vendors to understand what will happen and why. FIRST Vendor Sig produced "Guidelines for Vendor-Coordinators Relationship," which is good starting point on what should be done.

Again, this principle is also applicable in reverse, from vendors to coordinators. Neither side likes to be surprised, and both sides like to know how the other approaches the issue and what actions are (or are not) taken while handling vulnerability.

Summary

Global vendor coordination is a necessity, and its importance will rise even higher over time. The main reasons for this are code reuse and vulnerabilities in specification, rather than implementation. Global vendor coordination with the goal of coordinated notification publication helps protect the common user base. Multiple vendors working together to address underlying technical issues can produce more sound solutions rather than each vendor working in isolation.

Although almost anyone can claim to perform vendor coordination on a global scale, only a few organizations have actually managed to do that successfully. It is expected that many more organizations might want to enter that segment, but only a few would be successful. The main issue in coordination is the developing of mutual trust between vendors and coordinators, and the first step on that road is to keep surprises on both sides to a minimum.

References

Cisco, 2004. Cisco Security Advisory: "TCP Vulnerabilities in Multiple IOS-Based Cisco Products." Available at http://www.cisco.com/warp/public/707/cisco-sa-20040420-tcp-ios.shtml. [Accessed November 16, 2009].

Cisco, 2008. Cisco Security Advisory: "Multiple Cisco Products Vulnerable to DNS Cache Poisoning Attacks." Available at http://www.cisco.com/warp/public/707/cisco-sa-20080708-dns.shtml. [Accessed November 16, 2009].

Cisco, 2009. Cisco Security Advisory: "Transport Layer Security Renegotiation Vulnerability." Available at http://www.cisco.com/warp/public/707/cisco-sa-20091109-tls.shtml. [Accessed November 16, 2009].

FIRST, "FIRST—Improving security together." Available at http://www.first.org/. [Accessed November 16, 2009].

FIRST, "Vendor SIG, 2006. Guidelines for Vendor-Coordinators relationship." Available at http://first.org/vendor-sig/vendor-coordinators-guidelines-public-v1.0.pdf. [Accessed November 23, 2009].

ICAI, ICASI. Available at http://icasi.org/. [Accessed November 16, 2009].

Naraine, R., 2003. "Security Flaw Finder Severs Ties with CERT," InternetNews.com. Available at http://www.internetnews.com/dev-news/article.php/1577001/Security+Flaw+Finder+Severs+Ties+with+CERT+.htm. [Accessed December 14, 2009].

Index

D

H

I

O

P

W

CISCO.

ciscopress.com: Your Cisco Certification and Networking Learning Resource

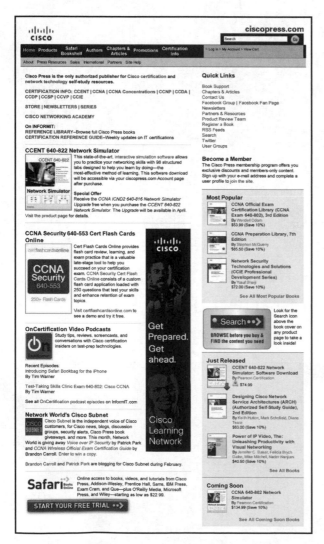

Subscribe to the monthly Cisco Press newsletter to be the first to learn about new releases and special promotions.

Visit **ciscopress.com/newsletters**.

While you are visiting, check out the offerings available at your finger tips.

– Free Podcasts from experts:
  - OnNetworking
  - OnCertification
  - OnSecurity

Podcasts

View them at **ciscopress.com/podcasts**.

– Read the latest author **articles** and **sample chapters** at **ciscopress.com/articles**.

– Bookmark the Certification Reference Guide available through our partner site at **informit.com/certguide**.

Connect with Cisco Press authors and editors via Facebook and Twitter, visit **informit.com/socialconnect**.

FREE Online Edition

Your purchase of **Computer Incident Response and Product Security** includes access to a free online edition for 45 days through the Safari Books Online subscription service. Nearly every Cisco Press book is available online through Safari Books Online, along with more than 5,000 other technical books and videos from publishers such as Addison-Wesley Professional, Exam Cram, IBM Press, O'Reilly, Prentice Hall, Que and Sams.

SAFARI BOOKS ONLINE allows you to search for a specific answer, cut and paste code, download chapters, and stay current with emerging technologies.

Activate your FREE Online Edition at www.informit.com/safarifree

> **STEP 1:** Enter the coupon code: GYAEHBI.

> **STEP 2:** New Safari users, complete the brief registration form.
> Safari subscribers, just log in.

If you have difficulty registering on Safari or accessing the online edition, please e-mail customer-service@safaribooksonline.com